Fighting the War on Terror

Fighting the War on Terror

Global Counter-terrorist units and their Actions

Judith Grohmann

Translated by Geoffrey Brooks

Pen & Sword
MILITARY

AN IMPRINT OF PEN & SWORD BOOKS LTD.
YORKSHIRE - PHILADELPHIA

First published in Germany as *In geheimer Mission – Was Polizeispezialeinheiten im Kampf gegen Verbrechen und Terror erleben* by RIVA Verlag, Munich, 2013

First published in Great Britain in 2018 by
Pen & Sword Military
An imprint of
Pen & Sword Books Ltd
Yorkshire – Philadelphia

ISBN 978 1 52672 745 9

Printed and bound in England
By TJ International Ltd.

Pen & Sword Books Ltd incorporates the Imprints of Pen & Sword Books Archaeology, Atlas, Aviation, Battleground, Discovery, Family History, History, Maritime, Military, Naval, Politics, Railways, Select, Transport, True Crime, Fiction, Frontline Books, Leo Cooper, Praetorian Press, Seaforth Publishing, Wharncliffe and White Owl.

For a complete list of Pen & Sword titles please contact

PEN & SWORD BOOKS LIMITED
47 Church Street, Barnsley, South Yorkshire, S70 2AS, England
E-mail: enquiries@pen-and-sword.co.uk
Website: www.pen-and-sword.co.uk

or

PEN AND SWORD BOOKS
1950 Lawrence Rd, Havertown, PA 19083, USA
E-mail: uspen-and-sword@casematepublishers.com
Website: www.penandswordbooks.com

"You're right. You're right. I don't know, if you're innocent or not. You could have done everything they say you've done. You could have killed that cop. I don't know and I don't care. There are ways to prove your innocence, but this is hardly one of them. And now you got hostages. So let me tell you this: you hurt one of them, you burn up any currency you have with me. They're all I care about. Getting you out of here alive... a distant second. Now, do I make myself clear?"

Kevin Spacey as Lieutenant Chris Sabian, *The Negotiator*, 1998

"A piece of advice: never keep a hostage-taker waiting. It pisses him off."

Samuel Jackson as Lieutenant Danny Roman, *The Negotiator*, 1998

For Dave, Marc, Martin, Scott, Christophe, Roland and Dominique, as well as all the men and women who risk their lives daily in the battle against terrorism and crime for security in our world.

For the surviving dependents and families of the victims of terror, and for Kevin Spacey, whose film *The Negotiator* inspired me to write this book and who, after the terrorist incident in Boston, visited the first responders and units personally to offer encouragement and express his thanks.

Contents

Prologue

The Visit of a Man Condemned to Death

The silence in the room seemed almost intolerable. Six heads were bent over the table, all had been staring for hours at the photo of a man with a black beard and gold-rimmed spectacles. The visit of this man, with the cover name Joseph Anton, required a quite special strategy. The planning for his two-day stay in Vienna had to be perfect. The operation had to remain a secret at all costs. There had to be no weak spots; one word too many would mean his death. The six men sweated. Smoking in the protected special operations room at the Ministry was not permitted, and the four cans of coffee had been empty for hours. The phrase 'a spectacular operation' had been hammered into their heads. Failure was not an option. Their tactics were to think in scenarios and their mantra was 'Live in the Situation', meaning to react as the situation demanded.

The preparations for the visit of Joseph Anton had been at full stretch for days. The six men had done the meticulous groundwork of tracing routes through the maze of streets in Vienna's city centre, puzzling out alternative routes and convoy formations, and committing the result to paper. The buildings to be entered had been examined from roof to cellar, equally the surrounding tramway housing; building plans inspected and emergency exits marked. Suspicious arrivals to Austria at the airport and railway stations had to be investigated, and also unusual movements at the embassies involved. The team that would be operational that day had been drawn up, together with their positions in and around the buildings to be guarded, their exact function during the operation: personal protection and surveillance teams, those responsible for tactics… The list was long, in all around 250 persons, for the analysis of the danger left no room for doubt; it was to be expected that an attempt would be made to assassinate the man.

The murder attempt could be carried out with bomb, firearm or sniper fire, as well as by knife, sword or bayonet. Every form of execution was possible. And for this reason the whole team had to be operational around the clock. Finally, a special kind of surprise had been thought out for the would-be assassin(s). The preparations were made in the usual efficient manner. At last nothing stood in the way of Joseph Anton making his entry into the country.

Whenever that elite circle, consisting of the leader of the Anti-Terrorist Operations Group and senior officials of the State Security Service and Office for the Protection of the Constitution, met with the special units for a conference, there was usually an 'atmosphere', for never before had it occurred in Austria that a man sought worldwide and with a price on his head was to be received as a guest of the State and to be honoured with one of the highest awards the State could bestow. From the outset, this operation had the highest possible risk level; an extraordinary situation for the small alpine republic of Austria.

The airport was wet with drizzle as Austrian Airlines flight OS460 from London approached Vienna International Airport at 10.50 am on Sunday, 15 May 1994. The control tower had the aircraft in sight and gave the pilot permission to land on a specified runway. The controller watched the landing through binoculars. Behind him, in the topmost floor of the airport tower, six large men wearing dark grey Cerruti suits, armed with a special version of the Glock 18 pistol, began speaking into their cabled ear microphones on a special frequency immune to monitoring. Only scraps of sentences could be made out: "Friends listen...Joseph Anton...ready...for landing." The term "Friends" was the agreed call sign of the personal protection team. OS460 landed punctually at 10.55 am, green beacons showing the pilot his way through the labyrinth of runways. A little later, the aircraft stopped at a previously arranged parking area some distance from other machines.

The men announced this into their microphones immediately: "Friends listen again...Joseph Anton...arrived...now." The Hollywood thriller scenario took over and scarcely had the aircraft landed than three armoured black BMW limousines raced towards it. Eight men jumped out of the vehicles and formed a cordon leading from the landing steps which had been pushed against the aircraft fuselage. The men did not look like bodyguards particularly, but rather a mixture of models, secret agents and military men. They wore black shades, jeans and grey sports jackets. Outwardly cool types. After a few minutes the passenger door opened and a stewardess emerged, followed by the first passenger; a man from amongst the police escort who looked around with curiosity. He was followed by a smaller man with a beard, balding with dark hair. He wore gold-rimmed spectacles, a dark lounge jacket, white T-shirt and jeans. Behind him appeared a woman, apparently a friend, dressed in a green summer dress and escorted by six well-built men of impressive appearance from the police escort. Other black vehicles arrived. Everything passed off very quickly. The escort vehicles kept their distance from the limousines. It was the first time that this kind of theatre had ever been seen at Vienna International Airport.

After the small balding man had been welcomed by a man from one of the limousines, he and his girlfriend got into a limousine, through which one could not be seen. The eight men who had awaited the guest were also back in the black limousines. The convoy now moved out at high speed from the airport to the autobahn lane for Vienna and headed for a helicopter pad sited centrally on the roadway. All lanes were free of traffic, the police having sealed off the stretch of road, as was usual for State guests. Police vehicles were stationed at every 300 metres along the route. Their officers saluted as the limousines drove past and relayed the message "Joseph Anton...just drove by."

The man with the cover name "Joseph Anton" had landed unharmed in Vienna where the mission began. His pseudonym was made up from the forenames of his two favourite authors, Joseph Conrad and Anton Chekhov. Already using the cover name for five years, he was the famed Indian-British writer Salman Rushdie, who had been forced to lie low and move constantly from place to place with an armed police escort because of the death sentence passed on him by the Iranian ruler Ayatollah Khomeini. Khomeini had pronounced a Fatwa against him and called upon the world's Muslims to execute it. In order to hasten the matter, he had placed a bounty of $3 million on Rushdie's head. His crime? To have written a novel entitled *The Satanic Verses* with the alleged intent to demean Islam, the Prophet and the Quran.

Salman Rushdie had come to the Austrian capital on 16 May 1994. He was on a two-day visit in order to receive the State award for European Literature from the serving Minister of Culture, Rudolf Scholten. In terms of importance, this placed his visit on a par with that of the President of the United States or the Russian Federation. The Interior Ministry had given the visit the highest level of protection on account of the Fatwa. This meant that an assassination attempt could not be ruled out. For this reason, a unit from the operational commando Cobra, the Austrian special unit used only for highly dangerous situations with particular difficulties, was appointed to protect Salman Rushdie. These seventy men guarded the author and his female companion around the clock during their entire stay in Austria. As his personal bodyguards, they put their lives on the line for his safety.

At the helicopter pad, where the Interior Ministry machine had landed, the security men who were positioned around the pad received the encoded signal "Joseph Anton arriving". There was no excitement in such a situation as this. For hours, the members of the unit responsible for observing the surrounding area had been checking every centimetre, every movement, every passer-by, every car with the greatest concentration. Aerial traffic over Vienna had been paralysed for an hour. Everything was under the control of Cobra and their police colleagues. When the convoy arrived, Joseph Anton and his companion left the vehicle quickly and, accompanied by two members of the special commando, within a minute had boarded the helicopter, which took off at once. The three armoured black limousines and the black cars with the other Cobra members set off southwards along the autobahn.

To have the author spend the night in a Vienna hotel or embassy was out of the question for the Austrian authorities on account of the Fatwa; the danger of assassination was too great. It had therefore been decided to provide accommodation at a much safer location, fifty minutes by car from Vienna; the headquarters of the Cobra operational commando. The centre is surrounded by a security fence 2.3 km long with perimeter security posts and cameras, and the entire Cobra team, men and women trained in all methods of defence against aggression, terror and brutality, inside it. No place in Austria is more secure. There and only there was the writer guaranteed his safety against a single assassin or gang of killers. That was certain.

After the helicopter had landed at the Cobra headquarters, Salman Rushdie alighted and was welcomed at the entrance by the Minister of Culture and his co-workers. Lunch followed. A tour of Vienna in convoy was scheduled for afterwards including a visit to the Burgtheater (Austria's national theatre) and the Museum of Historical Art. With a substantial back-up of Cobra agents the author was chauffeured in an armoured limousine into the city, unrecognised by the public, this time followed by several inconspicuous vehicles with Cobra agents in civilian clothing. While in the theatre, which was closed during the afternoon, the then Director, Claus Peymann, personally escorted Rushdie silently through the sacred halls. Another tactic was needed for the Museum of Historical Art, which was open to the public from all over the world. Ten Cobra members bought tickets and posed as a group of tourists, surrounding Rushdie and the Minister for Culture, and never strayed from their sides. Hours before, their colleagues had assured themselves that no bombs had been hidden, and then taken up positions in the picture gallery so as to screen and observe the visitors. They had contact with each other through their ear microphones, passing commands quietly and unobtrusively such as: "Friends…Joseph Anton in dialogue with Peter Paul" in order to indicate that Rushdie was near the paintings by Peter Paul Rubcns.

Rushdie then went with his 'group' to dine at an unusual venue, above the roofs of Vienna in a private apartment and in the presence of the Minister for Culture and his wife. As the diners discussed the Austrian culture scene, agents from the Cobra operational command spent several hours keeping a very sharp but unobtrusive watch on the flat, as well as the rest of the building, the neighbouring buildings, the street and practically the entire area of the Old Town. Towards midnight, when the convoy arrived at the headquarters of EKO Cobra to deliver its 'guest', the operation planners for all stages of this first eventful day of the visit by the State guest agreed that everything had gone to plan satisfactorily.

The award of the State Prize and the official presentation of Salman Rushdie in Vienna took place on 16 May 1994. On that day more than seventy members of Cobra, amongst them personal bodyguards and surveillance teams, the operational planners and command assistants, as well as those responsible for operational tactics, and police and secret service agents, were provided for the author. A total of more than 250 men. After breakfast Rushdie and his female companion left the headquarters of EKO Cobra in a helicopter for Vienna. An hour earlier, three black armoured limousines and twenty everyday motor cars had driven along the autobahn to the agreed rendezvous.

When the helicopter bearing Salman Rushdie landed in Vienna, the security force had already been there some time. Cobra agents were positioned to scrutinize all movements and persons on and around the landing pad. As Rushdie alighted from the machine, at the same moment a door of the first limousine opened and …out stepped Salman Rushdie. The agents of the special unit stole glances; the confusion lasted only a split second. How would the real Salman Rushdie react to his double? The author was clearly a man with a sense of humour and offered his hand admiringly to the Cobra agent with the code name 'Ossi'. Rushdie had never before experienced having a double for his personal protection. They were as alike as twin brothers and both wore similar attire: brown jacket, white shirt, yellow slacks and a yellow tie with a red, hot air balloon pattern. Optically it was impossible to tell them apart, even the height was the same. Both Rushdies got into their limousines swiftly. Suddenly, the back-up had doubled; the original convoy and a duplicate convoy with Ossi the Rushdie double. The duplicate convoy had the same destination, but would follow a different route to get there. Both limousine convoys headed for the Government district in the city centre through the narrow streets of Vienna, kept free by police and re-programmed traffic lights. It all went precisely to plan without a single pursuer.

The Ossi convoy stopped first before the Starhemberg Palace on Minoriten-Platz, the seat of the Ministry for Culture. After the agents had secured the street, surrounding roofs and houses, the entrance to the Ministry and the building itself, the false Salman Rushdie alighted from his black limousine and in no time was whisked away by security agents through a side door into the building. One hundred invited guests were already seated in the festival hall. They had all been subjected to a strict search and x-rayed, their mobile telephones confiscated and handbags searched.

The award of the State Prize began with an address by the Minister for Culture. Afterwards there followed a ten-minute speech by the Viennese Professor of Literature, Wendelin Schmidt-Dengler. There was a tense atmosphere as none of the guests knew to whom the State Prize would be awarded this year, although of course certain names had been circulating for weeks amongst journalists. The four photographers, camera and radio teams looked around at the faces. Nobody had an inkling that the Minister for Culture would award the State Prize to the author whose life was under threat by a deadly Fatwa. Nobody suspected that the author *The Satanic Verses* was in Austria and in the vicinity. Five minutes of high anticipation on the part of the guests and curious journalists passed. Nobody was allowed to leave the hall; the security agents and Cobra had sealed it off.

It was exactly 11.00 am when suddenly the doors opened and, to the astonished eyes of the public, Salman Rushdie entered, flanked by agents of the Cobra special unit. His double, Ossi, was already in an ante-room 'under wraps' for an hour.

The author showed no signs of fear and seemed relaxed as he took his assigned place at the table on the podium. At the same time several plain-clothed police and Cobra members spread themselves throughout the hall. Rushdie spoke a few words about himself, his work and how pleased he was to receive the award. He preferred not to say much about his work "for then I would not be able to stop myself." The still surprised public was then given the opportunity to ask questions, but nobody spoke up. Nobody on the hall had expected him, and so nobody had questions ready regarding his life and work; they were all still staring at the podium as if struck by lightning. Rushdie left the hall with the same friendly smile with which he had arrived, flanked by Cobra members. As he hurried down the steps of the Palace Starhemberg, his double, Ossi, got into the leading convoy. Unnoticed by the crowd, the real Rushdie left in a limousine from the second convoy. He had to attend a spontaneously arranged press conference in another palace before disappearing in the helicopter towards Wiener Neustadt. In the early afternoon he was taken unobtrusively by Cobra in a black limousine to the airport.

When the Austrian Airlines flight OS455 took off for London at 3.55 pm, the six men with the dark-grey Cerrutti suits and the Glock 18 pistols were once more in the control tower and watching the flight very closely. Beside them was the same controller who had been on duty the previous Sunday. He had given permission for the machine to take off and through his binoculars watched as OS455 headed upwards into a cloudless sky. After the aircraft had safely cleared Austrian airspace, before taking their leave, he heard the six men say into their microphones, "Joseph Anton has left Austria. We move away."

Introduction

"I am on a Mission, Baby."

It's 5.00 am as I put my black face mask over my head. I stuff my long blonde hair underneath it. Next comes the Ulbicht-Zenturio-TSO helmet with the full-cover visor. It weighs almost 5 kg, but I have to avoid thinking about it. Today I might be accompanying them on a mission.

I am really looking forward to my first operation with a counterterrorist unit. I am the first woman, the first female author in the world, to receive permission to travel with a team and observe an operation at close quarters. I am dressed in black, wearing an overall and bullet-proof vest. My clothing and equipment weigh 40 kg. I could not put it all on by myself, I had to be helped. The bullet-proof vest is almost crushing me. I clench my teeth. Now all that's missing are the gloves and black operational boots. I slip into them and tie the laces. They are a good fit. My photographer has given me his Victorinox Swiss knife. "For your safety. One never knows what might happen."

I want to learn from them, for they are something quite special; men and women whose job is to provide security for the people in their country against the world's worst criminals and terrorists. The first time I heard of them was in 1998. That year I saw the film *The Negotiator*, which changed my life. Kevin Spacey played the lead role as a member of the US-police special unit, SWAT. He was in charge of negotiating, and was therefore the man who spoke to blackmailers, kidnappers, terrorists and other major criminals. Spacey was a sensation as the negotiator, Chris Sabian. He was not only convincing, but also brilliant. All special units I have met say the same thing. Spacey is their role model, he is their absolute hero. And ever since the thing I most wanted to do was to learn more about these special units.

They are the higher echelon of the police and, simultaneously, their most dangerous weapon; the best of the best, resistant to stress and capable of multiple tasks in their work. When they talk to people they look them straight in the eye. Respect is important in their work. They even show perpetrators a limited respect. They are honest men of good character and perfect conduct; psychologically impeccable and intelligent. They have the body of an athlete through constant training; a precondition of their job. Their mission is the discovery and arrest of the more dangerous criminals and terrorists. They carry out operations that we never hear of, and it's because these operations can be so dangerous that we should be constantly concerned for them. However, they don't want this and consequently never speak about these operations, neither to the media, nor to their families or friends.

How Does One Become a Member of a Special Unit?

Their missions are as secret as James Bond would wish, and they are always dangerous. Each time can be the last. But the men and women of the special units know no fear; during an operation there is no time for it. As a result, they are perfectly trained. They will have started their careers as police officers and will be aged around 30. After a few years of police service they will have applied to join a special unit of their nation. The chance comes up once each year. From amongst hundreds of applicants, on average four or five are chosen per country. The best of the best pass the strict selection process lasting several days: physical endurance in sports, marksmanship, memory training and psychological tests, medical examinations, driving tests, interviews with the commanding officer and individual section leaders. Sport and shooting is a condition of the job and easy for those who train hard and have made up their minds to succeed. Not everybody passes the psychological tests, as not everyone is composed and imperturbable. Hysteria and aggression have no place in a special unit. Everything must be decided calmly, deliberately and tactically. During training which, depending on the country, can last up to a year, future members of the special units learn strategy, tactics, endurance, techniques and close combat fighting. Everybody must work daily on their physical deficiencies in the sports hall and work to exceed limitations by a healthy degree. Training is arranged to be as near reality as possible, and as a result accidents are not uncommon. One has to be constantly alert for dangerous moments. Training must never become mere routine for anybody. Members of the special units must be geared up mentally for every mission. Whoever can resist stress and strain is well suited to special unit work. In calmness lies strength, flexibility and endurance. Silent, rapid and efficient. Part of the team. In this calling, the team has great significance. On every mission the team must work together tactically and decisively. Every member of the team must be able to rely on every other member. Nobody goes it alone; the penalty is expulsion. Together the team is strong. They decide together what the next steps shall be. Politicians and company managers could learn something from them.

Women in the Special Units

Several commanders have been responsible for giving women greater importance within the special units. Women are accepted who are especially athletic, pass all acceptance criteria with bravura and can wear 40 kg of clothing and equipment without a grumble. Then they have to prove themselves to their male colleagues on operations. The reality of the team is that women often have to work harder and achieve better qualifications than the men before they will be accepted. Only once they pass this stage will they be recognised as team members.

Emotions in Situations

There can be no sympathy for the perpetrators during an operation. One can attempt to analyse the action taken but never approve of it. Emotions are switched off during an operation. This shows the professionalism of the team members of a special unit. Assimilate what is learned and carry out the task of subduing the perpetrator as quickly as possible; that is the stated aim of every operation. No fatalities are desired. Anxiety seldom appears during an operation, for working with the team provides strength. Nevertheless, caution is always called for on every operation. The unit's psychologists are always on hand for open consultation. These conversations with the psychologists are very important for team members in order to review difficult operations. Alone or in the team. Often a trauma does not appear for several years. Autogenous training and relaxation exercises are important in order to remain physically and mentally at one's best over long periods.

The Debriefing

The line is very thin between success and failure. Elite units are often openly criticised when perpetrators are killed during an operation, but not all the innocent can be saved. However, we cannot ask them for the impossible. These men and women are themselves in danger on every operation. They face extreme situations in which matters too often take an unexpected course. They know the importance of their mission and always strive to complete it to the best of their ability. In order to improve structures and methodology, debriefing meetings are held immediately after every operation in all areas of accountability. Those attending include the commanders and team leaders, down to operational leaders. They go over the details of each case with the unit chief, all taking note of lessons learned that will prove useful on subsequent operations.

Technical Terms on Operations

Through operations, teams arrive at a certain level of automatism. Every member knows his or her function, the task to be resolved and the methods required; additional measures will be ordered by the operational leaders and commanders. For every new situation, however, one may have to adopt a new approach.

In their work, special units employ many technical expressions. They may speak of 'tracking', 'camouflage', the 'platinum ten minutes', 'renegades', 'lawful killing' and 'dirty bombs'. I had these terms explained to me.

'Tracking' means pursuing a moving object.

'Camouflage' means disguise and assuming another identity for an operation.

'Platinum ten minutes' is the period of time after an exchange of fire when paramedics and emergency doctors arrive at the theatre of action; in these first ten minutes 90 per cent of the wounded can be saved.

'Renegades' are aircraft used by aerial pirates in terror attacks.

'Lawful killing' is the understanding that it may be necessary to shoot a perpetrator in order to save lives.

A 'dirty bomb' is one which, when it explodes, sprays radioactive material into the environment.

Never Say 'No': The Work of the Negotiators

In Kevin Spacey's film I took special note of a scene in which the SWAT agent Danny Roman, played by Samuel Jackson, holding out in a Chicago multi-storey building with hostages, told his rather unskilled police colleague Lieutenant Farley by telephone that a negotiator is never allowed to say no. This scene corresponds to reality. There are guidelines for negotiating teams when it comes to having conversations with perpetrators, including rules such as: never affirm or deny; listen, convince and be creative. This is for the initial communication. A good negotiator is all ears, the technical term being 'active listening'. He takes note of the tempo of speech, the intonation and nuances in the voice, the content of what is being reported, the intensity of the aggression or the calmness of his opposite number. Only in this way is it possible for the team of psychologists to assess the perpetrator and communicate information to the operational leaders. The most important things in negotiating are creativity and richness of ideas in order to find flexible solutions, because every perpetrator and every solution to a situation is different. The negotiator must never play a role or use empty phrases; he must be himself. The magic formula is 'be authentic'. Negotiating goes to the substance of a person. Therefore emotions must be discarded and 'the heart separated from the head'. The most important thing is and remains the task in hand; to solve the situation in an orderly manner, without fatalities, and achieve the release of all hostages.

Criminal Surveillance

The work of a surveillance team slightly resembles that of the spy; shadowing people and documenting in writing all movements of the target, with photographs, daily routine and all contacts which he may have. Often the surveillance team will have to adopt a disguise and follow perpetrators in specially modified vehicles in order to remain unobserved themselves, and so perform their task unobtrusively; they may be in a tourist camper, in a 'Smith's Installations Ltd' van that remains parked up all day, an innocent motorist refuelling at a petrol station, or a loving couple kissing in a car. Camouflage is everything. It must not be exaggerated or that will be spotted; it must remain realistic.

Snipers are always Prepared

Precision marksmen (snipers) in special units are not killing machines. Their job is rather to monitor the location of an incident from a high point and provide their colleagues with all necessary information for a perfect operation. The sniper will be patient, have a steady hand, and eyes which miss nothing. Most of all he is a good observer. Generally he will lurk on the roof of a building or in a flat on the opposite side of the street, together with a second colleague. Both will be in contact by radio with the operational team. The telescopic sight on the rifle and binoculars provide the best view of an event and give their colleagues cover. Important information: every situation has a chaotic phase in which even the perpetrator is not yet fully organised and at first barricades himself against the police. One round is sufficient to deprive the perpetrator of his power.

Security for Popes, Kings and Politicians

Amongst the more stressful duties for members of a special unit is personal protection. Whether a pope is coming, a member of a royal house or a high-ranking politician, first of all the degree of risk must be assessed and advised. The ranking is:

1. The person is in substantial danger, and an assassination attempt may be made.
2. The person is in danger, an assassination attempt cannot be ruled out.
3. Danger to the person cannot be ruled out.

Once the degree of risk is decided upon, the subject is never alone for a second after arriving in the host country. A watch is always maintained for would-be assassins. The surroundings are kept under constant surveillance by members of the special unit who have sight of each other and keep contact in this way. The protected person will always be followed visually, so that at any anxious moment he/she can be evacuated immediately.

High Tech in Every Situation

Terrorists often believe that they possess the most up-to-date technologies in order to frighten a country or politician, or inflict harm. This reckoning omits the special units, for self-evidently all of today's units are equipped with state-of-the-art technology in order to complete their assignments successfully. Moreover, cooperation exists with the most advanced development laboratories worldwide in order to stay ahead of the criminals. There are robots for every situation: GPS systems for navigation and marking of targets, as well as night-sight equipment. Using a special network system, operational leaders, psychologists and negotiating teams can obtain extensive information about the perpetrator(s), from family illness to the most recent telephone calls or e-mails and much else besides.

ATLAS – The European Anti-Terror Network

The need for better trained special units in Europe was identified during the 1972 Olympic Games in Munich, when attempts to free competitors of the Israeli Olympic team who were kidnapped by Palestinian terrorists resulted in a fatal outcome.

After this spectacular seizure of hostages, the majority of European nations decided to create their own special domestic force to be integrated into the military or police. In 1996, in order to avoid similar terrorist attacks in Europe in the future, the Council of the European Union decided for the first time to set up its own network, whose aim would be to bring the counter-terrorist units of each nation to the highest level of professionalism through intensive cooperation. After the Twin Towers attack in New York on 11 September 2001, at an extraordinary session of Interpol, the European Council arranged to take full control over such incidents in the future. At the same session the leading police chiefs were requested to organise and coordinate the cooperation of international anti-terrorist units. This led to the creation of the ATLAS networks with an initial fifteen member States. Until 2008, the Belgian unit DSU and the Austrian unit EKO-COBRA had the Presidency and Vice-Presidency. It's name comes from Greek mythology, in which the Titan Atlas carried the world on his shoulders. Its motto is 'All together to protect you'.

Over the years, ATLAS has become an informal network for cooperation between the special units of the European Union, as well as an informal association consisting of the police units of twenty-eight EU nations with a total of thirty-six units. These special units train regularly with one another in the framework of the European ATLAS Cooperation Agreement, so that all countries in Europe can guarantee their citizens protection of equal value. The network exchanges proven practices and procedures between nations.

Worldwide Operations

The security measures for the 2012 Olympic Games in London were planned meticulously for over three years. Every detail, every possible terrorist scenario was tested by the Metropolitan Police, from kidnapped hostages to bombings. The members of the British special unit SCO19, some of whose members were included in the organisational committee, left nothing to chance. Every possible horror scenario was taken into consideration and the appropriate counter-strategies practised for weeks. Over 40,000 security men, including 13,500 soldiers and 10,000 police officers (of which 1,000 were members of special units), were active between 25 July and 12 August 2012 in the Olympic zones. For the protection of the sporting teams, numerous working members of the special units posed as sportsmen and lived in the Olympic Village over the summer.

This kind of information fascinated me. Security at major events where politicians and members of royal houses are present – preferred targets for assassination attempts – is of great importance today. Consequently, I got into the special unit's operational vehicle wearing my 40 kg apparel to find out what was it like to take part in an operation. How organised was the work of these men and women?

The black van left the headquarters of the special unit and picked up speed. The speedometer read 120 km/hr. I knew what awaited us. While I trembled a little with excitement, I heard the others talking. I observed how they conducted themselves; they were calm and businesslike. Like scholars having to solve a difficult mathematical problem. I knew that I had invaded the holy of holies. I alone was tense. The men and women who had sat near me in the van and put on their masks exhibited no emotion. They were totally concentrated [on the matter in hand]. Their eyes shone, their whole attention was focused on the 'situation', a mission. Only occasionally did a smile flicker across their lips. They are highly professional, already planning in the vehicle the first steps to be taken on the mission. It is winter and we drink tea. That is to say, I drink tea. To calm myself. The others brood over their plans for the situation and mission. Within thirty-five minutes we are at the operational location.

I have crossed three continents to interview various special units. I have gone with them on training exercises, have seen how they prepare for operations, how they interact amongst themselves and with others, even how they train their dogs. I observed how nimbly and skilfully they climb high walls, for which even the legendary mountain climber Reinhold Messner would have respect for them. I saw them abseil down from towers and helicopters, silently, impeccably, tactically perfect. That is also their mantra. What follows now is what special units really experience on their operations...

"You? You want something? From me? You think killing a man gives you the power to negotiate with me? Why is that, Danny Roman? Cause you think you know me? Because you think you can trust me? Because you think you know what I'm going to do? That I'm gonna give you time? Don't you fucking count on it. Right now, I'm the only thing standing between you and an army that is just itching to walk in here and take you out. So, you tell me something, Danny: why should I get in their way? Ha? Make me believe, why I should deal with you ever again."

Kevin Spacey as Lieutenant Chris Sabian, *The Negotiator*, 1998

"I'm reading the eyes. The eyes can't lie. Didn't you know, what I was doing? A quick lesson in lying. See, this is what us real cops do. We study liars. Example: If I ask you a question about something visual, like your favorite colour, your eyes go up and to the left. Neurophysiology tells us your eyes go in that direction because you're accessing the visual cortex. So you're telling the truth. If your eyes go up and right, then you're accessing the brain's creative centres and we know you're full of shit. Now, let's try this again."

Samuel Jackson as Lieutenant Danny Roman, *The Negotiator*, 1998

Chapter 1

United Kingdom

Crime Scene on the Thames

Unit: SCO19 – Central Operation Specialist Firearms Command
(formerly known as SO19 and CO19)
Motto: *Legibus et Armis* = By Using Laws and Arms

Raid on the Provisional IRA

It had been raining for hours; a typical April day in London. All
parking places in the Lugard Road were occupied. In one of the many
cars washed by the rain, the passenger's side-window of a bright but
insignificant small car was lowered. A man in a black leather jacket
and black cap looked up cautiously, but with concentration, at a long
brick two-storey building with a front garden in bloom. When a head
suddenly appeared from the topmost window, the man aimed his camera
and pressed the shutter button. "That's it, we can go," he told his driver.
The car pulled away from 61 Lugard Road, Southwark, London SW1
and headed for Peckham. As they left, a dark, insignificant small car
took the parking space.

For months, Scotland Yard and MI5 (the British Secret Service) had
sent surveillance teams to this address to shadow the gang that was
holding out there, and to gather as much intelligence on them as possible.
On 14 April 1996 the watchers had completed their task and compiled a
comprehensive file on the movements of the suspects in and around the
location, and a good deal of information on the six men who lived there.
The suspects were members of one of the most radical terrorist groups of
the time and believed to be planning their next coup. Sixty-one Lugard
Road had three bedrooms and a roof terrace, but the six men, all in their
thirties, rarely left the house. They kept their heads down, which made
surveillance work difficult. Nevertheless, there were ways and means for

the surveillance teams to find out what the six men were up to behind closed doors.

Special unit SCO19 had been co-opted into the surveillance, and coordinated on a roster with colleagues from 'central', after it had been determined that the next attack by the Provisional IRA (the paramilitary organization which came into being in 1969 from the split with the IRA) was intended to paralyse the entire energy infrastructure of southern England through a bombing campaign, and the planners lived at 61 Lugard Road.

SCO19's plan was to invade the terrorists' dwelling house and arrest the six men. Great caution was required during the operation since it was not known how much explosive was to be found at the crime scene and in what form. Furthermore, there was no information available as to whether or not the house was being used as a storage depot for the explosives.

The concrete preparations for the operation were made on the night of 14 April. Fifty SCO19 members got ready to arrest the six Provisional IRA terrorists, glorified by their supporters as 'The Army'. The SCO19 team was made up of an advance and intervention party, explosives experts, technicians and dog-handlers. For safety reasons, SCO19 intended to enter the house via the windows, as it seemed probable that the front door would have been booby-trapped. The bomb experts gave very important advice to their colleagues not to use dazzle grenades, because it was not known if any unconventional explosives were stored in the house and to what extent the house might be prepared for, and protected against, entry. The leadership team therefore decided to surprise the terrorists in the early hours with tear gas.

At 4.00 am on 15 April 1996, the members of SCO19, wearing full working dress with face-masks and armed with Glock pistols and shotguns, climbed the outer walls of the house at 61 Lugard Road and then smashed the double-glazed windows. After tear gas grenades had been tossed inside, the men of SCO19 headed for the bedrooms with flanking cover while the house was surrounded and the street sealed off and guarded.

The six IRA terrorists were still asleep when SCO19 broke in. When they woke to the noise, the tear gas was having its effect and they could hardly see for the irritation. The gas also affected the nasal passages and lungs. It was an easy task for the SCO19 men to arrest the six men. They were led away immediately for interrogation at Metropolitan Police HQ.

Together with the Bomb Squad, the unit's bomb experts and the sniffer dogs combed through the whole house and cellars in search of any explosives which were to have blown up southern England, according to the IRA's plans. In the cellar directly below the house, the special unit discovered thirty-seven large wooden boxes containing material for bomb manufacturing, including batteries, electrical wires and detonators.

The police searched in vain in 7,000 closed garages and similar places of storage in South London for the 133 kg of plastic explosive to be used to paralyze London's supply of energy and electricity, but it was never found. Instead, the police came across around forty stolen cars and drugs amounting to an estimated value of £1 million.

The trial took place in June 1997 when one of the IRA leaders charged, 38-year-old Gerard Hanratty, explained that it had been impossible for the police to find any explosives because there were none. The IRA plan was to make bomb mock-ups using icing sugar which looked like plastic explosive when a light was shone through it. The idea was that the British authorities themselves would shut off the power so that their bomb experts could investigate the mock-ups thinking they had to be disarmed. Hanratty declared that the IRA had no reason to prejudice the peace talks with Northern Ireland that were being held at that time by setting off a massive bomb.

Hanratty's defensive ploy was not sufficiently convincing, and at the end of the fifty-six-day trial, an aggregate sentence of 210 years' imprisonment was handed down.

The Theft of the Millennium Dome Diamonds – 2000

It was to have been the world's greatest-ever diamond robbery with a perfect plan and a well-rehearsed team. But it turned out to be the greatest operation of the British special unit SCO19.

In the 1990s, the British Government, under the leadership of Prime Minister John Major, had signed a contract for the building of the biggest dome in the world in London. It was to be called the 'Millennium Dome' and its purpose was to create a worthy monument to celebrate the next 1,000 years.

Thus a structure resembling a UFO, which remains one of the world's largest domes, came to be built on the Greenwich Peninsula, a spit of land south-east of London on a bend in the River Thames, with the river on three sides. On 1 January 2000, the modern building was opened with the

'Millennium Experience Exhibition'. In fourteen different zones, numerous high-range sponsors displayed their products.

For this special occasion, De Beers, the greatest diamond dealer and producer in the world, had had a glass wall made, behind which many large and small diamonds were to be displayed. This included the Millennium Star which, at 203.4 karats, was the second largest diamond in the world, with an estimated value of £200 million. The glass wall was the most costly security measure ever envisaged and could withstand being hit by a blow of 60 tons force.

In the late summer of 2000, Scotland Yard received a tip-off from an informant that a very well-organised gang of thieves was planning to rob the Millennium Dome. A year before, the police had frustrated two major robberies at Nine Elms in South London and another in Kent. Each time brute force had been used by the robbers. They were heavily armed and used lorries in which they transported Christmas trees fitted with iron parts for use as battering rams. The gang escaped using speed boats to cross the Thames. A little later police found a lorry from which they were able to identify the would-be robbers, and they kept the plot of land where they had made their find under surveillance. The CID discussed this gang in connection with the tip-off. One of their colleagues had visited the Millennium Dome recently and suggested, "Perhaps they are after the Millennium Star." Since it was a possibility, the CID began its investigations there.

On 1 September 2000, Kent CID identified their three suspects as Lee Wenham, Raymond Betson and William Cockram. They were seen at the exhibition making videos of the display. It was immediately clear to detectives that the exhibition – and particularly the De Beers glass wall – was the main attraction and would be the gang's next target. From then on the three suspects and the Millennium Dome were placed under 24-hour surveillance while the CID requested De Beers to replace the diamonds with worthless imitations.

During the surveillance of the suspects, the CID discovered a fourth accomplice; Terry Millman, who was responsible for obtaining the speedboat. When Cockram and Betson were seen filming the Thames and the boats travelling on it, the surveillance was intensified. The suspects were often seen by the CID touring the Millennium Dome and taking photographs and, at the end of September, they were also observed making a test run with a speedboat in a Kent harbour.

Soon after, the London CID discovered the date for the coup. The date in October was communicated to De Beers and the management of the

Millennium Dome, but had to be postponed, however, when on the day in question the speedboat had engine trouble. The next date set was abandoned after the gang discovered that the tide at the planned hour would be too low for a fast getaway. The CID team were not idle during this time, and in view of the coup being imminent, as a precaution all Millennium Dome employees were replaced by armed undercover police officers. At the beginning of November, gang members were seen anchoring the speedboat at the chosen spot; an indication for the police that the robbery would soon be attempted. Furthermore, it was noted that the suspects were not only interested in the tides, but also the height of the water. The robbery of the century would have to take place when the tide and water level coincided with each other and were just right. The date would be 7 November 2000.

The CID operation was code-named Operation Magician and was led by Detective Superintendent Jon Shatford of the Metropolitan Police. Two hundred police officers were present in and around the Millennium Dome that day, including forty officers from special unit SCO19 and another sixty armed specialists from the Flying Squad, a branch of the Serious Organised Crime Command in the Metropolitan Police. Around twenty officers were positioned on the Thames to intervene should an attempt be made to escape across the river. Other officers were present in the Dome itself. The Dome control room had been taken over temporarily by the police as a tactical and strategic operations room.

The CID and SCO19 officers were briefed regarding the operation at 3.00 am on 7 November. Some of them posed as cleaners in the passageway that contained the imitation De Beers diamond collection behind the armoured glass wall, their arms hidden in cleaning buckets. Others were disguised as the Dome's general staff. Each officer had a precise role, took up their place in a pre-determined position in the Dome, and observed. The team functioned perfectly, cooperating at every step and communicating the situation constantly through ear-microphones.

At 9.30 am the time was ripe for the greatest jewellery heist of all time. Four members of the gang, dressed in protective clothing and wearing gas masks, were aboard a JCB digger with smoke bombs, sledgehammer and nail guns. The digger was to break through the fence and doors into the Dome and penetrate towards the 'money zone' in which the De Beers collection was supposed to be located. The raiders threw smoke bombs to the ground ahead of themselves and spread an ammonia solution.

It was William Cockram's job to fire at the glass wall with a Hilti nail pistol, after which his accomplice Robert Adams would use the hammer to smash the glass and steal the diamonds. They didn't get this far as members of SCO19 surrounded the gang in the vault. "The game is over, gentlemen. Come up at once and surrender," an SCO19 officer called out.

The four robbers were astonished to be confronted by twenty men dressed in dark blue overalls wearing protective helmets and carrying rifles. Within a few seconds they accepted the situation and gave in without resistance, laying on the ground covered by the armed officers. "Well, you reckoned without us, didn't you?" a member of SCO19 said to the robbers. Robert Adams could not help saying, "I was only 12 inches away from payday. That would have been a very happy Christmas."

"Hard luck, old man," came the reply.

SCO19 arrested the four men and brought them away from the Millennium Dome. Two other accomplices were arrested, one aboard the getaway speedboat on the Thames and the other in a car waiting on the north side of the river listening to the police frequency. Terry Millman was stopped in his van and also brought in for questioning with the others. The Dome was re-opened to the public at midday. As a result of statements made by the men in custody, a further six accomplices aged between 38 and 62 were arrested in the small town of Collier Street, Kent, and at Horsmonden.

Liz Lynch, spokesperson for De Beers, later stated that the diamonds had been substituted by fakes made of crystal after the CID notified the owners of the intended robbery. She said it would have been very difficult to sell the real diamonds because the international diamond market was small, easily monitored and everybody knew everybody else. The jewels had the value of the Mona Lisa or a Van Gogh and nobody would have bought them, for the collection was beyond price.[1]

The Kidnapping of Victoria Beckham – 2002

It happened in the year when the British singer Victoria Beckham, former Spice Girl and better known under the name 'Posh Spice', signed her £1.5-million contract with Telstar Records in order to give her solo career a boost. 2002 was to have been a super year. She was working feverishly on her latest single *Let Your Head Go/This Groove* while her husband, footballer David Beckham, had his best season with Manchester United, scoring sixteen goals in forty-eight matches.

Following the death of Princess Diana, the married couple rose to be the most-photographed personalities in Great Britain. Their every step was followed by a host of paparazzi. The more successful they became, the more journalists wanted to know about them and finally followed them across the whole country. The two superstars had almost no free time to themselves. They hired two bodyguards, but continued to be pursued by the British media. They often received death threats and were constantly beset by admirers.

At the end of October 2002, Mazher Mahmood, investigative reporter for the tabloid newspaper *News of the World*, received a tip-off that a criminal gang from Eastern Europe was planning to kidnap a prominent British woman and her children. Mahmood, who researched under the cover name Sheikh Mahmood, had been behind the prosecution of around 100 arms and drug dealers, paedophiles and killers. He put his team of reporters on the story and also informed Scotland Yard. He was known to work closely with the police. It was agreed with his co-workers that they should pose as crooks in order to infiltrate the Eastern European criminal gang. This required a certain amount of preparation.

The reporters created fictitious personal histories in which they featured as criminals. In these histories, a man was mentioned serving a life sentence at Manchester high security prison who would serve as a reference. This prisoner, a contact of *The News of the World,* was in on the secret and in the case of an enquiry by the criminal gang he was to confirm the information requested. One of the reporters was alleged to be an experienced driver of getaway cars, while another reporter was said to be 'a wealthy crook'.

Mazher Mahmood had been informed that a member of the criminal gang always carried a gun.

Therefore, any meeting with the gang might end in disaster for his colleagues. He told them of the danger and warned them emphatically to be watchful in the presence of the kidnappers and not allow the slightest suspicion to arise as to their true identities.

The gang consisted of two groups: four men and one woman from Romania, and three men with one woman from Albania. The 'wealthy crook' reporters met with the gang leaders, Albanian Luli Azem Krifsha and Romanian Jay Sorin, several times to discuss details of the kidnappings. It was immediately clear that these men were very serious about abducting the ex-Spice Girl: "We shall bring Victoria and her two sons, Brooklyn and Romeo, to a safe house in Brixton and wait there until the money arrives in our overseas account," Luli Krifsha stated. Jay Sorin briefed the infiltrated reporters: "If the children are with you that will be much better, as then

7

we can ask for £5 million immediately from the husband. He must pay the full amount and if he doesn't, then he will never see his family again and Victoria will die."

At these conspiratorial conferences the question repeatedly arose as to how far the gang wanted to go with the abduction. The difficult thing, so they said, was not kidnapping Victoria Beckham, but getting the ransom into their bank account. "What I don't understand is why she has such poor security. One of my friends works for her hairdresser and he told me that she only has one bodyguard standing outside." The plan was to ambush her as she was returning to her parking place after leaving the hairdressers, and to use a special chloroform spray they had bought in Italy which worked in three seconds. This was explained by Luli Krifsha to the others.

At a subsequent meeting with the kidnappers at the end of October, the Beckham's house and its surroundings at Sawbridgeworth in Hertfordshire were closely reconnoitered. This study was part of months-long surveillance of the couple. "We only have three seconds before she understands what's happening," Jay Sorin whispered to the others. A few days later the six men met again at a restaurant in Wandsworth, south-west London. "I'm going to relieve Beckham of £5 million, which is the same to him as paying fifty pence for a coffee," Krifsha said that day.

After each meeting with the criminals, the two journalists would inform Mazher Mahmood who passed the information to Scotland Yard. The day for the crime had been selected as Saturday, 2 November 2002. The CID specialists who dealt with serious offenses and organized crime, known internally as the 'Flying Squad', received information as to where the two gangs were hiding out.

One group was in Docklands, east London, the other at Morden, a district in south-west London.

The kidnappers were arrested in three raids. One raid carried out by armed men from the Flying Squad took place on a Saturday morning, the second in the afternoon and the third on the Sunday morning. On both days the kidnappers were in the process of loading chloroform sprays and weapons into their vans prior to driving to Sawbridgeworth, when they were surrounded by members of the special unit. "Police, hands up. You are surrounded. Get out of the vehicles slowly," the Squad's commander said. The kidnappers were totally surprised when they saw the arresting officers' dark blue uniforms and helmets with visors and quietly raised their hands. The two reporters maintained their aliases, posing as arrestees and following the Flying Squad's instructions.

"Damn, how could they have found us? How did they know where we were and what we were planning?" was the repeated incredulous question of the kidnappers. The police officers made no comment during the arrests.

The men and women were handcuffed and led quickly away to the Black Maria which would take them immediately to police headquarters. There the seven criminals were placed at the disposal of the investigators.

Victoria Beckham, who on the Saturday afternoon attended a football match at Old Trafford in which her husband was playing, had been informed of the raids in advance by Scotland Yard, but had decided not to tell her husband until after the game. After the arrests, the Beckhams increased their security precautions in collaboration with the police and Manchester United football club. Ever since, the former Spice Girl, her husband and four children have always been accompanied by twelve bodyguards, whatever their destination.

7/7: The Terror Attacks on London and their Consequences – 2005

The London Metropolis is much loved by the British people, but also by tourists from all over the world. Thirty million people come each year, six million alone in the summer months of July and August, for the cultural variety and the sights. July 2005 will always be specially remembered by the British, however, for in that month there occurred in London the hitherto worst terrorist outrage in British history, which led to other incidents and to a terrorist alarm remaining in force in the whole country for some considerable time.

The tragedy began on the morning of 7 July 2005. Shortly before 9.00 am explosions occurred aboard three moving London Underground trains at Liverpool Street, Edgware Road and King's Cross St. Pancras, set off by Islamic suicide bombers. The rucksack bomb which exploded at Liverpool Street claimed seven lives, while another six died in the Edgware Road explosion. The third bomb exploded on a Piccadilly Line train in a tunnel between King's Cross and Russell Square, killing twenty-six. Another thirteen people were killed when a bomb exploded onboard a No.30 double-decker bus at Tavistock Square at 9.47 am. On this day a total of 700 people were injured and 56 killed (including the four bombers). Many passengers were trapped in the damaged trains until the afternoon. All Britain was in a state of shock.

The suspected perpetrators of the terrorist attacks, Hasi Hussain, Shehzad Tanweer, Mohammad Sidique Khan and Germaine Lindsay had – unusually for suicide bombers – parking permits and return tickets, as well as carrying personal documents by which they were later identified. In a video claiming responsibility, Khan blamed the Labour Government of Tony Blair and British society in general for the attacks. His terrorist cell was mounting a war against democratic British society. He said he was a soldier.

The London attacks were given the abbreviation 7/7, borrowing from 9/11, the terrorist attacks on 11 September 2001 in the United States. As from 7 July 2005, Britain was in a state of high alert for those travelling by bus or on the Underground. Every day in London 3 million people use the Tube, another million take the bus to work. People taking public transport every day wondered what the Government could do in order to prevent such attacks. The police urged constant watchfulness. At a stroke, London life had changed: "You see somebody on the Underground who looks suspicious and you become uneasy that something might be about to happen. You realise that you're in the Underground and in the worst case scenario there is going to be no help," was a typical reply to media questions.

The Metropolitan Police and Scotland Yard turned their energies to investigating terrorist cases in order to find the suspects of an Islamic cell. Some arrests were made in subsequent weeks but the next attack was imminent.

On 9 July Birmingham city centre was evacuated following a bomb threat. Three suspects were arrested based on a video tape and statement by witnesses in Leeds and West Yorkshire after a raid on 12 July. The same day, 600 inhabitants of Burley (near Leeds) were evacuated from their homes for two days after a police tip-off led to several hidden bombs being found in areas of the city.

On 21 July, a fortnight after the initial terrible attack, the horror was repeated in the capital. On this occasion too, three Underground trains were the target of terrorists. Towards 12.30 pm detonators exploded simultaneously in the stations at Shepherd's Bush, Warren Street and at the Oval, Northern Line station, but not the bombs themselves. The explosions were much like fireworks, a small detonation and a lot of smoke, but this time no dead or injured. Passengers aboard the trains could be evacuated quickly. Some Underground lines, the Victoria Line, Northern Line, Hammersmith & City Line and the Piccadilly Line, were closed down for the day.

As with the 7/7 attack, there was a fourth explosion onboard a bus, a No.26 from Waterloo to Hackney Wick. Nobody was hurt. In contrast to 7 July, rescue services were quickly on the scene. Since the bomb did not go off, nobody was injured. Passers-by noticed that some men near the rucksacks containing the bombs had ran off. According to witness statements, one of the men appeared to be injured. Other witnesses reported smelling burning rubber. Although officials feared a chemical attack, on closer analysis it was determined that this must have been the odour of the explosive and no chemical weaponry had been used.

At 2.30 pm, University College Hospital was the destination for an SCO19 operation when, according to later eye-witness reports, around thirty members of the team were seen in pursuit of a fleeing man identified as a suicide bomber along Tottenham Court Road and into the hospital. A mail sent by Intranet ordered the entire team to search for a man of colour, possibly of Asiatic origin, 6'1" in height, wearing a blue top from which fine wires were seen projecting. Finally three rooms at University College Hospital were sealed off. The man was discovered in a passageway and arrested. He was held at the hospital for questioning for two hours by SCO19 men and then taken off to a police station by police jeep.

A second arrest was made the same day at 3.30 pm in Whitehall, near the Defence Ministry, when members of the special unit detained another suspect in the middle of the street. Encircled by police from the special unit he was ordered to, "Lay down on the ground slowly and put your hands slowly behind you." The event occurred 20 yards from Downing Street. Once handcuffed, the officers led the suspected terrorist away, unnoticed by passers-by.

The police had their hands full investigating the terrorist attacks. Their research, analysis and investigations were demanding and had to be as comprehensive as possible. From the beginning of July, immediately following 7/7, the search widened. The British intelligence network had discovered that other members of the terrorist cell were hiding out in London. The main focus fell on the four suspects who had set off the devices which had failed to explode fully in the London Underground and on a No.26 bus on 21 July. In this case the suicide bombers had escaped with their lives. There now began the greatest hue and cry in British history.

On 22 July a clue came to light; a membership card for a fitness studio found in a rucksack of one of the bombers gave an address in Scotia Road, Tulse Hill, a suburb of south London. A team was sent there at once to carry out surveillance.

That same morning, Jean Charles de Menezes, an electrician who lived in Scotia Road with his cousins, had to travel urgently to Kilburn in north-west London to repair the alarm installation of a Fire Brigade station. He set off at 9.30 am and once on the street was identified in company with three other men, of Somali, Eritrean or Ethiopian appearance, by the surveillance team.

One of the officers compared a photo of the bomber from a surveillance camera in London with de Menezes. He was of the opinion that de Menezes and the bomber were one and the same person, and followed him, but did not send a video of the suspect to his colleagues from Gold Command, the division of the Metropolitan Police which intervenes in catastrophe situations. On the basis of the officer's information, Gold Command authorised the surveillance officers to follow the suspect, but to prevent him going down into the Underground.

Plain-clothes officers now followed the suspect to the No.2 bus stop at Tulse Hill. He caught a bus and alighted at Brixton Underground station. When he saw that the station was still closed after the bomb scare the previous day, he made a brief telephone call and took the next No.2 bus to Stockwell Underground station. Meanwhile, the detectives shadowing him reported to their base that de Menezes – because of his appearance – was apparently one of the bombers being sought and bore a striking resemblance to the suspect reported to have 'Mongolian-looking eyes'. At some time the same morning, the detectives contacted Gold Command again. They received an 'Alarm Stage Red' which amounted to instructions to detain the man before he did anything, and SCO19 was also notified to send men to Stockwell Underground station. The local police now sealed the zone for a radius of 200 yards around the station.

At about 10 am de Menezes went into the station, took a free newspaper from the stand, bought a ticket, went through the turnstiles and took the lift to the platform. When he got there he ran for the train that was just entering the station. Members of the special unit followed him. He got into the carriage and occupied the first free seat. One of the three special unit officers ordered his colleague to, "Get on the train."

Calling out to the passengers, "Get off the train, quickly!" they took the suspect in their sights and told him, "Police. Show us your hands at once." The rucksack bombers had detonated the explosives attached to their belt by hand. While one of the officers blocked the train door, his colleagues covered the suspect with their rifles and told him to raise his hands. "I will do it," he replied. "If you don't do it, we will shoot you," he was told.

Jean Charles de Menezes was confused. The police were in civilian clothing. What would they want of him? He was just a simple electrician. At that moment he must have risen instinctively from his seat and gone for his jeans and belt, perhaps to adjust his trousers. Whatever he did, the special unit interpreted it as a movement to set off a bomb and immediately shot him. He was hit by eleven rounds of hollow-point bullets, which leave a mushroom-shaped opening in the body. The police closed the station and the emergency services, including a hospital service helicopter, arrived to attend to the seriously wounded suspect. The emergency doctor and his team did all they could, but de Menezes died while still at the Underground station. His body was later taken to pathology.

The following day the forensic pathologist determined that Jean Charles de Menezes, a native of Brazil, had not been one of the terrorists sought and was also not carrying a bomb. He was therefore another victim of the London bombers. The tragedy muddied the reputation of the Metropolitan Police and the members of the special unit for some time. A breakdown in the relationship between Great Britain and Brazil was a consequence, the man's family didn't know where to turn to and even the Muslim Council in England declared in interviews their dismay at the way this 'saving salvoes' policy had its unfortunate end.

The same day a mosque in Whitechapel Road was evacuated after a bomb warning was given during afternoon prayers. Nobody was hurt and the police later gave the all-clear. On the afternoon of 22 July, Scotland Yard acted on information they had received and launched several raids on houses in London. In Harrow Road, West London, near Paddington main line station, members of SCO19 defused a bomb using a specially-designed robot. On 25 July, bomb-making material was found during a police raid on a house at Ladderswood Way, New Southgate, in the north of London. Two suspects were arrested in the surrounding area.

The most important raids were carried out on 29 July in Notting Hill and North Kensington. Well-prepared in advance, the special unit acted on information from the Secret Service obtained from telephone tapping and the movement of terrorists.

In the early hours of 29 July, the special unit sealed off the two areas and evacuated the surrounding buildings. The team was in full intervention gear including gas masks and assault rifles. One hundred Metropolitan Police officers were also present. The suspects, who were asleep in the house, were ordered by megaphone to come out with their hands raised. At North Kensington one of the suspects shouted back, "We are British citizens and have our rights." Since the suspects did not obey the order, the SCO19 team used explosives to blow down the front door and enter. The special unit now had free access into the house where they arrested two suspects. Several small explosions were heard coming from inside; tear gas was also used.

At Notting Hill one of the terrorists, still in his underwear, entered into a discussion with the special unit: "How do I know what you really want with me? How do I know you're not going to shoot me?" The members of the special unit assured him: "As long as you follow our instructions and don't threaten anybody or ourselves, everything will be OK. Simply come out as you are, then we'll be sure that you aren't going to kill anybody and you've got no bombs on you." Meanwhile plain-clothes detectives monitored every step made by their SCO19 colleagues.

Three men arrested that day in London were amongst the bombers responsible for the second terrorist act; Yassin Hassan Omar, Ibrahim Mukta Said and Ramzi Mohammed were led away in handcuffs. A fourth accomplice, Osman Hussein, was arrested in Rome by the Italian special unit NOCS. All four men were tried at Woolwich Crown Court on 15 July 2007.

The Death of Terry Nicholas – 2007

The house with the noble address Huxley Gardens, Ealing, NW10 in West London was a typical suburban dwelling, with white window frames, a small front garden and a large garden at the rear with apple trees. On Friday, 20 April 2007 Terry Nicholas was not at home, but his wife and son were in the kitchen baking. When they heard the sound of breaking glass they ran into the living room. Seeing the broken window and a hole in the wall, they called the police. MPS Operation Trident, the jurisdiction of which lay in the area of armed criminality, sent two officers at once.

On Sunday, 22 April Terry Nicholas was standing with two MPS Operation Trident officers on the pavement in front of his house discussing the events of the previous Friday evening, when a stranger approached and opened fire at Terry Nicholas. He was hit four times. The stranger, 24-year old Jermaine Biddulph, ran to his vehicle and drove off. Terry Nicholas was taken to hospital, but the bullet-proof vest he wore had stopped all four rounds. His injuries were minor.

From this day on, his family were given several liaison officers to look after their safety but Terry Nicholas sent them away, observing, "I will deal with the man in my own way." Why he had been shot at remained a mystery for the police. However, through the Secret Service they discovered that Nicholas had asked a friend from the criminal underworld called Theo to get him a gun to protect himself or wreak revenge. The gun was allegedly to change hands on the afternoon of 15 May in the Italian Restaurant, 'Paolo' at Hanger Green, not far from the Nicholas family home.

Detectives immediately put together a unit of armed officers to observe Nicholas and his family. The team was supported by members of the special unit SCO19, who would intervene at the handover of the weapon and arrest Nicholas. The officers completed a risk analysis beforehand to weigh up the weak points of the operation and determine whether it would endanger members of the public. As a result, the SCO19 tactical unit was co-opted into the operation. Six options were examined, five of which were discarded and the following tactic adopted; the action would be carried out by armed SCD11 officers who would keep the man under surveillance. The role of SCO19 was to provide armed support.

At 8 pm Terry Nicholas arrived with his wife, Alida, and son at the restaurant. The family ate a relaxed meal. In the meantime, the officers had discovered that the family was planning to emigrate to Italy and start a new life there. At 9 pm a man arrived at the restaurant entrance to meet Nicholas. There was an excited conversation which the two men continued at the rear exit, where they disappeared behind a door. A quarter of an hour later Nicholas returned to his table to rejoin his family as though nothing had happened. The man whom he had spoken with was gone.

At 10 pm his wife and son left the restaurant leaving Nicholas in conversation with friends at the neighbouring table. Then he also left the restaurant to ride home on the motor cycle he had parked outside. He had just turned on its lights when six SCD11 officers and the special unit drove up in two vehicles. Nicholas dismounted and returned swiftly to the restaurant and from there suddenly pointed a gun at the two vehicles.

The SCD11 officers and the special unit looked on in amazement. What they saw was a sock in which a 9 mm Luger CZ 100 was concealed. Terry Nicholas wanted to shoot them with it, believing them to be his enemies arriving to kill him. "This can't be true, he must be crazy," one of the officers said. When they were only 5 yards away from him, one of the officers got out of the vehicle and called to his driver to pull up. At the same moment he heard a shot, felt a bullet whistle past and saw dust whirl up. There was no doubt that the shot had come from where Terry Nicholas was standing.

The SCD11 officer fired back. His colleague also got out of the vehicle intending to approach Nicholas and arrest him when he heard his colleague say, "He's got a gun." Instinctively, the SCD11 officer drew his pistol and fired three rounds. The vehicle with the special unit members was driving about 20 yards behind them. One of them saw that Nicholas was holding a gun and shooting at the officers. The SCO19 man fired six rounds at Terry Nicholas.

The officers ran to Nicholas and tried to resuscitate him. The ambulance service and an ambulance helicopter arrived very quickly but in vain. Terry Nicholas succumbed to his wounds a short while afterwards.

After a six-month inquiry into the Terry Nicholas shooting, Judge Deborah Glass concluded that "there was no evidence of a criminal offence by the officers of the special unit and SCD11." The officers had acted correctly. Jermaine Biddulph, who had fired at Terry Nicholas in the street in April, was arrested in June and upon conviction sentenced to twenty-four years' imprisonment for attempted murder.

The Chandler's Ford Robbery – 2007

The county of Hampshire on the English south coast is a popular holiday destination, with many tourist attractions such as coastal bathing, yachting harbours and even an automobile museum. With a population of 20,000, Chandler's Ford counts as one of the most idyllic communities of Hampshire and is easily accessible as it lies very close to Southampton airport. Chandler's Ford not only has a wonderful landscape, charming houses with beautiful gardens, but in 2007 it was also the target for a brutal robbery that was frustrated by the special unit SCO19.

For some time the Metropolitan Police special unit, the Flying Squad, had been keeping watch on a gang of robbers interested in security trucks carrying cash. They had carried out twenty-one raids at eighteen locations in southern England between Oxford, Bristol, Cambridgeshire, Reading, Croydon, Ipswich and Gloucestershire in the period between April 2006 and September 2007. The police had known of the activities of the gang for eighteen months and now the time had come to put an end to it.

The police knew that weapons had always been carried on these raids and that the gang would react brutally to guards who failed to comply with their instructions. In many areas the gang struck twice and during a robbery repeated at Colchester, Essex, one guard was a victim of violence on both occasions. The gang also rammed a Group 4 van coming from a shopping centre.

The gang leaders had been identified as 35-year-old Mark Nunes and Andrew Markland, 36, two dangerous men who would stop at nothing and would always resort to violence if the situation seemed to demand it. They selected the members for the individual robberies then drew up detailed plans and got to know the area.

The Metropolitan Police detectives listened in to the conversations between the leaders and their accomplices, keeping track of their mobile phones and getting to know and analyse their habits. Detectives noticed that whenever they committed a robbery, they would turn off their mobiles several hours beforehand and only restore them after the raid was over. Possible escape routes were identified and sites pinpointed where a changeover could be made between one vehicle and another.

Metropolitan Police detectives identified the tranquil town of Chandler's Ford and its HSBC branch as the next most likely target for a raid, and a strategy was developed to capture the gang there. It was important not to arrest the gang until there was sufficient evidence, and this was lacking at present.

The date 13 September 2007 was identified for the next raid. In the early hours of the day, the special unit proceeded in several vehicles to Chandler's Ford and took up position on the Bournemouth Road near the HSBC branch. Snipers settled on the roofs of the surrounding houses; the members of the special unit, some in civilian clothing, hid in and around various buildings along the high street, others even in the public toilet located near the bank. SCO19 officers awaited the gang hidden in their vehicles.

At 10 am the dark blue van of cash courier Michael Player parked on a spur road outside the bank on Bournemouth Road. An elderly couple passed, then a young man. The members of the special unit waited patiently. The information was relayed to the team, "The messenger is out again. He will be getting in immediately." Michael Player had collected the full cash box from the vault and was about to get back into his van when Mark Nunes, dressed in bomber jacket and jeans, wearing a black mask and carrying a 9 mm hand gun approached and told him to put down the money. The security man refused: "I won't do it. I'm sorry. I can't." At that, Nunes went up to the money courier and put the gun to his throat.

At that moment the operational leaders gave the order to shoot. The snipers were aiming at Nunes' head and fired, killing him immediately.

17

His weapon fell to the ground and slid near the security van. Nunes' accomplice Andrew Markland ran up, he bent down to retrieve Nunes' weapon and aimed it at the security man. Two shots rang out and Markland too collapsed and fell. The snipers had done their work.

The emergency medical team was quickly on the spot and attempted to revive Nunes and Markland. A third man slipped away apparently unnoticed by the police and sped off in a Volvo.

All help arrived too late for Mark Nunes, who died at the crime scene that had meanwhile been cordoned off with yellow tape bearing the words, "Police Line. Do Not Cross." Suddenly, at least thirty members of the police special unit appeared with machine-pistols. Police wearing protective jackets lined the cordon to keep onlookers away. Forensic staff wearing white protective clothing were also present to begin an analysis of the crime scene.

The seriously-injured Andrew Markland was taken to hospital, but died at midday of his injuries.

The third man who had escaped was later identified as 26-year-old Terence Wallace. A few hours after the incident at Chandler's Ford he was arrested at his address in Raynes Park, South London. Other gang members, including drug dealers Adrian Johnson, Leroy Wilkinson and Victor Iniodu, were also detained. Police discovered £500,000 at their addresses; the proceeds from several robberies.

Cash courier Michael Player told the media: "For the first time in my life I was looking into the muzzle of a gun. I have often wondered if it would be possible to throw myself to one side when I heard the click of the trigger mechanism."

London Westminster Attack: 82 Seconds of Terror – March 2017

It was a cloudy, spring day on 22 March. In London the thermometer rose slowly on this Wednesday afternoon to 9°C, while the sun made an effort to break through the overcast skies. Khalid Masood sat behind the driving wheel of a grey Hyundai Tucson SUV which he had hired a week previously from the Spring Hill Car and Van Hire Enterprise in northern Birmingham. He had informed the receptionist at the Brighton Preston Park Hotel, only ten minutes from the Channel coast, that he was visiting friends in Birmingham. He gave his occupation in the hotel register as 'teacher'. Masood was dressed in black. After lunch he had left his hotel room, climbed into the SUV, and taken the A23 trunk road to London. He had checked in as Khalid Masood and paid by credit card. Over the previous months he had continually changed his name. It was now 12.30 pm. On the radio they were playing Michael Jackson's *Thriller*. He juggled with the sound as he drove on the motorway. He gave a brief contented smile and scratched his forehead in embarrassment.

Masood was born as Adrian Russell Ajao on 24 December 1964, although in the Kent Register the entry read Adrian Russel Elms, his mother's maiden name. Two years after the birth of her son she married. The new man at her side was called Ajao and he adopted Adrian as his own. Adrian had a peaceful childhood. He attended Huntleys School in Tunbridge Wells, Kent, an elementary school for boys. His classmates remembered him as an intelligent, pleasant boy who was interested in sport. He liked to play football and took part in several charity tournaments. He was a very good player and considered one of the best at his school. Adrian was one of those children who are well-liked. In his childhood he had an easy personality and most of the scholars admired him. After he left school, however, his life was put out of joint when he got in with a bad crowd and became a thief and robber. For no explicable reason he lost his temper easily and at the age of nineteen, he went to prison for the first time.

Over the next ten years he seemed to calm down. He began studying at Sussex University for a BA in Economic History. After three years of study he married and had two daughters by his first wife, Jane. He lived with his family in a small, brick-built house with a garden in the village of Northiam, West Sussex. On the road to historic Hastings, it boasts many thatched roofs, orchards, a twelfth century church and roads which wend their way through gentle uplands. Many people there knew him as a man who liked to go into local pubs for a drink and to talk. Frequently, his changeable temperament came to light. One of the locals characterised him as a "right Herbert," meaning a silly or pig-headed character. People recall today that he had the reputation of liking to get into difficulties, but there were no indications then of the imminent catastrophe in March 2017.

Until 2000, Adrian Masood and his wife Jane ran a business selling cleaning materials and household products from Aaron Chemicals, initially from an office they had set up in their house, then later from a rented office in a business park near Bodiam. Masood seems to have played a less important role than his wife and so made a return to crime.

One day a citizen of Northiam was attacked with a knife in the car park near the Crown & Thistle pub. The assailant was Adrian Masood, who attacked a certain Piers Mott for a racist incident in his car. Piers Mott was a well-liked man in the village, who earlier that day had defended one of his co-workers in the presence of Adrian Masood. Adrian had taken what was said the wrong way and began shouting, slitting Mott's cheek with the knife and causing a wound 8 cm long which needed twenty stitches.

Adrian was sentenced to two years' imprisonment for the assault and after this his wife divorced him. Subsequently, Adrian never returned to the small town but settled on the south coast of England at Eastbourne. There he underwent a complete change of personality and took to hard drugs, mostly cocaine. Through his constant training at a fitness studio he had access to anabolics. An Eastbourne electrician got to know Adrian in a pub at Christmas 2001 where he was introduced to him as "Black Ady." He had just been released from prison and had also converted to Islam there. He seemed to have adopted a Jekyll-and-Hyde character and read the Quran constantly.

Most people in Eastbourne who knew him found him to be courteous, but one day in a pub he proved the opposite. He was seated at a table with a beer watching two men playing pool. At some point that evening an argument developed during which Adrian lost control and began to hit out with a pool cue. The men fled from the pub.

Adrian continued taking hard drugs and became increasingly more aggressive, although he was often seen in the company of women. He seemed to like one with pink dyed hair, as did his friends, resulting in Adrian warning his best friend that he would stab him if he stole his girl. In 2003 the threat became reality when he suspected that a stranger had had an affair with her. Adrian went back to prison for six months for assault and battery, inflicting grievous bodily harm and possession of a weapon. During his career Adrian was an inmate of three prisons: Lewes in East Sussex, Wayland in Norfolk and Ford open prison in West Sussex.

In 2004 he married a Pakistani Muslim at Crawley, West Sussex. At the time his surname was Elms, but he now called himself Masood. He spent two years in Jeddah as an English teacher and worked for their civil aviation authority from 2005 to 2006 and again from 2008 to 2009. When he returned to Britain he lived in Birmingham, but also spent time in Luton, Sussex, and in London. These wanderings seem typical of those men who convert to Islam; urgently seeking an opportunity to fit into the Islamic world as part of their effort to live the belief and lifestyle to the full.

Masood also lived in the East End of London with a woman of African roots. His eldest daughter from his first marriage lived with them.

20

Now he sat in a grey SUV driving along the motorway towards London, a journey of less than two hours. The traffic on that day was as heavy as ever. Masood soon found himself in south London. He drove from Southwark to Lambeth and from Kennington Road turned into Westminster Bridge Road. He was holding his mobile phone and while stuck in traffic sent a quick message via What'sApp. After that he concentrated on the traffic, passing the Marlin Waterloo Hotel and the Florence Nightingale Museum before eventually arriving at his target area: Westminster Bridge.

The bridge, built in 1739, is 275 yards long and 28 yards wide, and crosses the Thames resting on seven imposing cast-iron arches. It is painted the same shade of green as the upholstered benches in the nearby House of Commons.

At 2.40 pm he stepped on the accelerator, mounted the footpath parallel to the roadway and drove along it at a speed of 76 mph, giving pedestrians no chance to get clear. In thirty disastrous seconds he left many injured and several dead, amongst them Kurt Cochran, 54, and his wife Melissa, who were the first passersby to be hit by Masood's SUV. Mr Cochran was hurled from the bridge to the steps below, where he died of his injuries. His wife suffered a head injury, a broken leg and a fractured rib, but survived the attack.

Ayashe Frade, 43, was the next victim. She had just left her work as a Spanish language teacher at the DLD College near Westminster Bridge in order to fetch her two daughters from school. Masood ran her down. Leslie Rhodes, 75, a window cleaner and pensioner, was just crossing Westminster Bridge to catch a bus after leaving St. Thomas's Hospital at the south end of the bridge when he was run over by Masood. Andreea Cristea, 31, from Romania, was walking across the bridge with her fiancé, Andrei Burnaz, having made a short stop in London before returning to her home country. The SUV catapulted her over the guard rails and she fell into the Thames. The crew of a passing boat, the *Millennium Diamond*, saw her swimming for her life and brought her aboard using a boat hook. She was taken by a lifeboat for treatment by paramedics, but died fourteen days later in hospital.

More than thirty-five people were injured during Masood's attack, including three Metropolitan Police officers who had just come from an award ceremony. The injuries ranged from cuts and bruises to broken bones and head injuries. One victim lay in a coma for a day.

Countless people fled from the bridge for their lives, but Masood hadn't yet reached his actual target. After devastating the humanity on

Westminster Bridge in 30 seconds, he now crashed the vehicle through the railings of the Houses of Parliament gardens and ran, as if possessed, to the entrance. Guarding the door was Police Constable U-4157 Keith Palmer of the Parliamentary and Diplomatic Protection Squad. He had been in police service for fifteen years, was married and a father, but on this afternoon, unarmed as is the custom of British police, he stood no chance. Masood stabbed him to death using two knives. Seated in his service vehicle, the murder was seen by the bodyguard of Defence Minister Sir Michael Fallon. The bodyguard was armed. He ran from his vehicle shouting at Masood and then shot him in the chest from close range. The entire incident took 82 seconds.

While people ran blindly in all directions for safety, former Army sergeant Tony Davies, a coach with the British Lionhearts boxing team, had seen what happened to PC Palmer and ran to give assistance, but he was knocked flat by panic-stricken members of the public.

The whole area was now closed off for the uncertainty that other assassins might be preparing to attack, and MPs were detained in the Commons for four hours until the all-clear was given. Prime Minister Theresa May was brought from the lobby and, under the instructions of senior officers at Scotland Yard, was escorted by her bodyguards to a silver Jaguar which conveyed her to Downing Street. Besides PC Palmer, who died where he was attacked, five other people were killed on Westminster Bridge and fifty injured, thirty-one seriously.

The inquiry was led by SO15, Scotland Yard's Anti-terror unit. The police still believe that Masood carried out the attack alone, but continue to investigate whether he had background accomplices. The unit identified Islamic State as being the inspiration for the attack. Masood hid his extremism from his neighbours in private life so successfully that he was thought to be an enthusiastic gardener and devoted family man. It remains for MI6 to resolve why Masood, suspected of being an extremist of violent tendencies, should simply disappear from the radar.

Since this occurrence, the Metropolitan Police has put additional officers on the streets of London and lengthened the shifts from eight to twelve hours until further notice. The presence of troops outside London are there to guarantee security, prevent further Islamic attacks and also hate crimes against Muslims. The independent Police Complaints Commission has investigated the legal circumstances surrounding the shooting of Masood.

The Manchester Arena Terror Attacks – 2017

Ariana Grande-Butera is only 5 ft tall, but the voice of the 24-year-old singer is all the more powerful for it. In 2017 she returned from her 'Dangerous Woman Tour' to the Manchester Arena, used primarily for concerts since the year 2004. The Arena is in the north of the city, near Manchester Victoria railway station and 14,200 spectators were present that evening. The presentation concluded with the song *One Last Time* from the singer's album *My Everything*. After bowing to her audience, she waved and disappeared off stage.

The horror began on that Monday, 22 May 2017 at 10.30 pm, just as the audience rose from their seats and began to leave the concert hall. A loud explosion occurred in the arena's foyer. After minutes of uncertainty as to the cause, it became clear that people had been hurt. Distressed concert-goers began running in all directions in search of safety. Thick swathes of smoke drifted through the foyer above the injured and dead who were lying on the floor. The bomb devastated everything within a 20-yard radius of the detonation point.

The North West Ambulance Service had around sixty ambulances at the scene very quickly and began treating the first of the injured. The concert hall was a scene of carnage. Doctors treated people with more serious wounds, many with injuries caused by splinters. Fifty-nine seriously-injured were taken immediately to nearby hospitals. Time was of the essence. One of the first medical officers at the scene was anaesthetist Dr Michael McCarthy from the Manchester Royal Infirmary.[2] He raised the alarm about the bomb explosion, thus summoning several dozen of his colleagues to attend hospitals to see to the injured. Dr McCarthy referred to this reaction of his colleagues of various nationalities as a "masterpiece of medicine" as it clearly showed their sympathy, empathy and self-sacrifice when it came to rendering medical aid to save lives.

The police arrived in record time, secured the crime scene in the foyer and escorted the concert-goers out of the building. They also closed down Manchester Victoria railway station, which is very close to the concert hall, in case it might have been next on the terrorists' list. The police began to create a picture of the crime scene and question the first witnesses. One witness told police that he noticed "a large number" of nuts and bolts strewn on the floor of the foyer – important information which suggested that a shrapnel bomb might have been employed. Family members of the injured also confirmed to the officers that screws and nuts had been extracted during life-saving surgical operations.

The investigation was pressurised to identify the criminals as soon as possible. The armed police standing in the foyer, and who could have been outside helping with the rescue, were continually asked by concert-goers why help was not arriving faster at the scene. The police attempted to explain that the most important thing for them to do was to ensure that there were no other bombs in the concert hall. It is not always easy for outsiders to understand the work of police in such crisis situations and so it was all the more important for people to know the essential steps to take. The officers were there for the safety of the concert-goers and for technical reasons connected with the investigation. The safety of these people who had had the most terrible experience was their highest priority in the minutes that followed.

The experts of the Greater Manchester Police, including Chief Constable Ian Hopkins, in cooperation with the Anti-terrorist network, and Mark Rowley, Assistant Commissioner for Special Operations of the Metropolitan Police, and UK leader for counter-terrorism policy, began the search with other teams for those responsible for the Manchester bombing and any accomplices which may have been present. The National Counter-Terrorism Policing Network (NCTPN) is the British national collaboration of police forces in the United Kingdom. Set up under Section 22(a) of the Police Act 1969, it works to prevent, deter and investigate acts of terrorism in the United Kingdom. This body is accountable to the UK Government and the National Police Chiefs' Council Counter-Terrorism Coordination Committee.

Meticulous investigation work proceeded around the clock; statements were taken from members of the public and the concert-goers present that night, an analysis of all security cameras in and around the Manchester Arena, reports of scene of crime officers, forensic scientists and coroners.

On the afternoon of Tuesday, 23 May, Greater Manchester Police were able to make a statement to the public that the bomb, or bombs, were home-made shrapnel devices strapped to the body of 22-year-old suicide bomber Salman Abedi, and detonated by him in the foyer at the end of the concert.

A great deal of information about this killer had been gathered by police. Salman Abedi was a British-Sunni Moslem of Libyan origins. He was born in Manchester on 31 December 1994 to a Libyan Salafi family, who had fled to Britain as political refugees from the Gaddafi Government and settled in the south of Manchester. When Gaddafi was overthrown in 2011, the parents returned to Libya while Salman Abedi remained in England. The bomber had two brothers and a sister. He grew up in Whalley Range and his last address was a house in Fallowfield. From 2009-11 he attended the Burnage Academy for Boys, and Manchester College from 2013. In 2014 he enrolled at the University of Salford to study Business Economics and was a member of a student group that accused a tutor of Islamophobia for criticising suicide bombings. He abandoned his studies to work in a bakery. Neighbours described the family as very traditional and very religious. Abedi was considered to be an open-minded person and drank alcohol until 2012, even indulging in drug-taking, including cannabis. He often attended the Didsbury mosque with his elder brother and father. An imam at the mosque recalled that Abedi had given him a look filled with hate for preaching against Islamic State and Sharia law in 2015. Manchester police believe that he used his student loans to pay for his house and some of his trips abroad in order to learn the art of bomb-making; he didn't receive a bank loan until April 2017. Abedi was known to the British security services and police, but was not considered a high risk as even though he engaged in minor crime, he was not known to have professed radical views.

The house at Fallowfield in which Salman lived was searched by an anti-terrorist unit on 23 May 2017, the day after the bombing. Armed officers entered with the aid of a controlled explosion and conducted a thorough search. The bomber's 23-year-old elder brother was arrested in Chorlton-cum-Hardy in connection with the crime, while the police carried out other raids at two locations in the south of Manchester and shortly after at Whalley Range. These searches led to three more arrests. The police spoke originally of a network supporting the bomber, but later admitted that Salman Abedi had obtained all parts for the bomb himself and were now of the opinion that he had, for the most part, acted alone. On 6 July 2017, the police revised this statement and said that accomplices had known of his plans.

Police photographs taken at the scene of the bombing showed that the explosive had been fitted inside a light metal container carried by the bomber, under a black jacket in a blue Karrimor rucksack. Most of the fatalities had been in a circle around the bomber, presumably not suspecting that he had a bomb. His torso was catapulted through the doors to the arena, indicating that the explosive was in the rucksack and had blasted him forwards when it exploded. This meant that it must have been a small device set off by a detonator carried in his hand. The bomb material was the explosive TATP which had been used in earlier bombings. According to the police, the bomb would have been based on a manufacturer's design because it had a supporting detonation. The bomber had put the bomb together himself and had been alone during the execution of his attack.

On 28 May, six days after the bombing, the police published photographs of the bomber from the security cameras on the night of the attack. Other images showed him walking through Manchester carrying a blue suitcase. The bomber was identified from the bank card he was carrying and facial recognition technology by Metropolitan Police experts.

German police supplied information that four days before the attack, Salman Abedi had passed through Düsseldorf airport en route to Manchester from Istanbul. The French Interior Minister confirmed that Abedi had been in Syria where he had links to the Islamic State terrorist network. On 23 and 24 May respectively, Abedi's younger brother and father were arrested by Libyan security forces. The brother was suspected of having planned a bombing attack in Libya and had been in regular contact with his brother, Salman. He knew Salman's plan to bomb the Manchester Arena, but not the date. According to official Libyan sources, he telephoned his brothers about fifteen minutes before the bomb went off. On 1 November 2017, Britain requested the extradition of the younger brother, Hashem Abedi, from Syria on a charge of accessory before the fact to the murder of twenty-two persons.

The bombing at the Manchester Arena claimed the lives of twenty-two people, plus the bomber. Children were amongst the fatalities, the youngest being 8 years old. Twelve of the injured were under the age of sixteen and 512 people were treated in hospitals for their wounds.

The explosion coincided with the anniversary of the slaying of British soldier Lee Rigby, hacked to death on a London street on 22 May 2013. Rigby's murderer, Michael Adebolajo, gained worldwide notoriety after he was filmed by passers-by and was seen standing on the street with blood on his hands attempting to justify his crime.

In 2017, twenty-two people were arrested in connection with the Manchester Arena bombing, but all were released on 11 June when the police concluded that Abedi had acted alone, although others possibly knew of his plans.

In this connection it is interesting to note the following facts, made known with the passage of time:

Five years before the bombing, a social worker rang a hotline to warn police of Abedi's intention.

* *Members of the British-Libyan diaspora had been warning the authorities for years about the radicalisation of Muslims in Manchester. According to reports, up to five community leaders and family members had warned the authorities that Abedi was an extremist and had been banned from a mosque.*

* *The Chief Constable of Greater Manchester stated, however, that Abedi was not known to the Anti-radicalisation programme 'Prevent'.*

* *On 29 May MI5 began an internal investigation regarding the treatment of the warnings it had received about Salman Abedi, and also opened a second, more in-depth, inquiry into why the extent of the danger from Abedi had been underestimated.*

According to a veteran from the European secret service, Abedi had contacts with members of the Islamic State Battar Brigade at Sabratha, Libya.

A Terror Gang Strikes on London Bridge – June 2017

The evening of Saturday, 3 June 2017 in London was relatively warm at 14°C. That afternoon a white Renault delivery van stood in a parking lot at Harold Hill, north-east of London. The man who had hired the vehicle wanted something larger, a 7.5 ton truck, but his credit card had been rejected for insufficient funds and he had had to be satisfied with the smaller, white Renault delivery van. He drove it across London, jogging along in the direction of London Bridge. The concrete-and-steel bridge across the Thames, brightly lit each evening, was administered by the City of London Corporation. Open to traffic since 1973, the A3 arterial road ran across it to the south-west in the direction of Portsmouth.

At 10.06 pm, the Renault van headed northwards across London Bridge, then turned around to head south. The three men inside the van were 27-year-old Khuram Shazad Butt, 30-year-old Rachid Redouane and 22-year-old Youssef Zaghba. They were all looking through the windscreen at the pedestrians on the bridge pavements.

Butt was born in Pakistan and lived in Barking, a suburb to the east of London. He was a keen fitness-studio-goer and weight-lifter and the father of a small child and a baby. He had had a number of short-term

27

employments, most recently with Transport for London, with whom he had spent six months as a trainee in customer sales for London Underground. He was known to the police and MI5 and had featured in reports since 2015 as he was an ally of the hate-preacher, Anjem Choudary. In 2016 he took part in a Channel 4 documentary *The Jihadis Next Door* about Islamic extremists in Britain. He had once been ejected from the Islamic Centre *Jabir Bin Zayid* for interrupting the Friday sermon of an imam and for a verbal attack on the managing director of the Ramadhan Organisation, Mohammed Shafiq, calling him a *murtad* (traitor) for accusing the hate-preacher Anjem Choudary of being a supporter of terrorism after the murder of Lee Rigby in 2013.

Rachid Redouane was a Moroccan-Libyan pastry chef, who until recently had lived in Dublin where he had settled five years previously. Redouane, also known as Rachid Elkhdar, lived in a tower block in Dagenham, a few miles from the Barking house of his friend Khuram Butt. In 2012 Redouane had married Clarisse O'Leary in Ireland. She never converted to Islam and they separated on account of the major differences of opinion regarding the upbringing of their daughter.

The third man in the van, Youssef Zaghba, was an Italian national born in Fez, Morocco. He was listed in an international terrorist database after being asked the reason for his journey to Syria and declaring quite openly, "I want to be a terrorist." Zaghba had left Italy with his Italian mother for Morocco. In 2016 he attempted to travel to Syria via Bologna airport and Istanbul in order to join Islamic State, after being radicalised by material online.

Butt, Redouane and Zaghba were friends as well as accomplices in crime. They sat watching the pedestrian traffic on London Bridge for a few minutes through the windscreen of their van. They were armed with 12-inch kitchen knives with ceramic blades, secured to their wrists with leather straps. They wore belts with water bottles wrapped in duct tape to give the impression of explosives and so heighten the fear for passers-by.

At 10.08 pm their Renault van increased its speed to 50 mph and drove along the pavement running down the pedestrians walking along London Bridge.

The first fatality, who was rammed by the van, was Canadian Christine Archibald, who died in the arms of her fiancé, Tyler Ferguson. She was a 30-year-old social worker who worked in a shelter for the homeless and had left British Columbia to live with Tyler Ferguson in Europe. She lived in The Hague. Her cause of death was severe internal injuries.

The next fatality was 39-year-old Ignacio Echeverria, originally from Las Rosas in Spain and now living in Poplar, East London, working as an auditor for HSBC bank. He had hurried to render assistance to another casualty and attempted to hit one of the terrorists with a skateboard in order to save the victim. Reported missing, he was struck by one of the murderers and died from his injuries on the pavement.

Frenchman Xavier Thomas, 45, was walking in a southerly direction along London Bridge with his friend, Christine Delcros, when both were run down from behind. Christine was taken to hospital for an immediate operation due to her serious injuries; the body of Xavier Thomas was discovered days later near Limehouse, about 4 miles downstream from London Bridge. It is not known if he jumped into the river to save himself or was hit at such speed that he was catapulted off the bridge.

The emergency services were alerted by eye witnesses and the first rescue vehicles arrived on the scene within six minutes. Although the casualties were taken to hospitals in the area, they were only the first victims of the trio of killers, who now drove the vehicle further south towards Borough Market. As a result of its high speed, the van crashed through a traffic sign and into a column, at which the criminals abandoned the van. They then ran down some side-steps alongside the bridge towards the Café Brood and into Stoney Street, adjoining Borough Market. The massacre continued in this lively district of bars and restaurants on the south side of the bridge, the three killers using their knives to attack the customers. Running amok for about eight minutes with their 12-inch blades shouting "This is for Allah," they entered restaurants, pubs and bars simply with intent to murder; stabbing their victims at random. Those people sitting, standing or walking in the vicinity of these establishments along Stoney Street were attacked by the trio in cold blood. Four people collapsed after being stabbed in the Borough Bistro Pub. From there the terrorists ran along the street to continue their rampage against customers of the Mudlark Pub, before returning to Borough Market to attack people near the Brindisa Restaurant, the El Pastor tapas restaurant, the Wheatsheaf Pub and the Roast restaurant, stabbing those guests who happened to be nearest as they passed.

A number of guests defended themselves by throwing bottles and chairs at the attackers. A Romanian baker even struck one of the attackers on the head with a crate before offering twenty fleeing people refuge in his bakery in Borough Market. A 38-year-old British Transport Police officer was patrolling London Bridge railway station with a colleague shortly before his shift began when he saw a group of people forming up near a bar. He though it must have been a bar or gang fight that had spilled over into the street, until an off-duty Metropolitan Police officer called to him that he had seen somebody stabbing passers-by. Shortly after, the Transport Police officer saw people being attacked at the junction with London Bridge Street and almost at once an attacker confronted him. The police officer then found himself surrounded by the three terrorists: "It was like being in a Western," he said afterwards. The terrorist trio was constantly shouting "Allahu Akbar." The struggle lasted about ninety seconds. While one of them struck him in the face and he tried to ward off the attacker, another stabbed him in the right leg. After being stabbed in the right hand all he could remember afterwards was being involved in a life-or-death struggle for survival against three armed terrorists. He knew he could not surrender and must not fall unconscious.

Another of the evening's victims was 34-year-old Candice Hedge, from Queensland, who worked in Elliot's Café and suddenly became aware that guests were beginning to enter the restaurant shouting. Within minutes the attackers arrived. One attempted to slit her throat, missing the artery by a fraction of an inch so that she survived the murderous assault. The terrorists then circled the market and returned to Café Brood before continuing to the Black and Blue Restaurant.

Sergio Fariña, manager of Arthur Hooper's Restaurant, was alerted by passers-by running past and shouting. He had just dropped the steel roller-curtain to protect his clients when a knifeman, dressed in a striped top, attempted to get through the doorway. Fariña forced him back and skillfully blocked the entrance.

Eight minutes after receiving the first 999 calls, all three attackers were shot dead by armed police officers at 10.16 pm. Film from security videos show the three killers coming from Borough Market towards police and twenty seconds later they were dead. A total of forty-six rounds were fired by three City of London and five Metropolitan Police officers. After ending the massacre, the police evacuated people from Borough Market to Liverpool Street station to make statements and some were allowed to spend the night there for safety reasons.

The London Bridge attack was the second attack in London in 2017 and the third in Great Britain in three months. After Christine Archibald, James McMullan from Hackney, East London, was the killers' second victim. Xavier Thomas (45), Ignacio Echeverria (39), Alexandre Pigeard (27),

Kirsty Boden (28), Sebastian Belanger (36) and Sara Zelenak (21) also lost their lives in the killing spree.

Most of the surviving victims sought safety in nearby pubs and restaurants where they received care until the police restored the situation and the rescue services arrived. Oliver Dowling, 32, was in a coma after being struck on the head; his friend Marie Bondeville was injured. Another victim, Brett Freeman, was brought to hospital with four stab wounds. At least four of the fifty injured were police.

On Sunday, 4 June police raided the address in Barking where Butt had last lived. The result of the operation, which began at 7.00 am, was the arrest of twelve suspects in connection with the massacre in a flat above a betting shop on Barking Road, East Ham, by the Metropolitan Police Anti-terrorist Squad. The police also made a further eight arrests in the district. More police raids followed on 5 June. However, those arrested were released after a short while.

Prime Minister Theresa May asked for stronger precautions on the internet in the framework of the Four-Point-Plan for fighting terrorism "in order to deprive the terrorists of their secure space online." She also criticised technology firms for doing too little to combat terrorism.

Chapter 2

France

The Great Nation in the Mirror of Terror

Unit: Recherche Assistance Intervention Dissuasion (RAID)
Motto: *Servir sans faillir* – To serve without failing

Erick Schmitt: The Human Bomb of Neuilly – 1993

The man with the dark hair and dark bushy eyebrows stood for an hour in Rue de la Ferme in the noble 16th district of Paris observing building number 15, opposite. It housed a school named after the famous polar explorer, Jean-Baptiste Charcot. It was Thursday, 13 May 1993. At 9.00 am on the dot, the man drew a black mask over his head and put on a motor-cycle helmet, before hurrying across the street and entering the classroom of a nursery school. The female teacher, Laurence Dreyfus, was shocked when the masked man appeared in the doorway. He made his business clear. "I am taking hostages. Inform the headteacher at once." The young woman looked at him in horror, then went without speaking to the office of the headmistress, Suzanne Souilhé, and made her report. Both women ran back to the classroom, as all twenty-one children, aged between 3 and 4 years old, had been left alone with the hostage-taker. Now he issued his instructions; he required that the two women shut the windows and doors and hang a notice in the large window facing the corridor. It read: "No entry or I will blow everything up."

Suzanne Souilhé informed the police. Fifteen minutes later, the police director for the Hauts-de-Seine department, Aimé Touitou, arrived and began to negotiate with the hostage-taker for the release of the children. In response he received only letters, all signed "H. B."

Word about the seizure of the children in the Neuilly nursery school spread quickly. Parents and the media assembled off the Rue de la Ferme, which in the meantime had been sealed off by the police. Away from the commotion, Aimé Touitou continued negotiating with the hostage-taker; he needed to gain time so as to enable the special unit RAID, which had been called in, to prepare their plan of operation. The RAID team discovered that the criminal had planned his coup in great detail. H. B. had composed various letters for members of the Government, even one for the sitting Minister of the Interior, Charles Pasqua, all carefully written out on a computer. For the RAID lead negotiator it was soon clear that the man was educated, as there were no spelling or grammatical errors in his letters and he was painstakingly precise. The psychologists recognised signs of paranoia, and therefore a twisted perception of reality.

According to his own statement, H. B. was wearing a belt with explosives, and he had also fitted all doors into the classroom with them. The explosive had a detonation mechanism which he could operate by hand. He had set up a security system in the classroom so that nobody could enter it without setting off a bomb; the aim being to prevent any intervention by the police at all costs. The RAID technicians calculated that nobody could survive an explosion from this quantity of explosive within a radius of five metres. The next major problem for the negotiating team was that the man gave away nothing about himself. He remained mute the whole time and communicated only through letters and a few signals. So far officials had found out nothing about him, or his family, in order to identify him.

Towards midday, the father of one of the children, Pierre Narboni, was allowed to come near the classroom and was asked by the negotiators to support their efforts with H. B. When Narboni's 3-year-old son Lucas heard his father's voice he could not be restrained and escaped the hostage-taker. Lucas was the first child of the group to be freed. Pierre Narboni supported the lead negotiator and obtained the release of three more children before being relieved by the mayor, Government spokesman and Budget Minister Nicolas Sarkozy. H. B. was also informed that he had a new conversation partner. There were still sixteen children held captive in the classroom. Sarkozy's tactics were very efficient and he achieved the release of more children. Very well-known throughout France even at this time, he personally went into the classroom to lead out each child individually, even carrying many of them as they were too frightened.

H. B. was given a radio in return for releasing another child, meaning he was now able to follow the media's news reports. Towards evening he demanded to speak with a journalist from the state television station, TFI. Special correspondent Jean-Pierre About took on this task. Briefed by

RAID negotiator, a few minutes later he went into the classroom and spoke briefly with the hostage-taker, who now demanded 100 million francs (€15 million) in gold bars and foreign currencies and he wanted to be televised live leaving the school. The conversation was overheard by means of hidden RAID microphones and carefully analysed. The RAID team determined that it was the voice of a man who some weeks before had carried out a bomb attack in a parking garage. He had left behind a letter stating that he would soon carry out another attack which would kill ten persons. This letter was also signed "H. B."

Night fell over Paris and children continued to be liberated from the classroom until 1.00 am, for which the hostage-taker received money and food. There were now six children still held captive together with their teacher, Laurence Dreyfus, who did not want to leave them alone, and Evelyne Lambert, a fire brigade medical officer.

On the morning of 14 May, H. B. was very tense; he had not slept all night and was now showing typical signs of exhaustion. He requested a change of negotiators, and so Nicolas Sarkozy was replaced by Catherine Ferracci and then by Pierre Lyon-Caen. But H. B. had had enough negotiating. He told RAID and the State Attorney that his end was near. He simply did not want to go on. For the special unit it was now clear enough that something had to happen. Lyon-Caen suggested H. B. leave the school with him and the two flee together in a car. Towards 4.00 pm the hostage-taker declared that he would not surrender. He wanted to run away with the money he had already received. Two hours later he revised his request and now wanted a weapon and a child; a demand that RAID were obviously unable to comply with. No child was going anywhere with H. B. alone.

What the media was never told was that at this point in time, the hostage-taker was causing a great deal of concern for the special unit members, due to his increasingly disturbed conversations, in which he spoke of visions he was having, of figures coming from the walls. He was hallucinating and becoming ever more aggressive. The reason for this was probably the enormous tension to which he was subjecting himself, along with a lack of sleep. The RAID team planned to invade the classroom in the early hours of the morning. It was a quiet night, even the six little girls and Evelyne Lambert, still in the hands of H. B., slept peacefully.

On Saturday at 7.25 am, Evelyne was advised about the forthcoming assault. There was a hidden camera in the wall and she was to face it and undo several buttons of her blouse as the signal for the intervention. The plan succeeded. One section of the RAID team carried out the children.

Two of the girls began crying, waking H. B., who reached for the detonation mechanism. Three rounds and he was dead. When the special unit found his papers, his identity became clear; he was 42-year-old Erick Schmitt, an unemployed worker in the computer field. The initials H. B. stood for "Human Bomb."

Erick Schmitt came from Béziers, where his neighbours described him as a quiet, reserved young man with no special characteristics. At age 16 he had joined the French Army where he had learned to handle weapons and explosives. In the 1970s, after working for the SSI, the largest computer science company at the time, he started his own business with some friends, but the firm closed after four years. He had then been unemployed for a year, had separated from his wife and suffered severe depression. All three factors drove him into a diabolical circle from which he failed to emerge.

Mohamed Merah: The Bomber on the Motorbike – 2012

One morning towards 6.00 am, the chief negotiator of the French police special unit RAID was already in his office when the telephone rang. He took the call himself. A colleague from the Ministry of the Interior told him: "You must come to Toulouse as soon as possible, and bring as many men with you as you can." One hour later, thirty-five RAID men were heading for Toulouse by Air France, as yet unaware that they would soon be confronted by one of the worst-ever terrorist cases in France.

This case began more brutally than any US crime series. On 11 March, Imad Ibn-Ziaten, a 30-year-old French national with Moroccan roots, a paratrooper with 1st Parachute Logistics Regiment in Toulouse, was stopped by a masked motorbike rider dressed in black, wearing a dark helmet with visor and holding a weapon. The man on the stolen Yamaha T-Max 500 cc machine asked him, "Are you in the Army? Are you a soldier?" Then the stranger ordered him to lie face down on the ground. Imad Ibn-Ziaten refused: "I will not lie face down on the ground. I shall stand here. You want to shoot me? Then shoot." A shot was fired. Imad sank to the ground mortally wounded. The murderer left with the words "That is Islam, my brother: you kill my brothers, I kill you." He filmed the murder of the paratrooper with a GoPro camera.

A few days later, on 15 March, he struck again, this time at Montauban, a town in south-western France, 50 km north of Toulouse. There towards 2.00 pm he shot dead two airborne-unit soldiers, Abel Chennouf, 24, and

Mohamed Legouad, 26, as they stood with their colleague, Loïc Liber, at an ATM in front of their barracks. The men belonged to the 17th Parachute Engineer Regiment, the largest unit of the French military. Both units, at Toulouse and Montauban, had seen action in Afghanistan. Several witnesses saw the incident that day. The killer pushed an old lady to one side before pulling the trigger. Then he rode off.

On 19 March, when the RAID men were being flown to Toulouse, towards 8.00 am the same shooter arrived on his motorbike at the Jewish Ozar-Hatorah School on Rue Jules-Dalou and fired first at Jonathan Sandler, 30, a rabbi and teacher, standing with parents at the school gates. Then the killer left his motorbike, entered the school and randomly opened fire, killing both of Sandler's children, Gabriel, 3, and Ayreh, 6, and the daughter of the school's headmistress, Myriam Monsonégo. He had seized her brutally by the hair, but the gun jammed when he tried to shoot her. At that he drew a 45-calibre ACP and shot her point-blank through the temple. He then fled once more on his motorbike. All victims were French-Israeli persons of dual nationality. A pupil, Aaron Bijaoui, was seriously hurt but escaped the killer. It had been many years since a more brutal spate of murders had been seen in France.

When the aircraft landed at Toulouse, the RAID team were informed of the shocking news. It was clearly a terrorist event of enormous portent, as even children had been murdered. At this time the identity of the murderer was not known. Together with their police colleagues at Toulouse they began their research, reading through one police report after another, questioning witnesses, all in collaboration with the French interior and foreign secret services. In the course of this research, the experts came to two conclusions; either the murderer was a lone wolf, or was a terrorist from one of the extreme-Right or Islamic groups. The same day the 'Vigipirate Plan' was put into action. This is a special security measure for the protection of the French people against terrorism. Thus security forces, the military and police began patrolling with machine-pistols at railway stations and places with large numbers of tourists. In the meantime, France was at the tail-end of the presidential election campaign.

On Tuesday, 20 March 2012 the RAID team spent all night with the Secret Service and Interior Ministry working on the search for the perpetrator. The first indications pointing to neo-Nazi circles were discarded during the morning. Three men who belonged to a neo-Nazi group were initially suspected, but then no longer considered as perpetrators due to their alibis; confirmed stays abroad at the time of the murders in France. However, all at once there was an opportunity to resolve the case. During the day, the team interviewed a Yamaha dealer in Toulouse. He told the agents that fifteen days previously, on 6 March, a young man had bought a full hood for the head and asked how one could deactivate the GPS chip on his motorcycle. The Yamaha dealer was able to provide the police with the man's full name. This was checked by the Secret Service (the general directorate for internal security) and the National Anti-terrorism Office at the Ministry of the Interior. The investigators found out very quickly that the suspect had used his mother's computer to buy a motorbike. By 6.30 pm it was clear that Mohammed Merah was the killer.

The RAID team decided to arrest Merah at 3.00 am. They hoped he would be asleep at that hour, because if they went at 5.00 am he would be preparing for morning prayers. RAID and Toulouse police colleagues took up positions during the night in the Rue du Sergent-Vigné, in the Cote Pavée district, and at 3.10 am Merah's neighbours heard loud voices: "Open up, open up..." and then shooting. Merah had apparently been expecting them. He randomly opened fire again, hitting one of the members of the anti-terrorist unit, who fell unconscious on the stairway, but Merah kept shooting.

The chief negotiator, sheltering behind a *Ramses* (a giant shield), stood near the ground floor flat and addressed Merah through a megaphone: "Mohammed Merah. We are the RAID. Come out of your apartment, calmly." These phrases were repeated over and over, the intention being to de-escalate the situation. The neighbours were very worried. The front door of Merah's flat was quickly closed again and the shooting stopped, allowing the first of the neighbours in the block to be evacuated by the stairway and windows. They were then escorted to the nearby Pérignon barracks.

"Come out of your apartment calmly."

Merah shouted back: "Do you know who I am? I am a Mujahedin and am here to fight. What do you want of me? I am not going to leave my flat."

"OK, we understand you. Please come out of your flat, we won't harm you, simply come out."

Merah replied, "Just so you know, I have no fear of you, I have no fear."

This exchange ended the first phase of the operation, called the Stabilisation Phase, which had lasted until 7.00 am next morning. On Wednesday, 21 March towards 5.10 am, Merah heard a noise and in panic, fired through the front door, hitting a RAID member in the head and shoulder with two quick rounds. The wounded man at the lower entrance to the cellar called to his colleagues, "This man shoots to kill. I am hurt in the head and bleeding." Then he fell unconscious. Merah was obviously worried, explaining, "I thought you were going to storm my flat." The negotiator's voice said through the megaphone, "Not at all. On the contrary, we want you to come out and give yourself up quietly." Meanwhile, the special unit had sent a robot to the door of the flat in order to open it, but the killer was on his guard. He was becoming more cautious. The special unit knew what had to be done in such situations; try to keep the man calm. Towards 7.00 am Merah asked for a mobile phone to call his mother. This was refused, but he received instead a walkie-talkie with which to speak to RAID.

There now began the second phase in which Merah told the special unit why he had committed the attacks. He revealed what weapons he had hidden in the flat, gave the precise location where he had put them and – as a sign of goodwill – threw a Colt 45 out through the door. He said that he loved automatic weapons. "Give me time. I know that I will go to prison for life. I will come out of my flat, but give me time." The RAID psychologist recognised that the situation was moving towards a possibly fatality and warned his colleagues, "This man is drawing up his Will. It is similar to a suicide. He is admitting his guilt."

The special unit persisted in their attempts to convince Merah to leave his flat. "Are you ready to give up yet? Are you ready to come out of your flat?" The unit's psychologist recognised that Merah wanted to die a martyr and so leave his mark in the history books. Personalities who cover up their feelings of inferiority with immoderate craving for recognition suffer from what is known as 'Herostratus Syndrome'. In Ancient Greece, Herostratus made his name by setting fire to and destroying one of the Seven Wonders of the World, the Temple to Artemis at Ephesus, but Merah's career as a killer and petty criminal had little of interest in it.

Towards 11.00 am, Merah began talking about two well-known French murderers who were his role models; Jacques Mesrine, a rapist and Public Enemy No.1 in France in the 1970s, and the Roubaix Gang, an Islamic group which sympathised with Al Qaeda, who were caught and killed in 1996 by RAID after various bombings. Merah said repeatedly, "There is no way you will get me alive." It was clear to the police and RAID that he was attempting to manipulate them verbally. The conversation with him lasted into the night. Towards 11.00 pm he heard the voice in the megaphone say, "Mohammed Merah, we are waiting here for you. We are here." His answer came quickly. "No, no, I won't come out of my flat. I have told you a gigantic load of rubbish. I am not coming out of my flat." Mohammed wanted to know how many RAID men he had killed, but was told, "Our people are all alive."

"Shame," he replied, "I would have liked to kill a couple of you," and he warned that in the next confrontation with the special unit he would shoot to wound. He added that he would do it "not to land in prison, but to reach the end of my mission." He wanted to carry through his personal jihad, no matter the cost.

"Come out of your flat," the voice in the megaphone repeated, not knowing that Merah now had a small problem in his flat. "Don't shout so loud," he complained. "If only you knew how wet it is in here." The exchanges of fire had caused damage to the water pipes, causing the flat to flood.

"One more reason for you to come out of your flat," the voice in the megaphone persisted. It was almost midnight and time for the RAID team to take a rest. During the night a few stun grenades were tossed into the flat to keep Merah awake, but he had stopped communicating and was presumed to be resting.

Early in the morning of Thursday, 22 March, Merah was sitting on the toilet in the flat, asleep. The stun grenades had perforated an ear drum. The autopsy report confirmed later that he would still have been able to hear voices despite the injury. At 10.30 am the order was given to storm the apartment, a decision approved by Government legal and administrative processes. Over 100 soldiers stood ready around the block of flats.

The apartment was breached from outside, over the balcony and by way of the inner front door. The special unit infiltrated the flat room by room, at first the ground floor, the kitchen and bedroom. An exchange of fire began. Merah fired and hit two RAID members. When the men with a special, small video camera were inspecting the bathroom, the armed Merah ran from the toilet and jumped over the balcony bannister firing his weapon. RAID police posted outside the flat returned fire. Merah was hit and fell. He lay on the grass while a doctor and paramedic tried to resuscitate him, but in vain. The special unit gathered around the corpse. The RAID chief pronounced the usual words of finality after such a result: "Neutralised." The men were taken to a barracks where the French Interior Minister addressed them in person. Their wounded were attended to, the dead Mohammed Merah was taken to the morgue.

There was a great deal of media coverage worldwide about this case. Mohammed Merah, born in October 1988, was the son of an Algerian mother and French father. A single-parent family, his mother had raised Mohammed, his two sisters and two brothers alone according to strict

Islamic rules. He first came to notice in 2002 when he beat up a social worker. In 2007 he fired a gun at his brother's television and threatened both him and his sister-in-law, after that he committed violent burglaries and robbery. This earned him five months in prison, but he soon regained his liberty. In December 2008 he refused to stop for police and was returned to prison. A little later, at Christmas, he attempted suicide and was committed for psychiatric treatment. When his family visited him he laughed and explained, "I was just playing. According to the Quran one is not allowed to commit suicide."

After his return to prison at the end of 2009 he turned to radical Islam. From 2006 the French Central Intelligence Service had had a file on him. It contained the information that Merah had applied to join the Foreign Legion, but had not presented himself for the selection tests. He went twice to Afghanistan and Pakistan, maintaining to the last that he had received terrorist training. In July 2010 he was reported to the police by a mother for having shown her 15-year-old son videos of brutal murders. Between September 2010 and February 2011 he made 1,863 telephone calls, amongst them calls to Egypt, Algeria, Morocco, the Ivory Coast, Kenya, England, Spain, Croatia, Romania, Bolivia, Thailand, Russia, Laos, Kazakhstan, Turkey, Saudi Arabia, Taiwan, Israel, the Arab Emirates and Bhutan. In December 2011 he married a young Algerian girl who lived near Toulouse, and separated from her in January 2012. The marriage was dissolved on 20 March 2012.

In February 2012 he began to put his devilish plan into effect. He withdrew the last of his cash, €183, from his bank account and the day after bought a Go-Pro camera. In company with two accomplices, on 6 March he stole a motorbike and went to the Yamaha dealer that same day; a decision which was eventually to be his undoing.

Charlie Hebdo – Je Suis Charlie

On the morning of 7 January 2015, the temperature had fallen to zero and clouds covered the sky. It was freezing. Children had been back at school for two days, and their parents had gone back to work. The capital had lost its festive air and had returned to its usual traffic jams. In the 11th arrondissement, traffic was coping fairly well, but those employed in the neighbourhood had difficulty parking in the nearby roads. At No. 10, Rue

Nicolas Appert, a team of colleagues and friends had gathered in a happy hubbub for the first writing conference of the year. It was one of the last moments of shared joy. The editorial conference was to take place in a pale yellow building with white windows at the corner of the street, and although it resembled more of an artist's loft, it housed businesses and corporate offices. On the second floor were the headquarters of the audiovisual production company, *Premières Lignes*, and, since July 2014, that of the satirical weekly magazine *Charlie Hebdo*.

For the *Charlie Hebdo* team, the day began as it did every year after the holidays; journalists, artists and salespeople returned to work in a warm, friendly atmosphere. Sigolène Vinson, the judicial columnist, brought a cake; it was Luz's birthday. Lila, the little red cocker spaniel and mascot of the newspaper, was also there, and trotted down the hallway.

Around 10.30 am, the editorial team gathered around a large oval table topped with chouquettes and croissants: Charb, Riss, Fabrice Nicolino, Bernard Maris, Philippe Lançon, Honored, Coco, Tignous, Cabu, Elsa Cayat, Wolinski, Sigolene Vinson and Laurent Léger. From his chair in a corner of the room, Michel Renaud followed the conversation. As usual, Charb wrote down word clouds and scribbled on sheets of paper, listening to his colleagues discuss the latest novel by Michel Houellebecq, *Submission*, which was being released that day. They went through everything with a fine-toothed comb; news, literature, racism, the eviction of Eric Zemmour and the anti-Islam Pegida protests in Germany, and a drawing by Philippe Honoré caricaturing the leader of the Islamic State, Al-Baghdadi, which had appeared on Twitter. The drawing carried the message 'Best wishes, by the way.' It was a phrase that would prove to be key. It was now 11.28 am.

At 11.30 am, as the team prepared its new edition, a black Citroën C3 with the registration number CW-518-YV stopped in front of No. 6, Rue Nicolas Appert. Two men wearing black hoods and bulletproof vests, and equipped with pump action shotguns and Kalashnikovs, got out of the car. They entered the building alongside the postman, who had come to deliver a letter. They shouted at him and another employee of the building to sit down and asked them, "Is this *Charlie Hebdo*?," before firing a bullet through the glass door of an office. Stunned, an employee came out and, seeing the astonished look on his face, the two men quickly understood that they were in the wrong building. They went back to the car and drove to No. 10. In the reception area they meet two maintenance workers and asked the same question, before shooting one of them, Frédéric Boisseau. They then took the designer, Corinne Rey, as a hostage and brutally threatened her. They only had one obsession; to find the offices of *Charlie Hebdo*. Despite her fear, she tried to mislead them by taking them to the third floor, but was unsuccessful as they began attacking people in the corridor, repeating like a leitmotiv: "Where is Charlie?" At gunpoint, they forced Corinne Rey to enter the passcode for the armoured door, which finally gave them access to the editorial offices.

At this precise moment, the *Charlie Hebdo* team heard two shots, but did not identify them as gunfire. The two bullets pierced the lungs of webmaster Simon Fieschi, 31, who was to be the first victim of the brothers, Sherif and Said Kouachi. Seriously injured, he was later taken to hospital in a critical condition. In the newsroom there was a moment of hesitation, as everyone wondered where the 'firecracker sounds' were coming from. Franck Brinsolaro, one of the two policemen acting as Charb's bodyguard, left the back of the room and ordered everyone not to move. The team suddenly realized it was not firecrackers they had heard. At the same time, the door of the newsroom flew open. One of the two masked men shouted "Allahu akbar" then asked a single question: "Where is Charb?" The editorial team sat in stunned silence. Then the shooting began. The unknown men fired bullet after bullet. Slowly. Nobody screamed. Then followed a deathly silence and the smell of gunpowder.

Sigolène Vinson heard footsteps approaching. Then shots rang out again. One of the unknown men slowly walked along the wall. It was Said Kouachi. He said to her: "Calm down. Do not be afraid. I will not kill you. You are a woman. We do not kill women. But think about what you do. What you do is wrong. I will spare you, and since I have spared you, you must read the Quran." Staring into the killer's eyes, Sigolène nodded her head. Back in the newsroom, the youngest Kouachi brother did murder a woman; Elsa Cayat, a psychoanalyst and columnist. Saïd Kouachi shouted three times towards the big room: "We do not kill women!", before the two killers ran away.

In the conference room, the silence of the wounded echoed that of the dead. Bodies lay on the ground, face down. Philippe Lançon had been shot in the right cheek, and although his face had been torn off, his days were not numbered. Sigolène Vinson called the fire brigade: "It's Charlie, come quickly, they're all dead." The fireman asked how many bodies there were and the address. Sigolène Vinson repeated mechanically: "They are all dead!" It was then the man on the other end of the line understood the importance of the tragedy.

Every second seemed like an eternity. Help was slow in arriving and the wait was unbearable. Finally, the silhouette of the well-known Parisian emergency doctor Patrick Pelloux appeared in the doorway. He leaned over Charb's neck, took his pulse, then stroked his head: "My brother." Survivors of the attack now had to leave the crime scene. They were taken to the goldfish bowl; the large, glass-fronted office where Zineb, Laurent Léger and Gérard Biard usually worked. Luz and Laurent Léger were already there, followed by firemen, then by Riss. Cecile, Corinne and Luce were also there. Apart from Elsa Cayat, all of the other women were alive.

The cake Sigolène Vinson had brought was obliterated by the gunfire. Sensing death, Lila, the red cocker spaniel, ran from table to table. Far off in the street came the sound of more gunshots. The Kouachi brothers had returned to their black car to continue their barbarous killing.

It was noon when the commanders of the two elite French anti-terrorist units, the GIGN and RAID, each received a telegram from the main office of the Paris Judicial Police: "Attack on the premises of the *Charlie Hebdo* newspaper at No. 10, Rue Nicolas Appert in the 11th arrondissement. Eleven deaths currently counted. The two alleged perpetrators are on the run." The commanders conveyed the message, which for the moment was just this single piece of information.

Yet what followed would be a first in the history of the police and gendarmerie in France; for the first time since their founding, the two elite units would collaborate on several operations that ran for three consecutive days, both in and outside of Paris. Indeed, a convention called 'leading concurrent' has recently been signed between the two forces, stipulating that the territorially competent service – the one leading it – can ask for support from the other service, i.e. the competitor.

From noon, the threat level in France was raised by the Prime Minister as part of the Vigipirate Plan. This anti-terrorist system includes different elements of prevention, vigilance and protection, as well as an investigatory element, starting with a judicial enquiry which can be opened by the leaders. It covers 'Murder and assassination attempts, armed robbery, violation of weapons legislation, all in connection with a terrorist organization, and criminal conspiracy, that is, with the intention of committing a crime, or several crimes.'

The Vigipirate Plan's high alert was activated throughout the Ile de France region. All members of special units, whether on duty or not, were called back and prepared to mobilise. From pre-alert, they quickly moved to on alert. Hundreds of police, gendarmes and soldiers now proceeded to embark on a manhunt of unparalleled scope, in order to stop the terrorists who were still on the run.

Members of both the GIGN and RAID units have seen terrorism evolve using new forms of violence and have learned how to proceed. For these terrorists, it is less of a planned killing, but rather a 'solo' jihad. The perpetrators of the attack had attacked two symbols; democracy, through a satirical weekly newspaper that publishes caricatures they consider to be 'blasphemous', and the authority of the state, by attacking the police, who are symbols of order and security. Terrorists then take credit for their actions via the media. It had quickly become clear that these men, fitting the profile of indoctrinated psychopaths, had lost their own identity and had been radicalised by Salafist Jihadist organizations.

The members of GIGN and RAID were now in a race against the clock to avoid further catastrophe – that is, even more deaths.

While investigations continued, the two fugitives came face to face with a police car parked on Boulevard Richard-Lenoir and opened fire. They then came across a second police car and two policemen patrolling on bikes. One of them, Ahmet Merabet, fired at the two suspects. They fired back and wounded him, before proceeding to shoot him brutally at close range. They fled, chased by the police. At No. 45, Rue de Meaux, they robbed a motorist and stole his grey Renault Clio, yelling at him, "If the media ask, tell them it's Al-Qaeda from Yemen," before blending into the Paris afternoon traffic.

Thanks to several witness statements, DNA fingerprints and an identity card left behind in the black Citroën C3 that was found at Porte de Pantin, the two suspects were quickly identified; Chérif and Saïd Kouachi, two brothers who were well-known to the French intelligence services. They had symptomatic backgrounds; with French-Algerian parents, the two brothers were orphaned at a young age and placed in foster homes. Chérif Kouachi, 32, was radicalised in prison, where he met Djamel Beghal, who had been sentenced for participating in a planned attack against the US Embassy in France. Beghal would become his mentor. Chérif's brother, Saïd, 34, underwent terrorist training in Yemen and his involvement in jihadist groups had caused him to be spotted by the authorities.

The two brothers were listed on two US security databases; they had been banned from flying to the United States and were registered on the Terrorist Screening Center and TIDE's no fly list – a highly confidential list of known or suspected terrorists. Investigators discovered that the CNCIS (National Commission for the Control of Security Interception) had stopped wire-tapping the two fugitives in June 2014 due to lack of evidence linking them with terrorism. Gendarme and police forces quickly gathered all of their information and analysis together to find the two fugitives. In the afternoon, hundreds of police raided the flat in Reims where Saïd resided, and where Chérif regularly visited, then also Strasbourg, Pantin and Gennevilliers, as well as several towns around the Paris region. These operations continued until mid-evening, but did not give rise to any questioning. Although further DNA was found at Saïd Kouachi's home, the two brothers remained untraceable, even though it was certain that the fugitives had spent the Wednesday night in the forest near Vauciennes, on the edge of the Aisne and Oise rivers. Two days later, two chaise longue rugs, a car floor mat, a towel and a shopping bag with the two brothers' DNA on it were discovered in the woods.

At 9.21 am on Thursday morning, the Renault Clio was seen near Vauciennes, in the region of Villers-Cotterêts. Armed with Kalashnikovs and rocket launchers, they refuelled and stole money and food from the Avia petrol station in Vauciennes. The manager recognised the men and immediately alerted the police.

By 10.00 am, the GIGN and RAID units were on the scene, both engaged in multiple deployments. The men were divided into tactical groups to complete the systematic search of the area. As the Renault Clio resumed its way on the main road (RN 2), an important device was set up. Intervention brigades were mobilised due to the suspicion of a support network existing for the two suspects.

At the beginning of the afternoon, the Vigipirate Plan that had been put into action the day before for the Ile de France was now extended to Picardy as the search intensified. GIGN and RAID units worked together to the perimeter of the search area. The gendarmerie closed the roads permanently, particularly in the Villers/Chouy sector, with the aim of confining the fugitives. Despite the rain, they took refuge in the forest of Montagny-Sainte-Félicité, in the Oise, and slept in the woods. The night made them easy targets for terrorists, and so the gendarmes and police suspended their search.

In Nanteuil-le-Haudouin at around 8.00 am on Friday, 9 January, Chérif and Saïd Kouachi drove to Paris in a stolen Peugeot 206. However, hearing the warning messages on the radio, they stopped in the small commune of Dammartin-en-Goële, about 20 km from Paris Charles de Gaulle Airport. They parked in the car park belonging to the *Création Tendance Découverte* printing press and came across one of its employees, whom they let go. The man then proceeded to call the police. From the window of his office on the first floor, the manager of the company, Michel Catalano, saw the two terrorists arrive and immediately ordered Lilian Lepère, a young employee, to go and hide. He confronted the two Kouachi brothers as they entered the building, telling a deliveryman, who had just arrived, to leave. The terrorists claimed to be Al-Qaeda and said they wanted to, "fight the police, the state and all those who harm Muslims." A police patrol arrived in the car park and at around 8.50 am, Saïd Kouachi came out of the building and opened fire on the police, who fired back in return. Kouachi was hit in the neck and went back into the company building, where he was treated by Michel Catalano. Meanwhile, the gendarmes set fire to the Peugeot 206's tires so as to prevent any escape attempt. School pupils in the area were evacuated and residents told to return to their homes. Other gendarmerie patrols and members of GIGN and RAID units arrived on the scene. An emergency plan was put in place by the GIGN, with RAID units there in support, as well as doctors and an assault team of about sixty men. The plan also involved changes to flight plans at the nearby Charles de Gaulle Airport, whilst the police, supported by three helicopters, locked down the village and its 8,000 inhabitants. Snipers climbed onto the rooftops of neighbouring businesses, and the units deployed as they had been trained to do. Michel Catalano was released, but Lilian Lepère was still in his hiding position in the cupboard under the kitchen sink.

At 9.45 am, Igor Sahiri, a journalist at BFM-TV, called the company switchboard. Cherif Kouachi picked up the phone, then hung up. Igor Sahiri persisted and eventually managed to talk to him. Cherif Kouachi told him that he had been sent by Al-Qaeda to Yemen and that he had been trained by Imam Anwar Al-Awlaki, who had told him to shoot *Charlie Hebdo* journalists. A few minutes after this conversation, which was described by the special forces as a propaganda message, the national negotiating team from GIGN took stock of the situation and presented the strategy and objectives of how to make contact with the two terrorists. At 12.45 pm, it made contact with the two brothers, who, having already delivered their message to the media, no longer wished to communicate further.

At 1.00 pm on Friday, 9 January, 32-year-old Amedy Coulibaly parked his car in Saint-Mandé, a commune in the Val-de-Marne, two blocks from the *Hypercacher* supermarket at the Porte de Vincennes. From being a petty criminal, Coulibaly had progressed onto more serious crimes and, in 2005, had been incarcerated for seven months at the Fleury-Mérogis Prison, where he had met Cherif Kouachi. The two men became friends and after their release, they had met again in Murat, where their mentor, Djamel Beghal, was under house arrest. It appears that all three of them were involved in an attempt to rescue the terrorist, Smait Ait Ali Belkacem, but only Coulibaly and Beghal were arrested. Incarcerated in 2010, Coulibaly was freed in May 2014.

Amedy Coulibaly entered the *Hypercacher* supermarket at the corner of Avenue de la Porte de Vincennes and Rue Albert Willemetz, at 1.05 pm. Coulibaly instantly opened fire, first killing one of the clients, then a second man because his name sounded Jewish. Coulibaly also injured the manager, who was able to escape. As the rain of bullets flew, a customer who tried to enter the shop was killed and the twenty-five people inside were taken hostage. At 1.19 pm, the GIGN and RAID units were informed of the shooting and the hostage situation that was taking place back in Paris itself. In the event of a crisis, priority is always given to the most delicate situation, and so the taking of hostages in Vincennes was now the primary concern, due to the high number of prisoners involved. An assault team of forty men from RAID was redeployed from Dammartin-en-Goële to Paris, while a small RAID team remained behind at GIGN's disposal. The prosecutor's office opened an investigation "in response to the events near la Porte de Vincennes," which was entrusted to the anti-terrorist section (SAT) of the criminal brigade of Paris, supported by the sub-direction anti-terrorist (SDAT) of the Central Directorate of the Judicial Police and the General Directorate for Internal Security (DGSI).

Thirty-five members from the Paris Research and Intervention Brigade (BRI), which is part of the Central Office against Organized Crime, were already in position in front of the supermarket. Dozens of police cars, rescue vehicles, and firefighters were also on site. A security perimeter was put in place, from the Porte de Vincennes to the Porte de Vanves. The authorities quickly evacuated the shops near the supermarket and asked the teachers of the nearby Hélène Boucher secondary school to keep the students inside and block all exits. Meanwhile, the ring road was shut in both directions at the Porte de Vincennes.

An operational command post was set up to centralise all information, with the RAID commander taking overall strategic and tactical command of the operation, which included units from RAID, the BRI and hundreds of police. However, this did not prevent him from remaining in permanent communication with the GIGN concerning the situation at Dammartin-en-Goële.

Of Malian origin, Lassana Bathily was a shopkeeper at *Hypercacher*. Whilst busy stocking up the products in the fresh produce aisle, he suddenly heard gunshots and saw customers coming towards him calling "Help!"

He quickly understood the situation and took the first six customers to safety towards the basement, in the freezer room, which he disabled. Next, he climbed into the lift and escaped through the emergency exit, just as three customers had already done before him. When he emerged out of the supermarket with his hands in the air, he was handcuffed; he would remain handcuffed for an hour and a half until a colleague was able to confirm his identity. He was now able to collaborate with the police by drawing a sketch of the supermarket, and giving them the keys to the automatic shutter, which was lowered. Meanwhile, fourteen customers tried to hide in the second cold room, but were unable to close the door from the inside and so they returned to the store under duress. Another client, Yohav Hattab, tried to seize a weapon that was placed on a box, but it jammed and he was shot down by the terrorist.

At 1.27 pm, Amedy Coulibaly asked a hostage to speak to the police, saying that his interlocutor "knew everything" and "knew who he was", before hanging up. In front of his hostages, he announced he was fighting for the Islamic State and that he was "a friend of the two brothers who perpetrated the *Charlie Hebdo* attack." He claimed responsibility for the murder of a police officer carried out the day before in Montrouge, and explained his intention to confront the police force. At this precise moment, the RAID team knew that "Coulibaly would fight to the bitter end."

The hostages observed that the terrorist had a computer and was carrying a GoPro camera on his chest. Shortly after 3.00 pm, he turned on the television to retrieve more information and saw a banner on the BFM-TV channel indicating the number of hostages. He looked up the telephone number for the channel on the internet and called the journalists. Part of this conversation would be broadcast after the crisis had ended. He explained that he had 'synchronised' the launch of the operation with the Kouachi brothers and that they were "defending oppressed Muslims."

In Dammartin-en-Goële, Lilian Lepère was still in the printing shop. He sent his father an SMS, allowing the GIGN to locate where he was hiding. Meanwhile, the negotiator made contact with the Kouachi brothers who immediately declared: "We were Al-Qaeda fighters in Yemen." The negotiators quickly realised that the two brothers were determined to fight to the death. They expected the worst and so any assault had to be carried out quickly. The men in the GIGN team put their helmets on and stood ready to intervene. In a meeting room outside, the GIGN's chief operations officer went through the final details with his team, whilst elsewhere, the latest instructions were given to members of mobile anti-terrorist units.

Some men had hidden in the woods, others had taken up positions on the roofs, while others stood in front of and on a Sherpa Renault Trucks Defense assault vehicle, which was equipped with an assault ladder and a modular platform with hydraulic ramp. Meanwhile, three helicopters with onboard snipers circled over Dammartin-en-Goële.

At 4.40 pm, the GIGN team located Chérif and Saïd Kouachi on the ground floor of the printing works. The two brothers opened the door and looked outside. A three-point observation network on the transformer floor allowed GIGN members to follow any movements inside the building. Thirteen minutes later, the two terrorists opened the glass door and ran into the car park, firing in front of them as they went. At that moment, the assault was ordered and response teams returned fire. The snipers positioned on the roofs and in front of the entrance and on the Sherpa vehicles, fired at the two men. The attack only lasted for a few moments. Mortally wounded, Sharif and Saïd Kouachi collapsed in the car park, one having been hit in the back, the other in the stomach. On the ground, the units found a rocket launcher with a rocket already loaded, two Kalashnikovs, automatic pistols, a dozen grenades and smoke bombs. Afterwards, they freed Lilian Lepère, who was still hiding in the kitchen. A GIGN member was slightly injured during the operation.

At 5.12 pm, just after the operation against the Kouachi brothers in Dammartin-en-Goële had taken place, RAID and BRI members launched their assault on the *Hypercacher* supermarket. There was total silence all around Porte de Vincennes as a commando of fifty RAID members headed into the supermarket. Then shots were heard. A BRI lorry moved towards the supermarket entrance, followed by 100 members of special forces. RAID men were on the front line on three sides. A column burst through an emergency door and entered from the rear, but Coulibaly fired back. At the same time, another column raised the shop front's metal shutter and threw disabling grenades inside. A RAID member entered the shop first, covered by his colleagues, and he was injured as the shock of the Kalashnikov's bullet hit his bulletproof vest. Meanwhile, his colleagues opened fire on the front door and the windows. Realising he was cornered, Amedy Coulibaly rushed forward, weapon in hand, towards the entrance of the supermarket, but was immediately neutralised. RAID members rushed in to free the hostages, who came out screaming and crying in shock.

In total, four hostages had died over the previous hours: Philippe Braham, Yohan Cohen, François Saada and Yoav Hattab.

In the supermarket, the police found several weapons, including two Kalashnikovs, two automatic guns, eight magazines, a knife and twenty sticks of explosives. The hostage-taker had also tried to booby trap one of the shop's doors with explosives, and so effort was still needed to defuse what remained behind.

The toll of the attacks from 7-9 January 2015 amounted to seventeen victims, including eleven people in the Charlie Hebdo *offices, four among the hostages in the* Hypercacher *supermarket, a policewoman murdered in Montrouge and a policeman who was shot in Paris.*

The investigation carried out after the attacks established that one of the recovered weapons was the same as that used during the attack on a jogger in Fontenay-aux-Roses, on 7 January. It also established that it was Amedy Coulibaly who had murdered the policewoman in Montrouge, Clarissa Jean-Philippe, and injured her colleague. Hayat Boumeddiene, the companion of Amedy Coulibaly, and who was sought by the French authorities, is currently living in Syria.

In response to the Charlie Hebdo *attacks and the 'jihadist attacks' of 7-9 January, millions of people around the world demonstrated using the slogan: "Je suis Charlie"(I am Charlie). Given the exceptional level of mobilisation, by both the population and the heads of state, these attacks have had repercussions that can only be described as extraordinary. Many historians and political journalists agree that these attacks, as well as other recent terrorist episodes in Australia, Belgium, Great Britain, Canada and Tunisia, could one day be considered to be the dawn of a new era of terrorism, or as a trigger for a global alliance against a growing threat that requires effective action.*

Three hours of horror: Explosions at the Stade de France, Shots fired in Paris bistros and the Bloodbath at Bataclan - November 2015

Friday, 13 November 2015 was one of the last beautiful autumn days of the year in Paris; the temperature was 15°C, with broken cloud. That evening there was to be a friendly international football match between France and Germany at the Stade de France, the largest stadium in the country, in the suburb of Saint-Denis. The German Foreign Minister, Franz-Walter

Steinmeier, had travelled to Paris to watch the game in the VIP lounge with French President François Hollande.

That Friday morning, in the noble 16th arrondissement, there had been a lot of excitement and tension following a bomb scare at the Hotel Molitor where the German team was staying. An anonymous telephone caller had threatened to explode a bomb hidden in the hotel. The German players were evacuated at once to the safety of the nearby Roland Garros tennis centre, while police dogs searched the hotel for explosives. Two hours later the all clear was given. At this point the footballers were taking it all in good part, but this was how the day began which was later to send a shock wave through France in the next few hours.

The football match kicked off at 9.00 pm in front of 80,000 spectators and televised in sixty-six other countries. Normality seemed to have returned. Perhaps on account of the bomb scare earlier, the German side was not playing well. After fifteen minutes an explosion was heard from outside the stadium. This was noted by the players but did not interfere with play and the game continued.

The explosion was caused by one of three suicide bombers. After the match began, he had attempted to enter the stadium by Gate D in Avenue Jules Rimet. The security man on duty, Salim Toorabally, was very alert and stopped the stranger, who had no entrance ticket and was therefore directed to the main entrance. The stranger tried his luck at another gate. Here he had to submit to a body search where Toorabally found that he was wearing a vest with explosives and immediately informed colleagues at the other gates. The bomber noticed that Toorabally was excitedly making a telephone call and ran off to the nearby brasserie, *Events* where two minutes later the bomb exploded, killing the bomber and a passer-by.

The identity of the first bomber remains unknown. A Syrian passport was found at the scene issued to an Ahmad Almohammad, a Syrian Government soldier killed several months previously. The bomber was registered under this name on 3 October 2015 on the Greek island of Leros as a refugee, together with 200 other Syrians. He was finger-printed there and sometime later re-surfaced in a refugee camp in Serbia.

Back at the Stade de France, at 9.30 pm the second bomber exploded his bomb near Gate H of the stadium at the fast-food restaurant *Quick* and blew himself up. The second bomber also had a Syrian passport, this one issued to Mohammad Almahmod. The document, numbered 007773937, was one of a batch of blank passports stolen by the terrorist organisation Islamic State at Rakka in Syria. Almahmod was also registered on 3 October at

Leros as a refugee. According to passenger lists, both he and the first bomber travelled on 5 November by ferry to Piraeus.

A third bomber, Bilal Hadfi, set off his bomb at 9.53 pm in Rue Trémiés at the corner of Rue de la Cokerie in front of a McDonald's restaurant near the stadium. Hadfi was a 20-year-old French national who had recently been living in Belgium where he attended secondary school for six months before disappearing. Five minutes after the game had resumed after half-time there was some confusion amongst the spectators. After the first two explosions the gates had been shut and nobody allowed to leave, the reason not being announced. The game continued in the absence of the French President, while his German political guest stayed. The first details began to circulate in the eighty-fifth minute of the game as the first spectators anxiously began leaving their seats. When the game finished, a ghostly quiet prevailed in the stadium as the spectators slowly headed for the exits. When it was discovered that the exits were all shut, excitement and panic broke out and people now invaded the pitch in their thousands, waiting for the gates to be opened.

The Chief of the BRI and the members of his unit, the Search and Intervention Brigade, a special task force of the French police, had been informed of the three bomb explosions near the stadium and kept a close watch, for this spectacular beginning gave reason to fear that worse was to follow.

Another group of terrorists had meanwhile attacked bistros in different parts of Paris. Coinciding with the first explosion at Saint-Denis near the Stade de France, at 9.25 pm terrorists in a black Seat Leon opened fire with Kalashnikov assault rifles at diners sitting outside the restaurant *Le Carillon* in the 10th arrondissement, at the corner of Rue Albert and Rue Bichat. The same killers then concentrated on the Cambodian restaurant *Le Petit Cambodge* at 20 Rue Albert.These attacks resulted in the deaths of fifteen people and wounding a further ten.

The killers then drove on, and seven minutes after the first shooting they halted at a road junction and shot dead a man sitting in his car. After that they fired their Kalashnikovs into the *Café Bonne Biere* at 32 Rue du Faubourg du Temple, killing three people. Next they fired into the launderette *Lavatronic* near the café, and finally into the Italian restaurant *La Casa Nostra* at 2 Rue de la Fontaine du Roi, killing one and wounding eight. One of the killers now got out of the car with the intention of killing more diners at the latter restaurant, but his assault rifle jammed and as the car drove away, he contented himself with killing another passer-by in the street in a drive-by shooting.

At 9.36 pm the killers arrived at 92 Rue du Charonne where they fired from their vehicle at guests in the *Bar de la Belle Équipe*, shouting "Allahu Akbar" and the phrase "This is for Syria." Nine people were wounded in this attack.

Four minutes later, at 9.40 pm, bomber Ibrahim Abdeslan blew himself up after ordering a drink in the *Café Comptoir Voltaire* at 253 Boulevard Voltaire, in the 11th arrondissement. The bomb only partially exploded, but still wounded fifteen guests. This crime scene was only 900 metres from the *Bar la belle Équipe*. The black Seat Leon with Belgian plates that had been used by the killers was found twenty-four hours later in the Paris suburb of Montreuil, near the Croix de Chavaux metro station. Three Kalashnikovs, five full and eleven empty magazines were found.

The police were mystified by these attacks, but the evening was by no means over. The high point of a series of deadly attacks on Paris and the Stade de France would be one of the worst-ever attacks on French soil since the Second World War. The killers chose this as the culmination, and it happened a few minutes later.

The Bataclan concert hall, built in 1864 and once known as *Le Grand Café Chinois-Théatre Ba-ta-clan*, today boasts a colourful red-yellow façade with Chinese characters. At 9.40 pm on Friday, 13 November, the Californian rock band *Eagles of Death Metal* were the star performers. They had an audience of 1,500, and the concert was sold out. The mood was steaming and electric, most of the guests sweating after dancing to the hard rock sounds for half an hour. The atmosphere was good. A black Volkswagen Polo drew up outside. Inside sat the three black-clad terrorists Samy Amimour, Omad Mostafai and Foued Mohamed Aggad. They got out of the car armed with Kalashnikovs and immediately began shooting at passers-by. In front of the Bataclan they killed two young men on rented bicycles. Then they ran into the Bataclan over the bar and merchandising areas and shot down anybody in their path. Their purpose was to create a bloodbath in the concert hall. They entered the concert hall and suddenly the drumbeats of *Eagles of Death Metal* were matched by the sound of bursts of fire from assault rifles and exploding hand grenades. The band realised that this was not part of their repertoire and got to safety while their audience began a struggle for survival. Some of the guests succeeded in reaching shelter in rooms near the hall, or in the balcony areas, and from there managed to reach the street through the rear exit.

The first two officers of the Public Security of the Paris police (BAC) arrived at about 9.45 pm in front of the Bataclan, on Rue Oberkampf and the corner of Rue Voltaire. The Commissioner and his assistant had been sent to obtain first impressions. They discovered that in a hall near the Bataclan music hall were numerous people with gunshot wounds, many in agony. The Chief of the Search and Intervention Brigade received a text message at 9.47 pm from a colleague stating that there had been explosions in Saint Denis and much shooting in Paris. Because of the numerous crime scenes, initially there was confusion on the part of the police as to where the best place would be to assemble. The Chief Commissioner therefore ordered his men to meet in twelve minutes at the BRI base on the Quai des Orfèvres in the centre of Paris, which would be the departure point for the unit. By reason of the differing reports coming from their colleagues about the explosions around the Stade de France and the shootings in the streets of two arrondissements, the BRI decided to leave immediately, equipped with protective shields.

They went first to the *Bar de la Belle Equipé* in the 11th arrondissement, Rue de Charonne, where they saw there was nothing they could do as only the dead and seriously wounded were found there. Then came an indication from the Paris head of the Federal Criminal Police. "Many people. *Bataclan*. Shooting is going on…" The BRI Chief Commissioner knew at once what had to be done, but he did not know yet that two hours, thirty-eight minutes and forty-four seconds of a nightmare were to follow.

Meanwhile the two BAC officers escorted firefighters so that the wounded fleeing to the streets from the Bataclan could be brought to safety. Then they decided to enter the concert hall. Both men were armed only with their service hand guns and wore a light bullet-proof vest. They did not know what the situation was inside, nor how many terrorists were there waiting for them. They only knew that the black-clad terrorists were heavily armed and that as BAC officers, they had to handle a coordinated terror attack across the capital and in Saint-Denis. From the street they had heard a great deal of shooting coming from within the building and had no option but to go inside the Bataclan. In the foyer they saw the first evidence of the carnage, then they went forward into the concert hall. After a swift look around the Commissioner saw one of the terrorists. He was running around the stage and pointing his Kalashnikov at a particular person. The terrorist seemed very composed. The two policemen saw the bloodbath being carried out and began shooting at the terrorist on the stage until he fell dead. At that an explosion occurred and the police then assumed that there were other terrorists in the hall, perhaps rigged with explosives.

Through their actions, the two officers had saved the life of the hostage in the sights of Samy Amimour and prevented further butchery. They then became involved in an exchange of gunfire, without knowing how many killers they were facing. At that moment, despite the danger, both called their wives for a last farewell. They succeeded in leaving the hall when the rest of the BAC arrived.

It was 10.15 pm when the BRI team got to the Bataclan. They had an armed military surgeon alongside, who would enter the building with them. They took up positions and first secured the ground floor. The Chief Commissioner was present with his men. Every man counted here; it was still not certain what awaited them. The unit positioned itself along the wall and then went in quickly. Their first objective was to secure the bar area. Meanwhile, two terrorists had taken twenty hostages to the roof. The BRI team noticed that the shooting had stopped, which was strange. The concert hall had now fallen quiet. Four hundred people lay on the floor in pools of blood, unmoving. Those victims still alive were so terrorised they were unable to communicate.

It was very difficult for the operational team to filter out the living from the dead. Their principal task was to arrest the miscreants as soon as possible. That was the BRI's speciality. Nevertheless, in record time they had to establish if anybody on the ground was wearing a rig with explosives. As a victim was helped up, he had to show his hands and raise his T-shirt to prove that he had no explosives. The BRI doctors showed their colleagues which persons had to be brought out of the building quickly. First the wounded, then those literally paralysed with shock. The dead were left where they lay. After thirty minutes the concert hall had been evacuated sector by sector.

Towards 10.30 pm the first BRI reinforcements arrived. They made progress, but the work had to be done cautiously step by step. They searched every corner of the Bataclan in the attempt to identify places where terrorists might be hiding. Nobody knew that at that time they were on the upper balcony floor. The BRI men moved slowly upwards. Every time when the unit opened a door and peered around, they would find a group of terrorised people cowering in a corner. Each would be searched and then taken down to safety.

By 10.45 pm, every member of BRI was present in the Bataclan, and they were later joined at 11.50 pm by a team from RAID. They advanced slowly, as there was a constant danger that they might come across a terrorist who could kill them, and himself, by setting off a belt of explosives. At

11.15 pm the columns of the unit reached a door where a female hostage awaited them. She had been chosen by the terrorists as their spokeswoman and made it clear to the police that they should advance no further and to stand still. She also stated that two terrorists were waiting behind the next door wearing explosive belts. If the police took a step forward, the terrorists would set off the devices and kill the twenty hostages.

A negotiation was begun using a mobile phone. The five conversations with the two terrorists between 11.15 pm and 12.18 am were banal and superficial. They came from Syria, had no accent and were nervous and aggressive, but not panicked. Omad Moustafai and Foued Mohamed Aggad repeated the same phrase over and over, namely that they "as part of the Islamic State organisation were only replying to French aggression." What surprised the BRI negotiator during these conversations was that the hostages were never mentioned, nor was any readiness expressed to exchange hostages for something. It appeared that they represented nothing valuable to the terrorists. The terrorists did mention the media, however, and wanted to make a verbal statement, but the negotiator was not interested. They were wearing explosive belts and could blow themselves up in front of the cameras. In this way they would achieve their objective with countless onlookers. In any case it was a waste of time; the chief negotiator informed the BRI Chief that the terrorists were not planning to negotiate anything. The Chief Commissioner spoke at once with the Prefect of Paris Police and requested permission for an immediate attack on the grounds, declaring that the terrorists were unstable and that the situation was degenerating.

At midnight, the Prefect of Police gave his authority for the attack. The incident had to be brought to an end and the hostages freed. The BRI Chief and his men prepared for the worst. The worst case scenario could be that the terrorists were waiting behind the door and using the hostages as human shields. For the BRI, the situation was one of the most critical of recent years. Consequently, the Commissioner arranged his men into two attack columns. The first would enter with twelve men, and the second would climb over their bodies if they were killed.

A Ramses shield would protect the first BRI men to enter the corridor to the balcony. They opened the door quickly and an exchange of fire began. The shield was hit twenty-seven times, and countless rounds hit the wall. The shield was very important, protecting those hostages who could get behind it as the police advanced. As soon as the unit advanced, the wounded hostages begged for help while others asked the police to pull back and so prevent another bloodbath. The BRI men remained firm; a terrorist cannot aim at police and hostages at the same time. They kept shooting.

The hostages were brought out successively from the danger zone, and passed to the second column in a human chain. Behind the second column were the doctors who took charge of all hostages. Once all were safely out, the real operation began. The BRI forced the terrorists to the end of the passage. Suddenly they saw a shadow and started shooting. The first killer fell and released his explosive belt; he died where he fell, his explosion killed the other man.

The operation ended forty minutes later, but after the two terrorists were killed, the men of the unit uncovered much more. Other victims had hidden themselves behind wide doors and false ceilings and were so afraid of the unit figures clad in black that they were given their mobile phones and told to call the police emergency number and be told that these really were the police. The survivors were now led out of the concert hall, many of them keeping their eyes closed so as not to have to see the murdered bodies and the bloodbath. On the balcony were numerous victims still unable to walk or speak. What shocked the men of the anti-terrorist units the most were the numerous mobile phones which rang and rang hours after the incident, and remained unanswered. The units left the Bataclan at 2.30 am, but the operation would forever remain in their minds. The BRI men are used to crime and violence, but the scenes they saw on Friday, 13 November were cruel and cannot be erased from their memories.

In the series of criminal attacks occurring on Friday, 13 November 2015, more people were killed than in any other attack in Europe since Madrid in 2004. Altogether 130 people were murdered and 683 wounded, 100 seriously. The BRI Chief always emphasised in conversations with me that this was one of the most dreadful attacks ever to occur in France and that his men did not know its extent until it was all over. "Only then did they smell the blood and the death." Some of the wives of the BRI men told their husbands, "You're not going back to that unit. It is over. Finished. How many more people do you want to see die? Do you want to be the next?" But the BRI Chief *knew that his men would all report for duty the next day.*

The BRI is the primary unit for operations in Paris, RAID in other urban zones and railway stations, and the GIGN in the national départements *and airports. The BRI is unique in that on the one hand it is a special unit, and on the other has expertise in legal investigations.*

Bloodbath in Nice on France's National Day – July 2016

July 14 is a special day in France, recalling the storming of the Bastille and the end of the French monarchy. By a law passed in 1880, the day became a public holiday and it is celebrated with great joy every year throughout the country. On the Cote d'Azur, fireworks are let off along the Mediterranean coast and the population is exuberant. That particular night in Nice, 2016, was hot and festive. The Nice locals and tourists gathered along the famous Promenade des Anglais to watch the fireworks display. The promenade is 7 km long and is formed along the Baie des Anges, Nice Bay. The road along the shore has a wonderful beach promenade. That evening 30,000 people watched the pyrotechnics, including whole families from France and abroad. It was one of the finest experiences of the year on the Cote d'Azur.

The memory of the mass killings in November the previous year had gradually faded, although the violence of the attacks in Brussels in March earlier that year, and the murder of two policemen in Magnanville in June, were still in peoples' minds. That evening, however, for the French the threat was far away. The Government was confident too; that morning President François Hollande had announced the imminent raising of the state of emergency. Now the 14 July party was in full swing on the Riviera, and the people were relaxed and joyful.

At 10.32 pm, precisely after the last of the fireworks burst over the Mediterranean skies, terror returned to France when a white 19-tonne Renault Midiu lorry, coming from the Magnan district of Nice, turned into the Promenade des Anglais by the Lenval children's hospital, along the stretch normally reserved for pedestrians. The lorry driver was 31-year old Mohamed Lahouaiej Bouhiel, a Tunisian from the northern town of Msaken, near Sousse. Bouhiel was known as a drunkard and drug-addict who visited a fitness studio and liked to dance the salsa. His wife had left him on account of his inclination towards domestic violence. He didn't have strong Islamic convictions because he ate pork and practised bisexuality in southern France. On 1 July he had researched Islamic State on the internet, collecting photographs of dead people, as well as Osama bin Laden and the jihadist Mokhtar Belmokhtar. On 14 July he took a selfie with his mobile phone on the Promenade des Anglais, and after that went on his bicycle to rent the lorry, stowing the bicycle in the back of it.

From the moment he drove into the Promenade, Bouhiel was filmed by security cameras installed there. He was driving without headlights, and before the Boulevard Gambetta he increased his speed to 90 km/hr for 400 metres in order to break through a police barricade consisting of a police car, barriers and several highway partitioning segments. The barricade blocked off the street for pedestrian use only on the national holiday.

After breaking through the barricade, the lorry was filmed on a zigzag course before finally heading, in the most brutal way, into the crowds of people who stood on the southerly pavement ahead, and the three closed lanes of the Promenade road. Bouhiel tried to keep the lorry on the pavement for as long as he could in order to kill as many people as possible before being stopped. Obstructions he had to avoid included a bus shelter and a pavilion. Then he arrived back on the street, and for over 2 km the "crazy truck", as survivors referred to it later, attempted to kill as many people as possible on the Promenade by running them down. Scenes of panic and hysteria were filmed by hotel guests with their mobile phones from the balconies where moments earlier they had witnessed the fireworks display.

Near the famous Hotel Negresco, the lorry's speed dropped when 'Romain', a crane-driver, dropped his bicycle and ran after it. Once he'd caught it up, he attempted three or four times to open the driver's door, but found it locked. When the terrorist pointed a revolver at him, Romain was forced to desist.

At this moment 'Christophe' had been following the lorry on his motor scooter for 1 km at high speed. When Bouhiel drove the vehicle in a zigzag between the road and the pavement, Christophe cried in rage as he saw the lorry drive into the crowd, tossing people into the air, then leaving them to fall and lie lifeless on the ground.

Two agents from the special police unit BST (*Brigade spécialisée de terrain*) were on duty that evening in the front office of the police station in the Rue Meyerbeer. Elodie and Simon were alarmed by very garbled messages about a lorry breaking through a police barricade. They proceeded to the Promenade des Anglais and took up the pursuit, seeing Christophe running behind the lorry. The two police officers, who could now look into the driving cab at eye level, aimed at the driver with their service weapons but did not fire, unlike Bouhiel, who fired his weapon at them through the broken window. After throwing his scooter at the lorry, Christophe managed to run and catch it up. He got on the running board but then lost his balance during the ride.

More people were killed as the crowd ran in all directions. At that moment Christophe regained his footing on the running board on the driver's side and began to punch the driver while trying to open his door. As the lorry continued its course, Christophe saw the driver manipulating a 7.65 mm pistol. The driver hit him with it, and he lost his balance. While trying to follow the lorry again, Bouhiel began shooting in his direction. Another man, 'Michel', approached the cabin intending to enter it, but was forced to take cover when he saw the barrel of the weapon projecting from the driver's window. He shouted a warning to Christophe that they should both flee.

Christophe kept out of the field of fire near the lorry with Michel behind him, and at this point six members of the police BST unit appeared and surrounded the lorry. A team of three police officers arriving from the north of the city began shooting at Bouhiel, who wriggled out of the driver's seat but kept shooting. At the same time, Simon, the BST officer on the driver's side, emptied a full magazine of fifteen rounds into the cabin, and while reloading saw that the driver had collapsed.

From the right, female police officer Elodie approached holding her firearm. 'Eric', an information technician, who had made several attempts to open the cabin door when he heard the terrorist shooting, stated that Elodie hesitated, or perhaps tried to obtain cover before shooting, and he therefore offered to relieve her of her service weapon and use it himself. She refused, aimed her Sig-Sauer 9 mm pistol at Bouhiel and neutralised him.

The lorry drove for 328 yards and finally came to a standstill by the Palais de la Méditerrannée at 10.35 pm. Bouhiel was killed by dozens of police who stopped the lorry after it had murdered nearly 100 people on the Promenade des Anglais. A rain of bullets had poured into the driving cab, riddling his body which finished up leaning against the passenger door. He was dressed in a black shirt and blue shorts. Forensic scientists later counted sixty-nine hits on the lorry; the side windows were shattered, the fender was missing and one of the front tyres had been hit and burst. The medical examiner revealed that Boulhiel had been shot ten times.

After the shooting, suspicion and a certain disquiet reigned. 'Christophe' was arrested and handcuffed on the street as a terrorist. A passer-by called Pierre, 26, was also arrested as one of Boulhiel's accomplices, but was later released the same evening due to false information.

The police went over the lorry very carefully, fearing that the hissing from the burst tyre might be coming from a bomb. The head of the department for the intervention measures set up a larger security area and had the bomb squad informed.

A member from the Alpes-Maritimes Region's bomb disposal team, 'Bernard', was contacted at 10.46 pm and arrived at 11.20. He checked over the lorry for fifteen minutes, but found no explosives. In the driver's cab he cut open Bouhiel's Bermuda shorts to ensure he had not hidden explosives on his body. While he worked, the terrorist's mobile phone rang. It was his wife, and she continued to call a number of times until the following morning. Bernard completed his examination at 12.10, but on the Promenade des Anglais, the rescue teams and their helpers worked through the night.

The bloodbath on the Promenade des Anglais in Nice occurred over a distance of 1.7 km, between house numbers 11 and 147. The murderer, Mohamed Lahouaiej Bouhiel, was criminally responsible for the deaths of eighty-six people and caused panic in the whole city. Several of those injured had jumped over the promenade wall and landed on the pebble and shingle below in order to seek cover.

This terrorist attack was hard to digest in France. That evening television stations worldwide interrupted their programmes to bring the sad news, and the telephone networks ran hot as people tried to obtain news of family and friends. Social media giant Facebook *activated a security check. In Nice itself, chaos reigned. The sirens of ambulances howled incessantly, people on the streets cried. Some helped out by bringing medicines and dressings for the injured. All night long the survivors attempted to find their family members, while hundreds were tended in hospitals. It would be some time before Nice recovered from this terrorist attack.*

Apocalyptic Terror in Trèbes, southern France – March 2018

Friday, 23 March 2018 and the temperature was 14°C; a warm spring day in Trèbes, a quiet village in the *département* of Aude in southern France. Samia Menassi, the well-liked manager of the local supermarket *Super-U*, and wife of the mayor of Trèbes, sat in her office on the first floor discussing business with her executive director, Eric de la Jonquiere, and the new industrial medical officer. Suddenly they heard several very loud explosive noises, apparently coming from the supermarket hall. The time was 10.39 am. Irritated, thinking it might be a gang of children letting off fireworks, Mme Menassi stood up, apologised to the two men and left her office to investigate. She went downstairs quickly and, ducking low, looked through a window into the shopping hall. What she saw made her shudder. Very carefully she took a second look.

A young man holding a revolver fired it twice into the air before her eyes and shouted, "Allahu Akbar!" and declared to the frightened shoppers that he was a soldier of Islamic State. Then at cash desk 6 he shot dead the *Super-U* chief butcher, 50-year-old Christian Medves, who was just greeting cashier Julie. The killer then went to cash desk 2, said, "Watch, this is how it's done," and shot dead 65-year-old Hervé Sosna, who had just laid out his purchases on the conveyor belt. Fear and panic now broke out amongst the fifty or so other customers.

Mme Menassi could see that this was a terror attack in her supermarket and not a gang of children having fun. She knew she had to act quickly and told her two secretaries to inform the police immediately. Then with her two office partners, she set out to help her staff and customers leave the store from various sides. Some of the panicking customers took refuge in the refrigeration room, others lay themselves down behind the shelves. Most managed to leave the supermarket with Samia's guidance and ran across the street to the Peugeot car garage, begging the foreman for somewhere to hide.

Samia Menassi noticed that there were still four check-out girls in the supermarket. Meanwhile, the killer had walked to the *Super-U* bakery and shouted at a male customer, who fled in panic. The first gendarmes arrived at the supermarket at 11.00 am. The manager received them discreetly and asked them to come up to the first floor to see the surveillance film. The gendarmes could identify the two murdered customers, as well as the other customers lying on the floor near the shelves and the gunman holding a pistol, standing at the entrance. They knew that time would now be an important factor. The first fifty men of the special unit GIGN arrived from Toulouse to support the gendarmes.

Information relating to the killer had come from various ministries, and all pointed towards Radouane Lakdim, who was born on 11 April 1992 in Morocco, but had been a French citizen since the age of twelve. He lived with his parents and sisters in the poor Ozanam district, in Carcassonne. He had a criminal record going back to 2010 for illegal possession of a firearm and violent offences. In 2016 he had been sentenced to imprisonment for drug offences.

Lakdim was very active on Salafi social networks and since 2014 had been on a list of suspected Islamic extremists. He was considered a 'Fiché S' man, an indicator used both in France and Britain by law enforcement offices to note a person considered to be a threat to national security. He was being monitored by the authorities for his "radicalism and nearness to

Salafi[1] movements," but had given no indication of readiness to carry out attacks.

Early that morning, Lakdim had taken his little sister to school. Towards 10.00 am, in the Cité des Aigles, he had stopped a white Opel Corsa by aiming his gun at it, and thirteen minutes later shot its passenger, Jean Mazieres, the 61-year-old father of the driver and a well-known wine-grower in the region. Lakdim proceeded to throw them both out of the car and drive it towards the Caserne Laperrine barracks on Place Général de Gaulle. His first stop was the elite battalion of 3. Naval Infantry Parachute Regiment, where he intended to assault its administrative offices. Two hundred metres before he got there, however, he came across four policemen returning from their morning jog. He fired six rounds at them. One of the men received a bullet in the back and was taken to hospital with broken ribs and a punctured lung. Luckily, the bullet just missed his heart. The perpetrator crossed the Aude bridge and drove along Avenue du Général Leclerc, over the Rond-Point de l'Europe roundabout, along Avenue du 3e regiment de parachutistes d'infanterie de marine, and then took highway D6113 towards Trèbes. What possessed him to attack a supermarket will never be known.

Back at the supermarket, the gendarmes were hoping to detain the suspect without anyone else being wounded or killed. While the gendarmerie around the *Super-U* had sealed off the area, the GIGN decided to set up an assault column to free the four cashiers and fifteen customers who were still trapped in the supermarket hall, and to reason with the terrorist. The ten officers approached the supermarket entrance slowly from the outside. They negotiated with the terrorist for more than twenty minutes. Despite the tough talk he didn't weaken, and even threatened to set off three bombs which he had placed on the supermarket shelves. Together with the Toulouse GIGN officers, step by step the gendarmes managed to get all but one of the hostages out. One of the cashiers, 40-year-old Julie, had to stay back with the terrorist and act as his human shield with a gun to her head.

Lieutenant Colonel Arnaud Beltrame, deputy commander of the Aude Gendarmerie group, and one of the highest-ranking officers in the region, decided to hasten the release of the last hostage. He wanted to bring the drama to an end. Beltrame was known as an extremely courageous man who never gave in. He had had an epic career, both with the military and in police service, and had experience with the special unit of gendarmerie, even completing a dangerous overseas term in Iraq. He practiced various sports, was very religious, but was also a freemason, being a member of 'La Grande Loge de France'. He was happily married to Marielle, a veterinary surgeon. The religious rite of marriage was due to be celebrated at Vannes, where his mother lived, on 9 July 2018.

At the same time, three helicopters took off from the GIGN headquarters at Satory/Yvelines carrying the commander and several members of the unit to support their colleague at Trèbes. Beltrame now did something unique in the history of liberators; he offered himself to the terrorist in a hostage exchange. He ordered his people not to become involved until he gave them the signal. His team had no time to protest as he raised his arms and walked slowly to cash desk 2. When he reached the terrorist, he offered to exchange himself for Julie, who stared at him in fear. Beltrame looked into her eyes and nodded, a sign that she could go. He knew that he had gone voluntarily into the lion's den, as his GIGN colleagues would say later. He had accepted a danger that could result in his death. To the supporters of the Islamic State jihadist militia, a police officer was of greater value than a typical hostage. But the commander had made his decision. He laid his iPhone unnoticed on the cashier's desk so that his colleagues outside the supermarket could hear all that went on. The terrorist continued to speak with the officers of the GIGN branch in Toulouse, but his terms were the immediate withdrawal of the police presence from the supermarket. The discussion between the GIGN negotiator and Radouane grew ever tougher, after the latter confirmed that he was ready to die for Syria.

The GIGN officers knew what that meant; the terrorist wanted to die and would take his hostage with him. At the same time his demands now included the release of his 'arrested brothers'. Some time later he narrowed this down to Salah Abdeslam, the prime perpetrator of the Paris attacks of 13 November 2015, who was presently in Fleury-Merogis prison. This seemed to be important to the terrorist, who now disappeared with his hostage into the strongroom. The negotiations had lasted for well over two hours. The gendarmes and GIGN members at Toulouse did the best they could for Beltrame in their talks with the terrorist, but they knew there was no way out for him after putting himself in this trap. Beltrame continued to negotiate with Lakdim and liaise with GIGN.

At 1.10 pm, Lakdim appeared with his hostage in front of the strongroom. He held a gun to Beltrame's head, put an arm around his neck and threatened him with a knife. Beltrane continued talking to him until the negotiations broke down.

At 2.16 pm the GIGN team heard Beltrame shout: "Attack! Attack!" They ran in an assault column formation into the supermarket beyond the strongroom and then heard several shots. When they peered around the corner of the last stand of shelves, Radouane Lakdim confronted them using Beltrame as a human shield. This was insufficient cover for the terrorist. Several shots rang out and Lakdim sank to the ground, dead. Arnaud Beltrame, who had fallen beside him, was carried out by paramedics and taken by ambulance to the hospital at Carcassonne.

The GIGN commander had landed with his three helicopters, but unfortunately too late. Beltrame did not survive following an emergency operation in the early hours of Saturday. The bullet wounds to an arm and foot were not serious, but the terrorist had cut his throat and the loss of blood had been too great.

French President Emmanuel Macron honoured Arnaud Beltrame on 28 March 2018 by an act of State with full military honours in the courtyard of the Hotel des Invalides, after the coffin had been borne through the Panthéon. This official ceremony was held in the presence of the family and numerous members of the fighting forces, plus politicians and guests. After his address, President Macron awarded Beltrame a posthumous promotion to Colonel of Gendarmerie and the Commander's Cross of the Legion of Honour. The President had said: "To voluntarily die so that innocent persons may continue to live, that is the heart of the soldier's oath." Beltram's mother, Nicolle, stated in an interview to a journalist: "I know Arnaud was loyal, courageous and unselfish. Even when he was a small boy, he was always there for others. He often said: 'France comes before family.' Her son would not have seen it right to stand by doing nothing during such an act of terror. When she speaks today (i.e. a few months after the event) she does so only that his sacrifice would lead to us becoming "more humane, more tolerant. For a better world."

Four people died during this attack in southern France. Four too many. The French Minister of the Interior told the media that the terrorist was a "minor delinquent, known primarily as a drug addict. Nobody could predict that he would mutate into the kind of radical who would carry out the attack of 23 March." Lakdim was in the FGSPRT's database (Terrorist Radicalization Prevention) between 2016 and the autumn of 2017 when the watch on him was dropped.

On the evening of 23 March 2018, Lakdim's girlfriend, Marine Pequignot, born 18 November 1999 and 18 years old and also a 'Fichée S', was arrested for "criminal association connected to a terrorist enterprise."

When arrested she shouted "Allahu Akbar." She is a French national who converted to Islam at the age of 16. She is very active on social networks where she constantly praises the Islamic State and is known to the criminal prosecution authorities. During her detention she hailed the attacks in France as a good thing and even maintained that the Islamic State attack was a reprisal for fighters killed by the French Army. She also regretted "that there were not more deaths in Lakdim's attacks." She confirmed that she had been separated from him for a few weeks, however, and denied that she should be associated with Lakdim's project. At the same time she stated that she would not have reported him if she had known of his intentions. After her arrest she was arraigned for "participation with an association of terrorists preparing attacks on people" and was placed under interrogatory arrest on 27 March 2018.

Sofiane L., 17 years old and born in Carcassonne, was arrested between the Friday and Saturday for suspected complicity, but was released on the evening of 27 March.

During a search of Lakdim's parents' house at Trèbes, numerous writings were found in his room that were traceable back to Islamic State. A will was also discovered. The neighbours of the Lakdim family were unable to confirm that they had noticed any trend towards radicalism on the part of Radouane Lakdim. He had not attended the mosque for some time.

Why Commander Arnaud Beltrame bartered his life for that of the hostage Julie, and would not be deterred from doing so, remained a mystery for the police units weeks and months after the event. Ten days before the attack at Trèbes, Beltrame's father, Jean-François Beltrame, was buried in Trèbes at Grau-du-Roi. He had committed suicide and had been missing at sea since 16 August 2017. He left a note for his family. Arnaud Beltrame was very close to his father and had made a pilgrimage with him in 2015 to Sainte-Anne-d'Auray to pray for a wife. He subsequently met veterinary surgeon Marielle Vandenbunder and married her in a registry office ceremony in 2016. For his sacrifice he is a hero of the nation in the history of France. Jesus said (John 15:13): "No greater love hath man than this, that he give his life for his friend."

Chapter 3

Belgium

Kidnappers under Flemish-Walloon Pressure

Unit: Direction des Unités Spéciales du Commissariat Général
(DSU, previously CGSU)

144 Hours in the Hands of the Hostage-Takers – 1989

The nightmare for the inhabitants of Tilff, a romantic village in the Belgian
Ardennes in the Ourthe Valley, began on 16 September 1989, a beautiful
autumn day. Most of the villagers work at the Sart-Tilman campus of Liège
University in the hills nearby and enjoy the peace and quiet and remoteness
of Tilff. Guy Jeuris had been director of a branch of the Belgian Communal
Credit Bank in Liège for eight years. A qualified engineer, he was very
interested in information technology and commerce. He lived with his
family, wife Marie-Madeleine Jeuris and their two daughters Gaëlle, 10,
and Françoise, 13, in Tilff and had many friends.

That Saturday, shortly after his wife had returned from shopping, the
doorbell of their elegant villa at 5, Avenue Ardennes, rang. Thinking it was
her husband she called out, "No gangsters here" and opened the door. Two
young men holding hand guns quickly forced their way into the house.
Their names were Edward Dolecki and Tony Wagemans. An accomplice,
28-year-old Philippe Delaire, public enemy number one in France, arrived
later. At that moment, his face painted and disguised and wearing a false
nose, he was with Guy Jeuris at the bank branch.

Jeuris told him that it was not possible to open the bank safe without
setting off an alarm at the police station. It required a second key, which
was held by a colleague. He told the disappointed Delaire that he would
have to wait until Monday to rob the bank.

Delaire and his two lieutenants had been watching Guy Jeuris for
three weeks. They noticed that he always acted nervously in his car,

deducing that he was stressed and vulnerable. The opposite was the case, however, for he was a very self-controlled and clever man, a technician. He suggested to Philippe Delaire and his accomplices that they spend the weekend with the family and on Monday, he could then arrange for access to the safe. They concocted a plan. Jeuris would allow one of the perpetrators (obviously disguised with spectacles and a beard) to enter the bank as if he were a colleague of Jeuris. The other two would follow later with the first bank customers when the alarm was off, bringing their weapons, hand grenades, a machine-pistol, explosives and mines into the bank after opening time. A sign was prepared with the wording 'Closed for Renovation Work' to allay suspicion regarding the explosion if that were necessary to open the safe.

Delaire was much impressed by Jeuris and even fetched chocolate croissants from the baker's shop for breakfast. The Jeuris family and the hostage-takers apparently had a lot of fun together on the Sunday, so much so that Delaire had to warn them that "This is no laughing matter, it is a robbery." Everybody laughed. For Guy Jeuris,however, the good mood was a pretence. He wanted to charm them into taking the bait.

The intruders so enjoyed being in the Jeuris household that they allowed the couple to spend some time with them. Guy Jeuris was sitting on a window sill of the upper floor. He waited until a train was passing and then jumped down to freedom. He broke his heel bone in doing so and hobbled to his neighbour's house to raise the alarm, before being taken to hospital for treatment. There he provided the police with a precise description of Delaire and sketched the layout of the house and the situation.

The three perpetrators did not discover that Guy had escaped until they saw the police vehicles arriving. The street was sealed off and surrounded. The special unit CGSU (later DSU, *Direction des Unités Spéciales*) also came. The criminals' plan was now frustrated and they had to make fresh arrangements. They took Marie-Madeleine and her two daughters to the upper floor of the villa, imprisoned them together in a small cupboard and fortified the floor. Growing in boldness, they demanded a helicopter and an aircraft for their getaway. Initially the mayor of Tilff, Dr Bossuroy, talked with them until the CGSU lead-negotiator, Commissar Jacques Leonard, took over. Contact was maintained – as was usual at that time – via megaphone and walkie-talkie. The situation hit the village of Tilff like a bomb and left its traces. Neighbours of the Jeuris family offered themselves as hostages to obtain the release of the two girls, Gaëlle and

Françoise. The local school closed in solidarity. The hostage-takers then refused to negotiate further.

An unnatural silence reigned over the beautiful gardens of Tilff, lasting until the Wednesday morning when negotiations resumed. The directors of the Belgian Communal Credit Bank and Belgian National Bank agreed to pay the ransom that Jacques Leonard had negotiated with the kidnappers; 30 million Belgian francs (€743,680) for the release of the two girls. It was not an easy conversation. Meanwhile, Delaire's father had become involved via the media, calling upon his son to see reason: "Philippe, I implore you. This is your father speaking. I ask you to stop, release the hostages and surrender. That would be the best thing. It would be good, fantastic. I implore you Philippe."

Things grew worse on the Thursday. Delaire informed the negotiators that Marie-Madeleine had attempted suicide with pills and was in a coma. By the afternoon she had recovered, the negotiator informing his team that it had been a bluff. A little later a new arrangement was agreed with the perpetrators. In a press conference that evening, the representative District Attorney Pierre Romeyn stated that Delaire had agreed to the two following points:

1. The two children would be freed against the ransom of 30 million Belgian francs, in two stages.
2. After the exchange, the hostage-takers would be given free passage out in a car chosen for them.

The deal would be played out on the following day, the Friday. The next day, the two girls were freed against the two instalments of the ransom to negotiator Jacques Leonard, who escorted them to waiting ambulances. All of the streets in Tilff were cordoned off by police.

At 8 pm a black Mercedes 230 drove through the streets of Tilff in the direction of Liège. Inside were Marie-Madeleine Jeuris, who was tied to her tormentor, Philippe Delaire, on the back seat, a hand grenade resting between them. The two accomplices occupied the front seats and wore red capes with hoods. Five CGSU vehicles followed the black Mercedes. Shortly before reaching the Pontbarrage de Monsin, Marie-Madeleine was released in good health. The mission had now technically ended for the special unit CGSU; their principal objective having been the release of the hostages.

Now it was time for the showdown. In the afternoon, the police had arrested two persons of interest, discovering from them the identities of Dolecki and Wagemans, and also possible hideouts in Liège. On the Friday evening, while the special unit was still pursuing the Mercedes, their colleagues positioned themselves around the entrance to the main hideout. During the night, the perpetrators changed vehicles twice, intending to hide themselves in a tower block, the 'Match' in the Droixhe district of Liège, where they had a flat on the fifth floor.

As they arrived, towards 10.30, they ran into the CGSU ambush, opened fire and fled up the stairway towards the roof, always taking four steps at a time. They carried with them a bag full of money and an enormous arsenal of weapons, including a 9 mm pistol, a Smith & Wesson revolver, a machine-pistol, two hand-grenades, eight sticks of dynamite, sufficient ammunition and tools.

The media circus at the foot of the tower block was augmented by many onlookers as the pursuit inside continued. At the eighth floor, the CGSU came across the dead body of Philippe Delaire, who had apparently committed suicide by shooting himself upwards through the head, the bullet exiting through his skull.

On the twenty-fourth floor, an exchange of fire occurred in which a marksman fired twelve rounds at the two surviving perpetrators. Wagemans was hit twice, in the abdomen and spinal column. He lost a lot of blood, but both men reached the roof from where they showered the money down onto the onlookers, who had no shame in helping themselves.

"Show yourselves on the roof. Be realistic. It's over. Show us that you are giving in," came a voice through a megaphone below. Negotiator Jacques Leonard spoke to the two men again, but only Dolecki was able to signal their surrender to the police; Wagemans had collapsed.

The odyssey came to its conclusion at 1 am. "Lay down your weapons and lay yourselves on the ground," they were told by the CGSU. The two surviving perpetrators were arrested, blindfolded and led away, their heads covered with hoods.[1]

The body of Philippe Delaire was removed, leaving hundreds of citizens of Liège to grab what they could of the 30 million Belgian francs which had fluttered down from the roof. The numbers of the notes had been recorded and this also led to quite a story.

Crazy Farid: Hostage-Taker of his Own Family – 2005

Occasionally, the members of special units are put to the test, especially when the victims of a perpetrator are his own family. This happened in the case of French-Algerian Farid Bamouhammad, nicknamed 'Crazy Farid' by Belgian journalists. This man had a criminal past; assaults due to his angry temperament, as well as thefts and murder which were inter-woven into his life like a red thread.

In 2005, Farid was released from Arlon prison on compassionate leave. He was not only a dangerous individual but also a father. Soon after starting a new prison sentence, he had fought for visiting rights to his only child and obtained a licence to be absent from prison on 17 August for reconciliation with his daughter, Farrah.

It was shortly before midday when his mother, Zohra, gave him tennis shoes to take to his daughter, and two hours later he made his way to the agreed rendezvous in the St Gilles district of the city. His daughter received him reproachfully. She was very angry, scolded him for being an idiot and told him she did not love him any longer, returning the gift of the tennis shoes by throwing them at his head. This was how a deceived fiancée might behave, but not a 9-year-old child to her father. Farid knew that Farrah had been stirred up against him by his in-laws. He was desperate, recognising that his beloved daughter meant the words she uttered. After a few glasses of wine, Farid returned to his mother where he stayed only a short while. Upon leaving, he told her he would rather be dead, and then set off for the Café Albertine at 53, Rue de la Madeleine, an establishment run by his ex-wife's new husband. Farid had some more wine there and made a scene, making several telephone calls to his mother on his mobile in the meantime. She pleaded with him in vain to leave the café and come back home to spend a peaceful evening with her.

At six that evening a call was made to the police, answered half an hour later by two female officers attending at Café Albertine. Farid was on the first floor, in the flat of his ex-mother-in-law, Sylvia. Also living there were his sister-in-law, Chrystelle, his daughter, Farrah, and the latter's small half-brother, the offspring of the new relationship of Farid's ex-wife. When the two policewomen approached the first floor, Farid drew a hand gun and fired, hitting one of the officers.

Farid was beside himself with rage. His family had been broken up and he had lost all reason. Weapons were like toys to him. Having taken the four occupants hostage, he fortified the flat. He was armed with two pistols and a hand grenade. Where they had come from nobody knew. It was now a case for the Belgian police's tactical squad (DSU), who arrived with operational vehicles and men. The roads around the Grande Place quarter were sealed off, while the police and DSU evacuated the Café Albertine before occupying it themselves.

The leading negotiator sat with his colleagues in a box-type van in front of the café and began telephoning Farid. He was told that Farid had a Yugoslav hand-grenade with 50 grams of explosive, a starting pistol and a 6.35 calibre pistol. The negotiator discussed Farid's motives with him. He warned him not to harm his daughter, she was still a child, "a very irritated little girl thinking a lot about her father's life." The negotiator suggested it would be best to let the two children go. He made suggestions but made no criticism of the hostage-taker and let him talk freely, knowing at this stage of the negotiations, any upset could be fatal. The negotiating team also knew that Farid was a ticking time-bomb. He could fly into a rage very quickly and then panic. He had already proved perfectly capable of killing somebody out of jealousy or pure rage. Towards 9 pm, snipers moved into positions at the windows of the Hotel le Méridien opposite and on the side of the Congress building. Elite police units were also placed at the corner of Rue de la Madeleine and Rue Duquesnoy.

The DSU considered Farid capable of anything. Photos of an infuriated Farid and the family he had taken hostage and who stood at the windows, crying and afraid, went around the world, the media sparing no details of the horror.

Towards 10 that evening, the negotiators had their first success when Farid released the two children. The police brought them to the nearby Hotel Windsor, where a team of paramedics and emergency doctors were standing by. Upon examination, the children were found to be physically unharmed.

Although he was still raging, Farid was now tired and needed sleep. The night passed and towards 8 am, when he rang the DSU team again, he stood at the window in a violent temper holding up a hand grenade. He shouted at and abused the police on the street below and two hours later, when the hostages Sylvia and Chrystelle came to the window, they looked as if they had been driven to total despair.

Whenever the negotiator was in conversation with Farid on the telephone, his deputy would listen in and analyse Farid's answers. The two negotiators always worked together as the situation had to be constantly re-assessed. Often the deputy would hand the negotiator special questions to put to the hostage-take as an immediate follow-up. The keyword was spontaneity. Both negotiators had learned their profession with the best of the best: the FBI.

At 7.40 pm on the Thursday, Farid appeared at the window once more, holding a pistol and shouting incomprehensibly. Then he fired a shot in the

(*Above*) The SCO19 team is part of the Specialist Crime & Operations Directorate within London's Metropolitan Police Service. The unit is responsible for providing a firearms-response capability, and assisting the rest of the service, which is not routinely armed. Here the unit can be seen during a training exercise on a British Airways aeroplane. © *SCO19*

(*Right*) The SCO19 team uses a special car equipped with an extendable ramp, which can be used to scale high walls or, in this case, to board an aircraft. © *SCO19*

(*Above*) Counter Terrorist Specialist Firearms Officers are often called upon to storm buildings. The teams are on standby day and night to respond to a terrorist or major crime incident, both in London and on a national level. © *SCO19*

(*Below*) For maritime operations, the SCO19 unit is supported by the Met's Marine Police Unit, which operates a small number of Delta 1000TX rigid inflatable boats. These boats can reach speeds of up to 50 knots and are used to transport SCO19 team members along the Thames River network. This form of transport might be used to avoid gridlock on the city's roads, approach an objective alongside the river or to board a vessel. © *SCO19*

(*Above*) Author Judith Grohmann poses with members of the British unit SCO19. During the London Bridge attacks in 2017, the City of London and Metropolitan Police Firearms Teams were on the scene within minutes to stop the attacks; a testament to the unit's professionalism. © *SCO19*

(*Below*) A massive manhunt began immediately after the *Charlie Hebdo* attack in Paris on 7 January 2015. France raised its terror alert to the highest level and soldiers were deployed in the Île-de-France and Picardy regions. © *GIGN*

Following the attacks on 7 January, two days later a hostage situation took place at the Avenue de la Porte-de-Vincennes, Paris, in a Hypercacher supermarket. The Research and Intervention Brigade (BRI), often called the "Anti-Gang Brigade", was the first unit to arrive on the scene, followed by their colleagues from the special unit, RAID. © *Gil Tirlet, BRI*

The French National Gendarmerie Intervention Group (GIGN) was involved in neutralising the terrorists Chérif and Said Kouachi on 9 January 2015, outside an office-building on an industrial estate in Dammartin-en-Goële. The two men ran out of the building and opened fire on the police, intending to die as martyrs. © *GIGN*

A member of the BRI listens attentively to his commander and waits for the beginning of the intervention, reinforced by RAID colleagues, during the Paris attacks on 13 November 2015, which included assaults on the Bataclan theatre. © *Gil Tirlet, BRI*

Recherche, Assistance, Intervention, Dissuasion (Search, Assistance, Intervention, Deterrence), commonly abbreviated to RAID, is an elite tactical unit of the French Police. Here, members of the RAID unit are seen boarding the French high-speed TGV train in Calais, searching for three suspects that are supposedly hiding inside. © *RAID*

(*Above*) The Belgian special unit DSU travelling via helicopter and speedboat to Ostend, on the Belgian coast, to target criminals who are believed to be hiding on a ship. © *DSU*

(*Below*) In dangerous situations, members from the Mobile Medical Team, part of Luxembourg's special unit USP, provide assistance to those who have been injured. In an unknown area, such as the one shown here, the team are trained to use haemostatic compression bandages, as well as tourniquets and even blood transfusions. © *USP Luxembourg*

(*Above*) Hiding and observing in a camouflaged position in a wood in Luxembourg: the special unit USP in the wake of an attack by a kidnapper. © *USP Luxembourg*

(*Below*) Marksmen from Germany's elite police tactical unit GSG9 positioned on the roof of a building, ready for the operation. © *GSG9*

(*Above*) Members of the Italian special unit NOCS are training how to enter a house via the windows, balcony and doors, usually using explosives. © *NOCS*

(*Left*) NOCS dogs are used to storm buildings and sniff out booby traps. These dogs are indispensable to the work of the units because of their bravery and loyalty. © *NOCS*

(*Right*) Members of the Israeli counter terrorism unit Yamam climb down a building at night to face a dangerous criminal. © *Yamam*

(*Below*) Anyone who says they "can't do anything" about attacks by so-called 'lone wolves' or suicide bombers, is wrong. Every terrorist needs the right environment, the right preparation, as well as the right logistics, and often sends out warning signals in advance, either via the internet or word of mouth. It is the job of the special units – in this case the Israeli unit Yamam – to hunt them down and to bring them to justice. © *Yamam*

(*Above*) A short team briefing for members of the Austrian unit EKO Cobra DSE before an operation. Each member of the unit has to fulfil his/her role and protect their colleagues before being deployed. © *Michael Hetzmannseder*

(*Below*) Members of the Austrian unit EKO Cobra DSE showing how it is easier to target offenders from above than on the ground. Here, the unit is seen using a Eurocopter EC-135P2+ helicopter. © *Michael Hetzmannseder*

(*Above*) Armed Response Vehicles (ARVs) respond to spontaneous incidents involving firearms. To enable fast pursuit and arrival times, these cars are fitted with state-of-the-art satellite navigation and communications systems, and are the vehicle of choice for the Jordanian Special Unit 14. © *Special Unit 14*

(*Below*) Members of the Jordanian Special Unit 14 on a special mission high up in a residential area of Amman, where a terrorist is hiding. © *Special Unit 14*

(*Above*) A sniper from the Portuguese special unit GOE observes the situation in the house opposite. © *GOE*

(*Below*) Tactical service shields protect the team from the Russian counter terrorism unit SOBR during deployment in a garage in Moscow. © *SOBR*

(*Above*) It is already midnight and the suspects have been caught and are waiting for their removal. Here the Dutch Special unit DSI are seen at work in Amsterdam. © *DSI*

(*Below*) In this exercise by the Hungarian special unit TEK, a man has supposedly shot several people after escaping from prison. Stun grenades are thrown in his direction after he has taken up a defensive position. © *Michael Hetzmannseder*

(*Above*) In this training exercise, kidnappers and their victim are hiding in a demolished house in the Dubrovka area of Slovakia. Members of the Slovakian unit LYNX are on the scene. © *Michael Hetzmannseder*

(*Below*) Divers from the Lithuanian counter terrorism unit ARAS climbing aboard a ship, where dangerous offenders are hiding above. © *ARAS*

(*Above*) SWAT team members enter a suburban neighbourhood to search an apartment for the remaining suspect in the Boston Marathon bombings in Watertown, Massachusetts on 19 April 2013. © *BPD*

(*Below*) A K-9 officer and his police dog on duty on the streets of Boston. © *bdpnews.com*

In the air SWAT officers assigned to the NYPD Special Operations Division are constantly on the move. They are at the ready 24/7 to rescue those in need and to help protect New York City. © *NYPD*

The NYPD initiates preliminary security measures in response to a reported attack on certain government officials in Virginia. As a precautionary measure, the NYPD deployed directed patrols, including Critical Response Command and Strategic Response Group personnel, to certain government locations, including City Hall, pending further determination of any potential broader implications for New York City. © *NYPD*

A terror incident in Manhattan in 2017 shows the excellent, seamless response and coordination between the NYPD and their dedicated law enforcement partners and fellow first responders. © *Michael Appleton, NYC Mayoral Photo Office*

air. Finally it fell quiet in the flat at 53 Rue de la Madeleine. Next Farid requested food and drink for himself and his hostages. "Yes, of course, Farid. We'll have something sent up straight away." The negotiator smiled at his colleague. He had just had an idea how the DSU team could seize Farid without the use of firearms. The plan was thought through and everything calculated. Half an hour later, both negotiators were on the way up to the flat where Farid and the two hostages were awaiting the rations; a basket containing sandwiches, drinks and a large coffee can.

Time passed, and it was shortly after 3.30 am when twenty black-clothed DSU men armed with machine-pistols ascended the stairway and moved about the first floor with the softest of footsteps. The owner of the apartment had given the negotiators the key to the door. The negotiators swiftly unlocked it and entered, while from outside, their colleagues used telescopic ladders to climb up and break in through the windows.

Still asleep, Farid noticed the intrusion much too late and had no chance to flee. The two hostages were also sleeping. The negotiator was delighted with his success; the drinks had been drugged and a microphone installed in the coffee can.

Farid showed the symptoms of tiredness and defeat associated with a hangover, thus enabling the DSU to arrest him without the use of firearms. "Farid Bamouhammad, we are arresting you for the kidnapping of four persons. Hands up and follow us. It's over." the DSU man informed him loudly. Farid was tired and made no reply. Two DSU members put his arms behind his back and led him away.

An ambulance was waiting in the street to receive the two freed hostages. When the prisoner, now handcuffed and blindfolded, was brought downstairs, one of the DSU men heard someone on the radio say, "Is that it?"

"It's OK boys, stand down. Back to headquarters, please" came the commander's familiar reply.

In April 2008, Faris Bamouhammad was sentenced by a Belgian court to twenty-one years' imprisonment. As a result of his violent temperament, he has so far been transferred between thirty-four different institutions.

Kamikazes at Brussels Airport and Metro – March 2016

As was usual on every Tuesday morning at 7.45 am, the Director of the DSU held a briefing with his General Staff. This was a small team consisting of those leaders responsible for the operational areas of Information and ICT, (the communications technologies), and finance and logistics at personnel management level (GRH).

On the agenda were several management matters that were to be discussed over coffee. After a start was made there came a shout: "There's been an attack! Quick, hurry!" At once, the commander ordered the first convoy of men from his unit to Zaventem Airport to assess the situation. The head of the Intervention Platoon went himself with his team in the first vehicle. Normally the drive from DSU headquarters to Zaventem takes twenty-seven minutes, but on that day they got there in only fifteen. The sight that met their eyes on arrival was extraordinary and tragic. Chaos reigned. Thousands of people with their suitcases and travel bags stood out in the open, many were crying, some were shouting, whilst others stared at the airport building with shocked faces. When describing the operation, the leaders of the DSU teams recalled this shocked expression of the passengers. It was impressive and at the same time very sad for them and their men to see these many sad faces and knowing what had come to pass in the airport.

It was 7.35 am when 29-year-old Ibrahim El Bakraoui, 24-year-old Najim Laachraoui and 32-year-old Mohamed Abrini, all dressed in black, alighted from a taxi in front of the Zaventem Airport building with their matching black suitcases. Here follows a potted history of the lives of the three men.

Ibrahim El Bakraoui held up a Western Union branch in the centre of Brussels in January 2010. Surprised by police, he opened fire with a Kalashnikov assault rifle and wounded an officer in the leg. When he and his accomplice fled, they were forced to hold out in a house at Laeken, a district in which he had grown up with his brother. After being captured, at his trial in August 2010 he was sentenced to nine years' imprisonment for attempted murder. In October 2014 he was paroled, subject to not leaving Belgium for longer than one month. Ibrahim was arrested in June 2015 at Gaziantep, on the Turkish border with Syria, by the Turkish authorities who had identified him to the Belgians as a foreign terrorist, and at his own request, returned him to Belgium. Presumably he used the pseudonym Ibrahim Maaroufi from now on as a result of this arrest, because he used it to rent a flat in Charleroi, 40 km south of Brussels, in September 2015. The flat would be used as a safe house by some of the terrorists responsible for the Paris attacks on 13 November 2015.

The second perpetrator in the airport attack was Najim Laachraoui. He had attended a Catholic school and studied electrical engineering. His family swore by education and discipline. His brother loved the Belgian flag and was excellent at combative sport. None of that deterred Najim from membership of Islamic State and for whose purposes he dedicated his technical abilities to bomb making. Some of these devices were used for the attacks on Paris and Brussels. Until that day in March 2016, Najim was an invisible but central participant and one of the most important liaison men with the cell that had carried out the Paris attacks organized by Attelhamid Abbaoud. It was Najim who manufactured the bombs for the forthcoming attack in Brussels.

Mohamed Abrini appeared in a photo taken by the CCTV camera at Brussels airport and is known as 'the man with the hat'. He grew up in the Molenbeek district of Brussels with Salah Abdeslam, the only survivor of the group responsible for the Paris attacks. Belgian, but of Moroccan origin, he had been seen two days before the attacks of 13 November 2015 at a petrol station north of Paris. The principal suspect, Salah drove one of the two vehicles used for the attack. The Belgian authorities wanted Mohamed Abrini for "involvement in the activities of a terrorist association and terrorist murders," namely the Paris massacre. Identified by Belgian investigators as a radical Islamist, in the previous year Mohamed was thought to have been in Syria with his younger brother, 20-year-old Suliman, who was killed there. He was known to the security services for belonging to the same cell as Abdelhamid, one of the organizers of the Paris attacks who had fired into the bars, restaurants and the Bataclan concert hall before being killed in a shoot-out with police. Abrini was later accused of having left the airport without priming his suitcase bomb, after his alleged accomplices, Najim and Ibrahim El Bakraoui, made their debut, killing sixteen innocent civilians and themselves.

Back at Zaventem Airport, the three men had their home-made bombs hidden beneath the clothes contained in their large, heavy black suitcases. They did not want to carry or tow them through the airport, so loaded each onto a luggage trolley before heading to the check-in desk. In videos released later, they can be seen passing through the hall slowly, speaking to no one. One of the men, Abrini, is easily identifiable from his white jacket and large, black hat.

Towards 7.58 am shots were heard, followed by a shout and then the Arabic phrase "Allahu Akbar", after which the first two bombs exploded. The first nail-bomb went off close to the American Airlines check-in desk, where many passengers had already handed in their luggage and been given boarding passes for a flight to New York. The third suspect, Abrini, known to police as 'the man with the hat', had also placed his suitcase on a baggage trolley but fled, apparently in panic, without setting off his bomb. This meant that the catastrophic plan was limited to two explosions.

Passengers, their faces distorted with fear, abandoned their luggage and ran from the departure hall, from which huge amounts of smoke now billowed. During the next few minutes all aerial traffic over Belgium was diverted and the airport evacuated. The last aircraft took off at 8.13 am, and the highest anti-terrorist security measures – Stage 4 – were put into effect across all Belgium. The population was advised to remain in their homes or other places of safety.

While the police had to handle the chaotic situation at the airport, investigating officers attempted to obtain an initial impression of the crime from the eyewitnesses, but the situation was very confused. Many people were still in shock at their narrow escape from death. The commander and his men knew from experience that patience was very important in such situations, but they needed to obtain immediate statements before the initial excitement died down. Every witness was given a chance to tell his or her version of events; every witness was important, the commander said. It was vital for them to obtain information from the public, but they also needed a great deal of time for the experts to analyse and filter all of the information in order to reconstruct the exact sequence of events.

In the departure hall there were at least sixteen dead, including two terrorists, and ninety-two injured. The commander saw that the operations force was fully employed there and decided it would be better to return to headquarters. Perhaps he had a premonition, for the terror in Belgium on this day was not yet over.

Lacking a concrete job to perform at the crime scene, the DSU Anti-terrorist unit attempted to reassemble at headquarters, but just eleven minutes later, another bomb exploded in the Metro station at Maelbeek, on the Rue de la Loi, in the Europa quarter close to the city centre. The Anti-terrorist unit remained at full alert at headquarters, prepared to react when necessary. Meanwhile, the Brussels Metro and also the main line railway stations were closed down and their staffs evacuated. Buses and trams were also affected and controls at the national frontiers stepped up. An emergency number was set up for family members to call.

It later transpired that the fourth bomber was 27-year-old Khalid El Baraoui. He grew up at Laken, a residential district north-west of Brussels. His father, a pensioned-off butcher and pious Muslim, had emigrated from Morocco, whilst Khalid's mother was described as conservative and reserved. On 27 October 2009, Khalid was a member of a three-man gang which took part in a bank raid. They kidnapped an employee and forced him to take them to his branch in Brussels to disconnect the alarm, then made off with €41,000. About two weeks later, Khalid stole a vehicle and was later discovered at a warehouse with other stolen vehicles. Although arrested, he was not charged with a crime at that time. In 2011 Khalid was arrested again for possession of a Kalashnikov assault rifle. In September that year he was sentenced to five years' imprisonment for car theft, illegal possession of a firearm and for the 2009 bank raid. After serving most of this sentence he was released conditionally.

In May 2015 Khalid was rearrested for consorting with a former accomplice and prison inmate, but was released by a judge because he had otherwise complied with the terms of his conditional release.

In August 2015 Interpol issued a warrant for his arrest, and a further two were issued on 11 December 2015, one global, one European, by a Paris judge investigating the November 2015 attacks in that city. Khalid had rented the house at Charleroi using a forged document, and the fingerprints of Abdelhamid Abaaoud, the mastermind of these attacks, and the suicide bomber Bilal Hadfi, had been found there.

On 15 March 2016, Khalid and his brother Ibrahim avoided arrest during a police raid in Brussels. The following day the FBI provided the Dutch authorities with information relating to him, and the New York Police Department also informed the liaison officers at the Dutch Embassy in Washington that the two brothers were being sought for terrorism, extremist activity and recruiting terrorists.

In Brussels the enquiries over the next hours and minutes bore fruit and led the Anti-terrorist unit to descend upon a Brussels address in the Schaarbeek area to conduct a house search. A taxi driver had remembered collecting three passengers for the run to the airport, but had not been allowed to touch their bags or suitcases upon arrival at the departure hall; they preferred to unload it all themselves. The pick-up address was a building with many glass windows in the Rue Max Roos. It was not known if another terrorist might be there, or if the flat was empty. The greatest caution was therefore needed by the DSU men; after all, the flat could be booby-trapped. The security forces therefore sealed off a block of streets in the Schaarbeek district.

Only 150 metres from where the second operation was under way, a motorist was stopped and questioned. This man provided the DSU with the first information regarding the day's events. A flat was entered and the DSU found an Islamic State flag; the terrorist organisation had already claimed responsibility for the attacks in the afternoon through its mouthpiece *Amac*

An examination of the flat soon revealed that the bombers had originally planned to take more luggage. The bomb squad quickly discovered the third airport suitcase with its unexploded bomb, and that evening more bomb-making material was found including 15 kg TATP, 150 ltr acetone, 30 ltr hydrogen nitride, detonators and a case filled with nails. A laptop was also discovered on which one of the bombers had drafted his will.

Information showed later that the intention of the three men had been to hire a minibus to transport all of their bombs to the airport, but finally a simple taxi was used which probably prevented the attack from being carried out on a much grander scale.

That completed the work of the DSU for the day. Having made an important house-search, they secured the crime scene and left it to the investigating officers before returning to headquarters.

The airport and Metro attacks in Brussels that day claimed the lives of 25 people and left another 300 injured. Sirens howled, helicopters and drones circulated above empty streets in the city centre. The mobile telephone system had been disconnected. The city was noticeably in shock. The crisis centre recommended that citizens remain in places of safety, or their own homes, as the possibility of more explosions was too great. Students were confined to their campus for hours, white-collar workers in their offices.

It required weeks and months of house searches to unearth the supporting criminals and finally draw a line through the affair. Proof was found that many of these suspects had also been involved behind the scenes in the Paris attacks.

Also worth a mention here was the development of a special code between the police and the citizens of Brussels. In fact, a new Twitter hashtag aimed at preventing suspects from obtaining information regarding current anti-terrorist measures appeared, which involved posting cartoons and pictures of cats using the phrase #BrusselsLockdown.

The Belgian police urged social media users to stop posting photographs or details of the police operation which might alert any suspects, and instead encouraged them to concentrate on being more 'creative'. Suddenly, hundreds of cat images started flooded in, accompanied by the #BrusselsLockdown hashtag, making it more difficult for the suspects to uncover information.

Some of the Tweets proved to be very comical, such as those depicting cats as 'prime suspects', or posing as members of Belgium's National Security Council, or cats 'on a mission', as well as people's response to police advice to stay away from their windows.

Chapter 4

Luxembourg

Alarm in the Grand Duchy

Unit: Unité Spéciale de la Police (USP)

A Kindergarten taken hostage at Wasserbillig – 2000

It was 3.40 pm when the telephone rang. Jacques, the lead negotiator of the Luxembourg special unit USP, lifted the receiver. "USP, good afternoon…" The excited caller interrupted him: "Jacques, you are requested to go on a mission urgently. Hostages in the Wasserbillig kindergarten." At that the man hung up. The negotiator was irritated. What was this, a test by the new commander?

The amalgamation of gendarmerie and police had been approved in the spring of 2000 and carried out straight away. Combining the forces also resulted in an expanded team of lead negotiators. All members of the new team had been given an additional four month's specialist training, which had been completed exactly one day before; the freshly signed certificates lay on their tables.

The lead negotiator therefore assumed that this summons on 31 May could have been a test by his commander, but he notified his colleagues and within three minutes all were ready to leave. They boarded the negotiators' vehicles and headed for Wasserbillig, a town in the east of the country, about thirty minutes drive from the city of Luxembourg.

Neiji Bejaoui had withdrawn into a small room with a washbasin in one corner and a stack of children's chairs in another. The 38-year-old Tunisian with a Luxembourg passport had worked for several years as a pastry cook, but had now been unemployed for many months. He had no family; six years previously, in 1994, he had lost custody of his two children, the court having found that he beat them. He was known to the local police as a violent individual, and they often had to be called to violent domestic disputes at his home. The children were now 9 and 14 years of age and lived with their mother at Wasserbillig, whilst he lived at neighbouring Manternach.

Neiji's life was not a happy one. Since losing his job he had kept his head above water with occasional work, often as a doorman. A thick-set man, he spent a lot of his time playing football with neighbours, who described him as an innocuous outsider but not to be provoked. Now here he stood in this kindergarten room, flushed, sweating with excitement and threatening a teacher with a knife. The slender young woman stood trembling before him. He shouted at her to remove her blouse and called her "a piece of shit."

Jacques' operational vehicle was just turning into Rue Duchscher in Wasserbillig when a local police colonel approached him. "Thanks, Jacques, for having come so quickly. We need you today very urgently. We have a catastrophe on our hands," the colonel told him. The lead negotiator was still unsure whether or not this was a test set by the commander, but his police colleague came at once to the point.

Towards 3.35 that afternoon, Neiji had taken forty-seven children and five teachers hostage at the Speitennascht kindergarten. It was a colourful two-storey house at number 30. Neiji had already called the Commissioner's office. He seemed to be motivated by an enormous feeling of hatred against the police and the staff of the kindergarten and so now Jacques knew that this was no test, but something much more serious. Set up with his team in the police station kitchen, Jacques reached for the telephone and prepared to negotiate with the hostage-taker.

Neiji left the room in a rage. The telephone had rung and he had had to stop what he was doing to the teacher, go to the administrator's office in the next room and lift the receiver. The caller was Jacques, his telephone linked in to colleagues at police headquarters. He asked how the hostages were. Neiji answered in a rage that they were "all right" and struck the desk with his weapon. He made known his demand to be flown to Libya next day, telling Jacques that he had a pistol, five hand grenades, a knife and a can of petrol. He was prepared for any eventuality and was threatening to blow up the kindergarten by pouring petrol everywhere and igniting it with a hand grenade. The police believed him capable of it. Neiji then abruptly terminated the conversation.

Jacques called him again an hour later asking when he would be prepared to release the hostages, Neiji replied that only once he had the aircraft. The negotiator assured him that he would speak to the Interior

Ministry. During this conversation he learned that Neiji had lived without his children for a considerable time and had been receiving psychiatric treatment since losing custody. The purpose of his actions was to make others feel what he had had to endure for years; being alone, without his dear children. In order to 'protect his family', any expedient seemed justified to him: "Give me a chance to get away from here so that I can bring up my children."

Jacques remained stubborn; he wanted a *quid pro quo* for organising an aircraft for the hostage-taker; aircraft cost money to hire and a flight for a single person in a jet was a very expensive matter. The man had no money, but what he could do, Jacques suggested, was free hostages. The negotiation was now coming to a head, but Jacques knew exactly how far he could go with this man.

Conversations with criminal psychopaths was trained for at length at the police academy. There are words which a negotiator should avoid. Outright refusals. Promises are not to be given unless definite. A good negotiator fishes for information from his opposite number – from his medical history to hobbies – in order to see his objective more clearly. The goal is always the positive conclusion to the case. One must therefore get to know as much as possible about your opposite number in order to assess him correctly and be able to predict his reaction. A negotiator is never to use phrases he has been practising; he must always be himself, an authentic conversationalist holding "a normal spontaneous telephone conversation." In Neiji's case, his own psychiatrist also had to be called in to assist.

Neiji felt superior. The police were ready to organise a flight for him to Libya and in return he had agreed to release sixteen children and two teachers. That left thirty-one children and three teachers in the hands of the hostage-taker. By now it was 8 pm and the streets of Wasserbillig were dark.

While Jacques negotiated with the hostage-taker, the police provided information to the media. Suddenly the small tranquil town of Wasserbillig, on the German border at the confluence of the rivers Sauer and Moselle, had become a venue for the international press. The children's parents were staying in a room made available to them at the community cultural centre, where they were being looked after by volunteer helpers and doctors. It was a major responsibility for the police to keep them continually updated as to the progress of the negotiations and the well-being of their children, without involving the media. The next of kin were always the first to hear of any developments. The most important quality in a good negotiator is to remain in constant touch with the hostage-taker, checking that all remained in order and to gather as much information as possible about the hostages and kidnapper, including how all were bearing up under the strain. It is important too that a negotiator never lies to his opposite number.

Towards 10 pm, the TV and radio evening news programmes carried the first interviews on the incident. Prime Minister Jean-Claude Juncker spoke to the nation about the hostage situation and the first steps in the negotiations. An over-zealous radio station reporter made clear in his account that the kidnapper was 'mentally ill'. Hearing this report, Neiji became disturbed and began to rant and rave on the telephone. Jacques and Neiji's psychiatrist tried to calm him down. Neiji then asked to speak to a female judge at the family court. "It is very late, we'll try early in the morning," Jacques told him.

Neiji was at the end of his tether. Some of the children were crying, others were very restless. He did not like that. The police assured him that there would be no activity during the night, but he was doubtful. He did not trust these periods of quiet. In every police series he had seen on television they always came at night and it had always resulted in the death of the perpetrator. He didn't want to die. He wanted his children back and to leave the country with them. He had had enough of Luxembourg. The people around him had no idea how he was suffering, and all that he had gone through in the last few years. He wanted to shout it out so that everybody knew how low his spirits were, so that people understood why he had taken the steps he had. While in deep despair at his situation, the phone rang.

When Jacques rang Neiji just before midnight, he noticed his rage and despair at once. Neiji was set upon giving an interview. Jacques said he would try to make this possible, there were sufficient media people close by. Neiji made it clear that he was panicking because he feared the police were going to make an assault. Jacques calmed him down: "We are attempting to resolve the whole situation by talking to you. There will be no assault," and then remained in frequent telephone contact with Neiji throughout the night. Next came a fresh demand for a delivery van for his escape. If he got that, he promised he would do no harm to the children and their three teachers.

Behind the scenes, Jacques' colleagues deliberated on how they should proceed. The hostage-taker had called his relations and attempted to interest the media in his statement of discontent with the justice system and police of Luxembourg. As a result, Jacques arranged an interview for the following morning with the RTL television station.

Towards 9.30, the RTL interviewers arrived at the kindergarten, but when Neiji opened the door he saw the fire brigade vehicles and emergency doctor's car on the other side of the street. He assumed from this that the police must have already positioned the snipers. Throwing the interviewers out of the building, Neiji persisted with his demand for a vehicle to make his escape until midday. Thanks to the skill of the negotiator, Neiji was persuaded to release two more children. By six that evening, Neiji was very tired. He had invested two days in his 'action'; he was tense and wanted no more negotiating. Jacques tried to help him control his emotions; because the first television interview had not taken place, Jacques arranged a second one.

Shortly before 10 pm, the RTL television bus arrived at the entrance gate to the kindergarten. Two reporters got out and went to the door. It opened to reveal the hostage-taker, grey-faced and hardly able to keep his eyes open. The tiredness and strain of the last two days were obvious. He invited the reporters to enter with a welcoming gesture. At that moment snipers fired two rounds into his head, wounding him seriously, but not fatally. He fell at the door. At once the emergency team came forward to stretcher him away. He spent the period until his recovery in a clinic. The USP police members left for their headquarters. Thanks to their negotiator, Jacques, the case had come to a successful conclusion.

In November 2001 Neiji Bejaoui was tried and sentenced to twenty-two years' imprisonment for the rape of a female teacher and offences against the weapons' legislation. The court accepted a plea of mitigation for a lesser sentence on account of the mental state of the accused. The judge also ordered that he undergo anger management therapy.

The head of the kindergarten told the media next day, "We can live with the sentence."

Raid on an Al-Qaeda Cell – 2003

The man with the moustache stood beside a silver-coloured Volkswagen Passat smoking a Gauloise. He rested his foot on the bumper and looked at the house in front of him. It was his twelfth cigarette of the day; the afternoon was very cold, a typical 28 February with snow and some sunshine. The man had already spent several hours in the cold vehicle, now he had to have a few hours' fresh air whilst his female colleague sat waiting in the vehicle. Smoke-breaks in official vehicles were strictly prohibited.

83

Four narrow streets away, a couple walked hand in hand. The young man wore a black cap and looked with loving eyes at his blonde friend wearing pink ear muffs. They stopped before No. 22 Rue Louvigny for a long, passionate kiss, nobody noticing his glances at the house opposite, No. 21, during this charade. The couple spent quite some time embracing.

No. 8 Rue d'Eperney was directly opposite Luxembourg railway station and various hotels. With so much coming and going, hardly anyone would have paid attention to the van bearing the slogan 'Dupont Installations, always there for you.' The two men sitting in the van wearing blue dungarees were conversing in an excited manner. Now and again one of them would look towards the building on the corner. Spread out in front of them were sketches of bathrooms.

The motto of the police teams throughout this operation was: "Keep a low profile." Six months earlier, the USP members had been given advance notice of a dangerous operation. The man with the moustache, the couple in the Rue Louvigny and the two bathroom installers opposite the railway station were all members of the approximately seventeen tactical groups that day observing members of a cell belonging to arguably the most dangerous terror group in the world: Al Qaeda. The tactical teams had gathered information about the suspects under surveillance: who was married, who had children, who left the flat or house when and how often. What did that person wear on each occasion? What was their routine, whom did they visit and who visited them? The daily life of a suspect filled many pages of a dossier. Now and again the unit's files crossed when meetings occurred between suspects. All the dossiers stacked together would probably have reached the ceiling.

This operation was amongst the most difficult for the USP. It is a complicated business keeping a particular person under observation for days to study his or her behaviour. To observe several people presents a quite different challenge, with an additional problem being if one of the targets only leaves home occasionally, usually to attend the mosque on a Friday. All persons under surveillance were male and married – therefore had wives and probably children. This operation was known as 'Danger of Terrorism'.

This kind of difficult surveillance required precision and efficiency from the officers. If they assumed another identity and went under a disguise, their appearance had to be perfect. One error, any inattention to detail, could lead to their being detected, endanger their own lives and that of their colleagues. The Luxembourg special unit knew that the men were members of an Al Qaeda cell and were in constant communication with their contacts abroad. At last the six month period of surveillance ended and 'X-Day' approached. The day set for the destruction of the cell was 1 March 2003.

Before a mission of this kind takes place, many precautionary measures have to be taken in hand. For example, whole blocks of streets have to be cordoned off, motorists and pedestrians requested to go by another route for their own safety. Police vehicles and officers in civilian clothing had taken up seventeen different posts awaiting the signal from the commander to act. All participants must concentrate and be on the alert, and act in accordance with the previously agreed plan. Again, the smallest inattention to detail could lead to a fatal end for the endeavour. Every member of the team had his or her job and knew what had to be done; they had to be personally responsible, or otherwise the operation would not succeed.

Shortly after 5 am the teams dressed up with masks, protective helmets and vests, black overalls and boots. They readied their weapons and were driven into the streets where the Al Qaeda members lived. The teams entered the buildings in question, unobserved by neighbours or the suspects. They moved silently up the stairs and waited in position in front of the suspect's flat, awaiting the commander's signal. The commander was seated in a service minibus with members of his tactical team. A glance at his watch, a telephone conversation, and then he bent his head towards the microphone before him.

"Team, assault now." With these words the physical operation began. USP broke down the doors and within seconds were inside the suspects' dwelling. In the seventeen flats and houses the occupants were still asleep. The shock effect can be imagined when six to eight masked figures in black approached the bed and gave the order at gunpoint, "Hands up, police. Give up. You have no chance." It's a scene from every TV crime series.

The women of the house now realised that it was a police raid. Many became hysterical, screaming and crying and even attacked the members of the special unit with their fists. Children who had just woken up started to cry. The suspects, shocked from their sleep, had no chance to resist. With tired expressions they left their beds, raised their hands and knelt, many murmuring something comprehensible only to themselves. They allowed themselves to be handcuffed and led away, their women too.

In all seventeen flats and houses, representatives from the Interior Ministry, negotiators and child care services attended. The neighbours had very little understanding of the operation and received reassurance from the officials present. This operation was a milestone in the discovery of radical terrorist cells in Europe. The operation was perfectly organised. The suspects were driven away quickly for interrogation and within thirty minutes, at 7 am, the operation concluded with the commander's words, "Operation ended. Teams return to your vehicles."

The Blackmail of a Scrap Dealer – 2008

Although originally from Belgium, Albert Syler had lived in Luxembourg with his wife and son for over forty-five years. In the late 1950s he and his father Michel had crossed the frontier in a simple caravan and opened a business 'buying and selling damaged cars'; basically a scrap dealership. They gradually became established over the years so that by the age of 70, Albert had made a small fortune. He owned a beautiful single-family house with garden in the Pfaffenthal district, near the Kirchberg plateau, whilst his garage housed an Aston Martin and a Ferrari, although these were used only for excursions at the weekends. Otherwise, the family had a very modest and rather innocuous lifestyle. Albert was particularly proud of his son, Antoine, an industrious worker in the business and married to a young lady of noble birth. The family felt very much at home in Luxembourg and had made many friends there over the years.

In September 2008, after finishing a hard day's work, Albert and his wife Monique left for home. She got out and waited while her husband garaged the firm's car, then both went indoors together. Monique headed for the kitchen where she lit the gas oven to prepare a soufflé. Suddenly, she became aware of a cold draught coming from the living room. She was just thinking of telling her husband that he had not shut the window properly that morning when three masked figures crept up to her without a sound.

The intruders demanded that Albert open the safe. He obeyed, fearing for their lives. The criminals stole jewelery and documents from the strongbox, but strangely decided to leave a Swiss IWC watch behind. Before leaving by the front door, they bound the couple with curtain cordage, pushed them into the bathroom and locked them in.

After two hours, Albert managed to free himself and called the police. Gendarmes went over the house for fingerprints and noted down every detail of the raid. The description of the intruders was rather vague since they were masked and had left few clues before departing. The police search for the trio in the following months bore no fruit.

At the beginning of December, Albert and Monique had just returned home from work when they received a mysterious telephone call. The caller's voice was threatening and made it clear to Albert that he was, "talking too much about the theft," and warned him that if he did not desist, he and his grandson would pay with their lives. After he hung up, Monique called the police, then handed Albert the receiver saying, "You must provide them with every detail, do you hear, Albert?" He obeyed. From this time on, the police tapped the Seyler family's telephone line.

A few days later, on 19 December, another call came in which the perpetrator demanded the sum of €300,000. Albert admitted defeat; he was prepared to pay up to get the blackmailers off his back. The local police now advised their colleagues of the USP, whose strategists worked out a plan with the family. If the perpetrators demanded Albert should bring the money alone, he was to tell them that he had heart disease, and therefore could only walk very slowly and needed two family friends to accompany him. The money would be paid over in the presence of the friends or not at all. Furthermore, he needed the weekends free, as "since his heart operation, he spent almost every weekend in Nice for special health checks."

Albert was the ideal lead negotiator. He was a good, convincing talker and could develop ideas which did not betray the least suspicion of his being coached by the USP. Everybody who had contact with him said they were pleased with his performance. He was not only clever, efficient and liked talking, but above all he had intuition; whenever the USP suggested a storyline, he had already thought of it himself. There was an unusual affinity between victim and special unit. The final test, X-Day, was 14 December when the money was to be brought from the town to the waiting blackmailers. That morning, Albert went to his branch of the bank and withdrew the €300,000 from his account. He was accompanied by Carla, a USP officer assigned to him. She spent the whole morning going over all possible dialogues with the blackmailers, and so Albert was well prepared. After they both left the bank, the blackmailer called Albert's mobile phone and told him to drive into France. Albert proved his skill as a tactical negotiator and convinced the suspect to agree to meet him in the car park in front of a petrol station 100 metres short of the French border. Albert also mentioned that he had been experiencing serious heart problems for several days and therefore had to be accompanied by Carla, the family's best friend. The blackmailer agreed to this.

Carla and Albert got into the firm's vehicle, which USP had fitted out with listening devices, and set off. Leaving Luxembourg City, they drove along the A3, also known as the Diddelenger autobahn. Albert, who had been loquacious all day, now fell strangely quiet, his face white as chalk. Carla, who had known him for some time, noticed and asked how he was feeling. Albert was fearful. Fearful of being pursued by murderers, that they would harm his family and finally that his vehicle would be blown up. In short, he wanted to turn back. Carla had difficulty in keeping him from doing this and talked to him calmly. The suspects were not known, but the aim was to arrest them. Albert was indecisive, but accepted her argument and drove into the car park at the petrol station. The special unit had been in position there long before. They had various disguises: the married couple having a snack in the petrol station's cafeteria; the over-tired long distance lorry driver drinking a Red Bull whilst filling up his vehicle. Other officers in plain clothes were spread here and there around the petrol station.

Carla and Albert got out of the van. Albert pulled a face; he was still doubtful. Leaving the bag containing the money in the vehicle, as the extortioner had stipulated, together they made their way slowly to the petrol station. The watching USP officers soon struck gold. About five minutes after Carla and Albert had left the vehicle, two powerfully built, unkempt men in dark leather jackets approached it. In the act of taking the money bag, they suddenly found themselves surrounded by members of the special unit. "Police! Down on the ground!"

Taken by surprise, both men obeyed and offered no resistance. The handcuffs clicked and the pair were led away. Albert fell around Carla's neck with relief. They had done it. The blackmailers had been overcome; Albert and Monique could sleep peacefully at night.

Two years later, in 2010, Albert and Monique Seyler were threatened once more by blackmailers. The police only discovered several weeks later that this time the perpetrators were family members of the imprisoned criminals. Albert and Monique decided to pay up this time, without informing the police, and finally had peace.

Chapter 5

Germany

Men in Black on Travels

Unit: GSG 9 (Grenzschutzgruppe 9)

The Last Shot of the Red Army Faction

RAF: the initials of the terrorist organization sound like three shots fired one after another. These three letters stand for *Rote Armee Fraktion*, the most notorious left-wing extremist terror group beyond the borders of West Germany.

Its origins were in the student movement of 1968 and it was founded by Andreas Baader, Gudrun Ensslin and Ulrike Meinhof among others. They acted against the Establishment, rebelled against authority and in Frankfurt, in April 1968, carried out two arson attacks on commercial businesses in order to protest against the Vietnam War. The fire damage caused amounted to DM 675,000 (€345,122). Nobody was hurt, and the arsonists, sentenced to three years' imprisonment, were set free in 1969 on appeal. Andreas Baader went underground for a while in Italy and then in France. Upon his return to West Berlin he was identified by an informer, arrested at a sham police check point and incarcerated in the Tegel penal institution to serve out the rest of his sentence. On 14 May 1970, during a planned research date for a book, Baader absconded with Ulrike Meinhof. This escape marked the birth of the RAF, also known as the Baader-Meinhof gang, after the surnames of the leaders.

In the following weeks, twenty RAF members were trained in shooting and bomb-making by Palestinian Al Fatah guerrillas in Jordan. The first bomb attacks were made against the Axel Springer publishing house in West Berlin and the headquarters of the US forces in Europe at Heidelberg. After the 'May Offensive' Andreas Baader became the most hunted terrorist worldwide. In 1972 police arrested the entire RAF leadership squad.

The RAF organization was not brought to its end, as a second generation of terrorists continued the 'anti-imperialist struggle'. The high point of terrorist activity was reached in 1977, when the State Attorney General Siegfried Buback, the head of the Dresdner Bank, Jürgen Ponto, and President of the Employers' Federation Martin Schleyer, were kidnapped by the RAF and brutally murdered. A Lufthansa aircraft was hijacked to Somalia in order to extort the release of the RAF members in custody using hostages, but this plan failed when a special unit of the Federal Border Protection Service (GSG 9) was called in and successfully completed its mission. Reacting to the news, the terrorists of the first RAF generation, Gudrun Esslin, Andreas Baader and Jan-Carl Raspe, committed suicide in prison. Ulrike Meinhof had hanged herself a year earlier.

The RAF lost support during the 1980s, many members leaving to reappear in the DDR, the Soviet-occupied zone of Germany. A few more attacks were made, including the spectacular bombing of the newly-built prison at Weiterstadt, in Hesse, in March 1993. The cost of the damage was €50 million.

In June that year, the last members of the RAF at command level were arrested. The 'Weinprobe' campaign put the investigators on the trail of Birgit Hogefeld and Wolfgang Grams. An agent of the Federal Office for the Protection of the Constitution Rheinland-Pfalz, Klaus Steinmetz, had been admitted into Germany's autonomous and anti-imperialist scene. For ten years he had informed on activities in the Rhein-Main area and had gradually worked his way into the inner circle of the RAF.

On 17 June 1993 the men of the special unit GSG 9 were given a new challenge. What happened that summer Sunday was to be retold in countless books, newspaper and magazine articles and film scripts. Witnesses, alleged witnesses, collaborators, genuine and not-so-genuine experts....all had their version of the event. However, only those members of the special unit GSG 9 who were present that day in the village of just 3,000 inhabitants know what really happened.

Two months earlier, on 17 April 1993, and barely a month after the attack on the prison at Weiterstadt, Wolfgang Grams, Birgit Hogefeld and Klaus Steinmetz met up for the first time in the town of Cochem. A further meeting was planned for 24 June at Bad Kleinen, in Mecklenburg. It was at this point that preparations began for the capture of Hogefeld and Grams, both of whom had an arrest warrant out for them. They could not be allowed to elude the police again, but it was uncertain whether the meeting between the two RAF leaders and Steinmetz would take place. On 24 June, Birgit Hogefeld and Klaus Steinmetz took a train from Bad Kleinen to Wismar, where they rented a holiday flat, only leaving it occasionally over the next three days.

On 17 June, towards 11.00 am, Hogefeld and Steinmetz left the holiday flat to take the train for the agreed meeting with Wolfgang Grams at Bad Kleinen, near the Schwerin lakes. When Birgit Hogefeld was saying goodbye to the owner, he was curious and asked if her holiday was over and she had to return to work. She replied that she was going to meet friends. Hogefeld and Steinmetz then took the bus to Wismar railway station and then the train to nearby Bad Kleinen. They arrived around 1 pm and went into the Billard Café, an inn at the railway station. Towards 2 pm, Birgit Hogefeld met RAF leader Wolfgang Grams from the train. He was 1.8 metres tall, 33 years old and had dark, curly hair and a moustache. He wore a T-shirt and jeans. Both went to the Billard Café where Steinmetz was waiting for them. There were some other guests in the inn, and besides the serving staff, a female officer from the local BKA and two GSG 9 surveillance experts. At this time there were also GSG 9 agents in the vicinity to eavesdrop on the conversation between the three subjects, and several GSG agents positioned in the railway station. Altogether, there were more than 100 agents positioned around the grounds of the railway station.

At 3.13 pm Hogefeld, Grams and Klaus Steinmetz left the Billard Café and headed in the direction of the railway underpass, their every step closely monitored by GSG 9 agents. A seven-man special operations squad was waiting to seize the trio in the tunnel. The plan stated that the 'target persons' were not to be allowed to leave the tunnel once inside it. After a few metres, Birgit Hogefeld stopped to consult a railway timetable on the wall. Grams and Steinmetz went on and waited in front of the stairway leading up to platforms 3 and 4, a single platform reached by four steps. Suddenly, communication between the GSG 9 agents encountered difficulty, and only a 'broken' message came through due to the transmission being distorted in the underpass.

The message sent was: "If the seizure is successful, control the red cadet." This was heard as: "Seizure successful, I control the red cadet." For the GSG 9 agent in the tunnel this meant that the seizure had gone ahead successfully and he was to provide support. As he ran down the stairs he saw that the seizure had not yet taken place. Another GSG 9 observer in the tunnel saw Wolfgang Grams react to his colleague, look briefly left and right and then run up the stairs to platforms 3 and 4. In the same instant,

Birgit Hogefeld and Klaus Steinmetz were arrested by members of the special unit.

GSG 9 agent Michael Newrzella gave chase to Wolfgang Grams along the platform, closely followed by six colleagues. "Stop, police! Drop your weapon! Surrender!" Immediately after reaching the platform, Grams turned and began shooting at his pursuers, hitting Michael Newrzella, who had not yet drawn his weapon, with several rounds. Newrzella reached the platform but then collapsed and died in front of his colleagues. Another GSG 9 agent was also hit. A third colleague drew his weapon and opened fire. Meanwhile Grams, now under constant fire, moved from the left side pillar at the top of the stairway and approached the edge of platform 4.

To this day, the GSG 9 officer does not know whether he hit Wolfgang Grams or not. He threw himself to the ground instinctively and reloaded his weapon. An exchange of fire occurred over the next eight to ten seconds. When the officer raised his head, he saw Wolfgang Grams lying on the rails, having fallen backwards from the platform. GSG 9 now ran forward to capture the RAF man where he lay. Paramedics arrived and attended to Newrzella, as well as his other wounded colleagues and Grams. The latter received a blood transfusion and was given artificial respiration.

The media had a field day regarding this operation, alleging that Wolfgang Grams had been executed by GSG 9. Anonymous witnesses told the press their version of events. There was much speculation on how Wolfgang Grams had died: who had shot him? Had he committed suicide? It was a long time before these questions could be answered.

Experts were called in from the Zurich city police forensic department and the University of Münster's Institution for Judicial Medicine. After several months they confirmed that Grams had committed suicide, thus absolving the GSG 9 agents. After looking through 1,800 pages of documents, including 140 witness statements, and based on the experts' findings, the Schwerin State Attorney came to the conclusion that following the wild exchange of fire on 27 June 1993, Wolfgang Grams was hit by four bullets on platform 4. The fatal round was fired by Grams' own weapon, a CZ 75 pistol from the Czech weapons factory at Brünn.

After this, Bad Kleinen would hold a bitter after-taste for GSG 9.

The *Hansa Stavanger* in the Hands of Pirates – 2009

The Hamburg shipping company Leonhardt & Blumberg had had a successful 106 years in business, with more than 150 of its ships to be found worldwide on the high seas. The fleet consisted of reefers and primarily container ships. The German undertaking was headed by Frank Leonhardt, a grandson of the founder. On the morning of 4 April 2009 the company's fortunes changed when the unimaginable had happened; at 9.14 am, about 400 miles off the coast of Somalia, the container ship *Hansa Stavanger* was seized by pirates. Bound for Dar-es-Salamm, it had been travelling from Jabal Ali, in the UAE, via Mombasa, Kenya. The 20,000-ton *Hansa Stavanger,* 170 metres in length, was carrying goods from Asia with a value of several million dollars.

The pirates approached the ship aboard speedboats, firing rockets, and climbed aboard taking Captain Krzysztof Kotiuk and his twenty-four-man crew hostage. The international crew included five Germans, as well as Russians, Ukrainians, and men from the Philippines and Tuvalu. Towards 9.30 am, Frank Leonhardt received news that the ship was in the hands of Axadu, the leader of the pirates. He demanded $15 million "Immediately or we will kill everybody here."

Axadu had nothing more to lose. He had become a pirate for money; his regular job as a builder in Somalia was no longer enough to support his family. The crew were made to kneel and were held continuously at gunpoint; it was the start of what would be the worst hours of their lives. The region where the container ship had been seized was at the centre of a so-called 'risk-zone', which international anti-terrorist organizations had been warning shipowners about in the weeks before the capture.

It was clear to Frank Leonhardt following his telephone conversation with the pirate that he must act fast. He immediately dialled an emergency number and was connected to the police chief. "Please help me, my container ship *Hansa Stavanger* has been captured by pirates off the coast of Somalia. They are asking for an impossible ransom to release the hostages. Please come quickly." The Federal Government Crisis Staff called upon members of the Interior Ministry, the office of Foreign Affairs and the Defence Ministry to take part in talks and the meeting was held in the Foreign Affairs Office in Berlin. German Federal Police has jurisdiction for freeing German hostages abroad, even having trained units who board captured ships on the high seas to save hostages. In warlike situations the Bundeswehr, with its corresponding special forces, known as *Kommando Spezialkräfte*, KSK for short, can also be involved, but because the military in Germany requires parliamentary assent to act abroad, the police's elite troops were chosen for this operation. The Crisis Staff was at once in agreement; this time nobody would pay, neither the shipping company and certainly not the Federal Republic. As a result, the Crisis Staff decided to dispatch the police special unit GSG 9.[1]

GSG 9 could be ready for a mission in the nearest port within ninety-six hours, but in this case the pirates could have reached Harare within twenty-four hours. Time was a decisive factor in this life-and-death struggle for money and power. Everybody knew that as soon as the captured ship reached port it would be too late for a successful operation.

On Easter Sunday 2009, two Antonov An-124, three Ilyushin Il-76, a Transall and an Airbus flew explosives and six Puma and Bell helicopters to Mombasa. More than 200 elite GSG 9 police travelled with their special equipment to Kenya, Somalia's neighbour. From there they went on to Mombasa to occupy the 'Bahari Beach' hotel. They soon came to the notice of the holidaymakers present, who could hardly believe their eyes when a number of trained, muscular men with shaved chests were suddenly swimming lengths of the hotel pool at a speed close to that of world champions. That evening the same men sat at the bar drinking mineral water or orange juice. No alcohol. The Federal Interior Ministry sent medical doctors and co-workers of the Technical Relief Organization to Kenya. Each individual military carrier was reported by the German Embassy in Nairobi to the Kenyan Government by verbal note, with a vague mention of military equipment and thanks for their cooperation. The US Navy made its assault ship USS *Boxer* available in support of the operation.

Meanwhile, the men of GSG 9 set themselves up in the hotel, their command centre being on the floor above the reception desk, while below them technicians erected satellite dishes.

While GSG 9 prepared for its special mission, scenes took place within the container ship that might have been from a horror movie. Axadu and his pirates threatened the crew with their lives: "We will shoot you if your shipping company will not speak with us or not pay the ransom," and then proceeded to carry out mock executions. Captain Kotiuk and his crew experienced pure horror: "At first we were told to kneel, then they pointed the muzzle of their guns at our temple or head and told us, that 'these were our last minutes.' Sometimes they fired after aiming a little away from the head so that the bullet passed close by. Then they would aim at us again, but not fire. This made me so fearful that I thought I was going to die within a few minutes, either from a bullet or heart attack caused by the stress."

After two days, on 6 April 2009 – as the Federal Government Crisis Staff had feared – the pirates towed the ship towards the port in the bay of Harardhere, about 400 km north of the Somalian capital Mogadishu.

Nothing could be done about this. All attempts to free the *Hansa Stavanger* from the clutches of the pirates were to no avail. When the German frigate *Rheinland-Pfalz,* with its 200-man crew and armed with guns, rockets and helicopters, sighted the *Hansa Stavanger*, it was forced to turn away. Upon sighting her, the pirates forced the Captain to signal to 'his people' to keep their distance, fearing as he did for his own life and that of his crew. The *Hansa Stavanger* now lay at anchor near several other captured ships, monitored from offshore by the German frigate *Mecklenburg-Vorpommern*. In the darkness, eighteen frogmen parachuted down from the Transall aircraft near the *Mecklenburg-Vorpommern* to be collected by inflatables and brought aboard. They were naval frogmen, the elite of the Bundeswehr,[2] holding themselves at readiness to board the *Hansa Stavanger*.

Meanwhile, the shipping company had agreed with the Federal Government not to give into the ransom demands. The Crisis Staff was prepared to order a warning shot to be fired near the ship or at her rudder, to bring the hostage crisis to an end. The question of how the elite of the Bundeswehr were to free the hostages remained open.

Matters deteriorated on the night of 11 April when the pirate leader Axadu, with his own crew and taking along the crew of the *Hansa Stavanger*, attempted to assist other pirates to take hostage the master of the *Maersk Alabama,* who was being held prisoner in a lifeboat. This crazy project came to nothing, however, as even despite hours of searching, Axadu and his crew were unable to contact the other pirates or find the lifeboat.

As a precaution following the storming of the captured yacht *Tanit* by the French Navy, twenty of the twenty-four-man crew of the *Hansa Stavanger* were brought ashore in Somalia, four crew members being obliged to remain behind on the ship. On the night of 18 April, the pirates returned the twenty crew members to the ship, which had meanwhile been moved to a new anchorage 9 miles off the port of Hobyo.

The frigates *Rheinland-Pfalz* and *Mecklenburg-Vorpommern* had been joined by the frigate *Emden* and the supply ship *Berlin* – a total of 800 crewmen – and now lay off Hobyo, all observing the comings and goings aboard the *Hansa Stavanger*. Aboard the ship, the original number of pirates had fallen to six, all armed with machine-guns, pistols, Kalashnikovs and bazookas. A network of sentries were on duty and the ship was lit up at night. The kidnapped crew was accommodated in rooms below deck.

There were now several possibilities to save the *Hansa Stavanger* crew; sending in helicopters was the first option under consideration, but had the drawback that the pirates would hear them and open fire at once. Divers could be sent in on inflatable boats to climb the sides of the ship using special ladders or suction cups.

The Crisis Staff discussed it at length but could not reach a satisfactory decision. The operation would have to be played out by GSG 9 on the spot. The commander needed a further day for surveillance and requested the responsible Ministry to grant his team this day's delay. Then came the decisive telephone call. The US security adviser, James Jones, told his colleagues in Germany that the US military advised against any forcible action to free the hostages and wanted to withdraw the warship USS *Boxer* from the scene. They did not wish to become involved in a suicide mission; the prospects for a successful operation were too slim.

Toward 6 pm the competent German Secretaries of State were informed. Even before the next session of the Crisis Staff, it had been decided to call off the operation by the last week of April and to order the GSG 9 men to come home. "That can't be true. We are so well prepared and ready to act, and then they call us home. It's not right," a member of the special unit complained.

"Don't get excited about it, that's the way things are," a colleague replied.

While the special unit was in the air returning to Europe, the negotiations regarding the size of the ransom continued between the shipping company and the hostage-takers.

The breaking-off of the GSG 9 liberation operation shows that this kind of mission – despite similar operations by France and the United States – cannot be the solution for such acts of piracy. The risks are simply too high and the operations too costly. Until now the international community has seldom found an alternative solution to paying the ransoms demanded.

The captain and crew of the *Hansa Stavanger* were in the hands of the pirates for 121 days. After two months the ship was in such a filthy state that many crew members fell ill. For three weeks, contact between the shipping company, pirates and ship was cut off; a period of sheer horror for the captives. The psychological stress was enormous. In an email on 3 July, the captain wrote that he had "neither water, medicines nor food."

On 3 August 2009, the pirates departed having agreed upon a ransom of $2.75 million. Intermediaries dropped the money on the *Hansa Stavanger* from a helicopter. The next day the media considered it a questionable deal.

GERMANY

On 8 August 2009 the Hansa Stavanger *reached the port of Mombasa with a German Navy escort. The ship's master and his five German crewmen returned to Hamburg on 11 August. For the Hamburg shipping company Leonhardt & Blumberg this – and the relatively mild end to the kidnapping – was the great success in 2009.*

Chapter 6

Italy

Kidnappers in the Land of Leonardo da Vinci

Unit: Nucleo Operativo Centrale di Sicurezza (NOCS)
Motto: *Sicut nox silentes* = As quiet as the night

The Red Brigades Kidnap a NATO General – 1982

It was 17 December 1981. In a noble Verona penthouse, four men wore blue suits and caps bearing an unknown logo. One of them was looking at the water level gauge. First impressions would be that they were workmen, but this was not the case. General James Lee Dozier, the highest ranking NATO general in Southern Europe, stepped back, seeing at once that instead of tools they held guns, which were pointed at himself and his wife, Judy. Their intention could not be mistaken and they had nothing to do with repairing the water leak. They had wanted to gain access to the flat, for these four men were counted amongst Italy's most dangerous terrorists; members of the Red Brigades, a Communist underground organization founded in Milan in the 1970s. Judy was quickly tied to a chair, chained and left alone in the flat. The general was bound by the hands and led down the staircase to waiting Red Brigades vehicles. They left Verona for Padua in a convoy. There the general was locked in a flat with a tent, in which he was to spend the next few days. He was fitted with headphones playing loud hard rock music so that he could not overhear the terrorists' conversation. The nightmare had begun.

The days passed with the Red Brigades questioning him about NATO operations and playing him loud music. The kidnapping had caused worldwide surprise. In the Pentagon, the general opinion was that the Cold War was responsible. Very recently NATO had made public its plans to instal Pershing II rockets in Western Europe, including Sicily, to confront Soviet SS-20 rockets. Statements such as this could have triggered the kidnapping of the general. However, it was clear to everyone that the NATO general was one of the biggest fish to have been hooked so far. Something had to be done to free him from the terrorists as quickly as possible.

Every day the Red Brigades would send the Italian media documents bearing the general's signature and their symbol; the red five-pointed star. The general negotiated with them on his own and they granted his request to be played George Gershwin instead of hard rock. Furthermore, he requested daily information about his wife and requested his abductors oblige him by bringing news of her, sometimes including photographs they had taken of her shopping or walking down the street.

Meanwhile, the efforts to rescue the general were running at full pace. The Italian police left no stone unturned in their attempts to discover the Red Brigades' hiding place. A month went by.

Then came the decisive clue as to where the terrorists might possibly be holding their kidnap victim. It was clear from the outset that members of the Italian special unit NOCS would take over this operation, since it was unknown what weapons they had, or whether there were explosives in the flat and the condition of the hostage. It had to be a well-planned action with no mistakes; the victim was a US citizen and the United States had already sent a team of commandos to Europe in order to free him from the terrorists' clutches.

The operational leadership and the NOCS crisis staff sat together in a secure room and discussed what form the operation should take. Next morning, 28 January 1982, the members of the special unit drew up to a building where the hostage was thought to be being held, in a furniture van. Unnoticed by passers-by and the occupants of the building, the NOCS members, dressed as furniture removers, got out of the vehicle. First, the team had to determine whether the entrance door to the Red Brigades flat was fitted with explosives. To find out, a NOCS member and a female police officer were sent into the building pretending to visit the dentist who had a practice there. The entrance to the surgery was on the same floor as the terrorists' flat. Once on the correct floor, the two officers had the opportunity to test the door for explosives. Fortunately, it was not fitted with them. This information was relayed to their colleagues and now the operation could go ahead.

A twelve-man operational team began to climb the stairs quietly to the Red Brigades flat. Its team included a world boxing champion and a wrestling world champion. The greatest caution was required, nothing had to be left to chance. The special unit burst into the flat and the operation went off in a flash. A member of NOCS broke down the front door with a battering ram and used a female terrorist as a shield in order to force the other terrorists back. The members of the Red Brigades were armed with heavy weapons, bombs and rifles, but they had no chance to use them as they were swiftly disarmed by the special unit. One of the terrorists had held a rifle pointed at the hostage. A NOCS man struck him in the face with a rifle butt. At the same time, one of his colleagues found General Dozier in a tent, unable to understand the commotion. Dozier had mistakenly assumed that a rival terror gang had invaded the flat in order to kidnap him from the original kidnappers. When the NOCS men declared who they were and let him know that he was free, he said, "Wonderful. The police." These were his first words to go round the world. For NOCS, the liberation of the general was one of its most important operations, and it is still hailed today as an outstanding achievement, particularly because the operation was concluded without any of the five terrorists being killed.

General Dozier was taken in haste to police headquarters where he held a press conference. News of his release spread like wildfire and the media fell over themselves to deliver the positive news. The members of NOCS who took part in the operation were awarded the silver star by the United States and the US President, Ronald Reagan, made a telephone call congratulating the general on his release. He had agreed with the NOCS to request the Texas entrepreneur and presidential candidate Ross Perrot to send his personal security team to Italy to secure the general's release. Perrot's team had actually been on the way to Italy when the NOCS operation was successfully completed.

The five terrorists arrested, including Antonio Savasta, were each sentenced to sixteen years' imprisonment. After ten years Savasta was given amnesty. When General Dozier was asked for his reaction, he replied in his emphatically diplomatic manner: "If this man has been punished enough in the eyes of the Italian authorities, then that is OK by me."

General Dozier is now retired and living in Florida, but continues to work with the US Air Force. For years he has given courses on the way to react to hostage-takers and the correct attitude to adopt if kidnapped.

Augusto de Megni: 112 Days in the Hands of Kidnappers – 1990

It was the evening of 3 October 1990. Dino de Megni and his 10-year-old son Augusto were alone in their villa, perched on a hill opposite the city of Perugia, the capital of the Umbrian region. Dino's father, also named Augusto, was a renowned lawyer and banker, having founded the Bank of Perugia and other Italian financial institutions. He was also a Freemason. The family was known for being industrious and assiduous and enjoyed a very good reputation in Perugia. Dino worked in one of his father's banking institutions.

A fire flickered in the hearth. Dino sat at a writing desk working on customers' particulars while young Augusto was reading. Suddenly they received an unexpected visit. Four armed and masked men bound Dino to a chair and taped his mouth. Another covered Augusto with a weapon. "We'll take this young one here with us," were their last words. Then before the eyes of the despairing father, they took the boy and disappeared into the night.

Dino de Megni found it difficult to hide his tears. With the last of his strength he attempted to move his chair forward to the writing table, remembering that he had left a pair of scissors there. He hoped he could use them to free himself. He was successful and after cutting away all the cording and wire wrapped around himself, he got to the telephone to report the kidnap of his son. The Perugia police responded within a few minutes and took details. "Could you remember anything, Sr. de Megni? Any detail could be of help to us." He was still in shock and the only thing he recalled was the deep voice of one of the kidnappers and the frightened face of his son. "If we hurry, perhaps we'll still have the chance of catching them on the road."

The same night the police blocked off some of the roads in the neighbourhood and checked vehicles passing through. Amongst them was the kidnappers' car, but it passed the control unnoticed, whilst Augusto lay on the floor of the vehicle in the back. The kidnappers then drove more than another 160 km with their victim. They wanted to take Augusto de Megni away from his family to a place where he would not be known.

Meanwhile, several police officers searched the area for the kidnappers and their vehicle. Neither were found in the next twenty-four hours. It was a severe blow for Augusto's father. Days passed and nothing was heard from the kidnappers.

The de Megnis were a strong clan, but they were extremely worried for the safety of the missing boy. The longer he was absent, the worse it was for his family. After twenty-seven days the demand was made for twenty thousand million lire – about €10 million – to be paid into a bank account in Rome. Augusto's family would have paid up at once if they had been allowed to, but at that time a new law had come into force in Italy which made it illegal for the families of kidnap victims to pay a ransom. The background was clear; the Government wanted to prevent kidnapping.

The Italian Government introduced a special method of preventing ransoms being paid: by legally freezing the family's bank accounts. This was the path followed in Italy to stem the endless cases of kidnap and to make it as difficult as possible for kidnappers. The method was meant to protect everybody. Naturally, this was of no interest to the de Megni family, who only wanted Augusto freed and didn't care how that was achieved. They sat together in the evenings considering a new tactic, until they finally made contact with the special unit, NOCS.

The taking of Augusto concerned not only his own family; his classmates were sad and wanted to stand by the family. One day they organized a demonstration in the centre of Perugia, publicly demanding the boy's release. The whole of Italy held its breath. Then NOCS received the decisive clue that the child might possibly be being held at a hideout in the province of Pisa, in Volterra. The special unit headed there. They searched the area using four helicopters and finally found what they were looking for. It was the 112th day since the disappearance of Augusto de Megni and there was finally light at the end of the tunnel. It was early morning when the helicopters landed near the Poggio la Rocca farmstead, supported in the search by around 200 police officers. They found a wood nearby; a perfect place for a hideout. NOCS went into the wood while police searched the farmstead. After combing through the trees they came to a rock with a cave beneath it. It was surrounded by dense vegetation, meaning that it was scarcely visible from a distance. Two men were standing in front of the cave. Realising they must be two of the kidnappers, the NOCS men suspected that young Augusto de Megni was being held captive in this cave.

The two kidnappers were overpowered and arrested. Then a NOCS member discovered another of the kidnappers in the cave, the entrance to which was completely covered by vegetation. Augusto de Megni stood near him. This third man, Antonio Staffa, was already known to police, having planned kidnappings before and having been living underground for years.

While the arrestees were being led off to a police vehicle, a terrible scene was being played out in the cave. NOCS had blocked the entrance and begun negotiating with the kidnapper, who was holding a gun to Augusto's head. He declared he would not go back to prison and demanded a vehicle for his escape. The special unit and detectives who had been called in stood firm. First, Augusto de Megni must be released, then they could discuss the vehicle. As time went on the negotiations became ever more difficult and were broken off several times by the kidnapper. Then he spent an hour debating with the special unit's lead negotiator. In the end, Antonio Staffa couldn't negotiate any longer and so dropped his weapon and surrendered. As he was being arrested and led away to a police vehicle, NOCS entered the cave and freed the boy. He embraced the members of the special unit with joy.

The photographs of Augusto, wrapped in a jacket that was too big for him and surrounded by masked NOCS police, later went round the world. NOCS arrested four kidnappers, all from Sardinia. Amongst them was one man whom Augusto called 'the good Genoven' because he was there when the other three were planning to cut off Augusto's ear to send it to the family. All were handed down prison sentences from twenty to thirty years.

Augusto de Megni survived the experience rather well. At age 15 he left the family to be a footballer. Years later, in 2004, he was a candidate for the television show Big Brother, *but not selected. Nevertheless, he began a career in television, appearing in numerous series, and studied communications science.*

Chapter 7

Israel

Zoff in the Town on the Border

Unit: Yamam

Destruction of the Tayyibe Terror Net – 2000

The Israeli special unit, Yamam, has to deal with 900 operations annually, many of them in the most diverse areas of Israel, and so several operations may occur the same day at the same time. Tactical and strategic flair is required of the commander and his men in these interventions, together with strength and endurance. Cooperation with the country's other secret services (Mossad, Aman, Shabak) is particularly important; much of the information received about terror cells lands there first, is then analysed for its truthfulness before being passed on to colleagues in the special forces unit. As was the case in this story.

March 2000 had been quiet, with no major occurrences between Israelis and Palestinians. It was the time when Bill Clinton was personally advocating a new beginning in the Middle East and wanted to meet the Syrian President, Assad, in Geneva. His aim was to try and pave the way for serious talks between Israel and Syria.

The day after he announced his travel plans to Geneva, on 20 March 2000, at 3.00 am the telephone rang in the home of the Yamam commander. His operations leader was calling. He informed his chief that the secret service Shabak, responsible for Israel's internal security and counter-intelligence, was apparently in possession of information concerning a group of Palestinians who had left the Gaza Strip three days before and were now heading inland. So far it was not certain if they might just be illegal workers using a criminal platform. The information came from a young female soldier who had made the observation in the area near

Tayyibe, a small Arab conclave in the centre of Israel, located within a small triangle of Arab-Israeli towns.

The commander was used to such telephone calls, usually receiving around five per day. He left home and drove to the operations centre, where the Police Director and the rest of his team were waiting for him. A conference was held at 1.30 am, at the end of which it was agreed that the possibility could not be ruled out that Hamas[1] had sent out five suicide bombers in five different directions.

The commander decided to contact an estate agent in Tayyibe in order to find out if there was a large empty house which might have been rented temporarily by the group. The house was soon found and blocks of streets in a 150 metre radius were sealed off. Buildings were evacuated in case of an exchange of fire or bomb explosions. Anything was possible. The important thing was to prevent whatever criminal act they might be proposing to carry out, and by any means available.

More information began to flood in to the operations leader and the Yamam commander; all the signs pointed to there being a group of five men in the house, with terrorist intentions. The operations leader took up a megaphone and shouted in the direction of the house: "This is the police. We have your house surrounded. Come to the door with your hands raised." He repeated these sentences several times. After fifteen minutes, one man came out and was led away by members of the special unit for interrogation. He declared that he was an illegal immigrant, but not a terrorist. The commander now instructed his men to be especially careful, because illegal immigrants, as well as terrorists, might be present in the house. He was anxious to avoid innocent people being harmed.

A second man now left the house carrying a bag and ran off. From now on, the whole team knew that something was definitely wrong. The street barriers were strengthened and the whole town put on high alert. The operational leadership decided to send a dog into the house to sniff out explosives and, if possible, restrain the accomplices. A few seconds after the dog reached the front door, it exploded. "This is an incredibly awkward situation. We have to think of some better way of getting these people out without sacrificing another dog or a member of the team," the commander stated.

After further consideration, he decided to bring up several IDF-Caterpillar-DP-bulldozers to demolish the house. Only in this way would he be sure of not putting any member of his team at risk. While the special unit waited for the equipment to arrive, a crowd of curious onlookers began to gather. They were difficult to disperse and proceeded to take photographs and ask the police what was going on. Even some journalists had turned up, knowing that wherever Yamam was in action, a story would be there somewhere. Everybody waited with interest to see what would happen next.

Information finally arrived from the operations centre that other members of the terrorist group were hiding in five other locations in Israel and were preparing suicide bombings. The commander now had to act quickly in order to prevent a tragedy. He decided to send members of his unit to the five localities. He felt sure this was going to be one of the major operations against suicide bombers in Israel.

The Interior Ministry informed him that one of the suspects could be holding out in the town of Shefar'am, in the north of Israel, east of Haifa. With helicopters and the support of Israeli naval forces, the five suspected localities were occupied by Yamam and a watch kept on the suspects. Once again, whole blocks of streets were cordoned off and local inhabitants evacuated for their own safety.

The bulldozers for the Tayyibe operation arrived towards midday. Naturally the team was glad to get to work. The operations at the various other places were variable in length. While the bulldozers began demolishing the house at Tayyibe, snipers had set up in other buildings and the operations team had surrounded the suspects' house, whilst helicopters circled and observed overhead. The time needed to knock down a house depends on its size and the building materials. The crowd waited to see what, or who, would eventually show themselves from behind its walls. Many helped in their own way by throwing stones at a suspect.

The action at Tayyibe ended at 6.00 pm, with two terror suspects being taken into custody. At the other locations it would be the early hours before members of the terrorist cell were captured. Towards 4.00 am the mission at the first location ended with five suicide bombers detained and four Hamas members killed. The leader of the group, who had concealed himself in a Hamas house in Shefar'am, was also captured and interrogated. Hamas has a special tactic of breaking off negotiations and providing their counterparts with a *fait accompli*. It is naturally not the fine English way of doing things, but is still a clever strategy.

ISRAEL

The terrorist cell was detained but the operation was not yet over. In the following days, Yamam, along with colleagues from the Interior Ministry, found further hideouts belonging to the group of suicide bombers and arrested those involved. Yamam was lucky; in all of these operations over the following days, a whole series of terror cell chiefs were caught and taken away for interrogation. The members of Yamam sighed with relief, as this was an important and successful coup against a diabolical network of suicide bombers.

Chapter 8

Austria

Operation in Red-White-Red

Unit: EKO-Cobra DSE — Einsatzkommando Cobra
Motto: *Melius semper* = Always Better

Death Threat in a Village – 2001

The woman was frightened and sobbing, her face swollen unrecognisably. She had grazes over her whole body and numerous injuries from which she was bleeding. Her clothing was torn. Neighbours stood around her. What the police discovered that spring day in 2001 when called to a single-family house on the main road at Strasshof was more than tragic.

Strasshof is a small, tranquil spot with well-tended gardens, about 20 km from Vienna. But the idyll is deceptive. If the police are called to Strasshof, officers are particularly on their guard, because this Austrian village is renowned not only nationally, but sadly internationally as well, with the tragedy of Natasha Kampusch, the girl who was held here for years in a cellar by her abductor and whose story half the world knows.[1]

The woman told the officers that she was obtaining a divorce; her husband was an alcoholic. After an argument that afternoon, he had beaten her brutally then thrown her out of the house and barricaded himself inside with a pistol and several rifles. He was threatening to kill himself and his own son, a boy of five. He had cut the telephone line and drawn the blinds. All contact with him had been broken off for hours.

The police tactical unit EKO Cobra was alerted and it was clear to them that they would have to storm the house and quickly subdue the perpetrator. The twenty-two members of the unit analysed the situation without delay; the house was single storey, with a cellar, and was reached by ten steps leading into a narrow hallway. The surrounding garden was well laid out with bushes and flower beds, and an apple and cherry tree. You could hear the television from outside; the husband had fortified the living room. He did not react when the police knocked on the door.

The members of EKO Cobra didn't want to lose any time; an action plan and several alternatives were ordered by the commanders. Present at the time were an operations leader, a tactician, a technical aide, a leadership assistant and a large operational team with a negotiator. The plan involved an assault on the house through the windows and doors to overcome the perpetrator and take him into custody.

The commander leading the operation was not comfortable with it. He went over the situation in his mind; here was a married man who had assaulted his wife and then barricaded himself in his own home with his son, and had allegedly threatened to kill the boy and commit suicide. Under Austrian law, the only crime which he was guilty of so far was assault and battery. The man was with his own child in the house. The child was suffering from the stress of the situation, not to mention the conflict between his parents and the resulting violence. How would the boy react to the entry of the police tactical unit into the home and the subsequent arrest of the father? Would he not be further traumatised?

The commander made a spontaneous decision. Beyond Plan B and Plan C there had to be a Plan D. His senior tactician uttered objections. EKO Cobra existed for extraordinary missions and attacks which they carried out as a special unit. As he knew from his own experience, the 'soft plan' was not the desired option, nor was it appropriate to the situation. The commander was firm however for a "swift solution to the case" for both the legal and tactical standpoints as far as the child's welfare was concerned. The members of the special unit reconsidered the situation. Did the allegations match the reality? How did the situation really look?

The television inside the house could be heard on the street. The members of the unit thought about the wife's statement, comparing it with what the police and various neighbours had said. The team went over several ways of entering the house unobserved. They always carried a special ladder for opening doors and windows, thus enabling the team to enter the house at the same time. The perpetrator had to be taken by surprise, making it impossible for him to react – i.e. draw his weapon and shoot. The analysis of the situation lasted three-quarters of an hour, during which time checks and re-checks were made. A tactical plan was drawn up quickly to include the legal components. Operational tacticians are old warhorses with a great deal of experience, which helps them in awkward situations such as this one. Nevertheless, the Cobra members was not happy;

a 'soft operation' was a contradiction in terms and something for which the unit was not called out for. This was something the police could do. The commander remained steadfast; he was aware of his responsibility and he knew that his decision could have repercussions. He did not want to risk breaking the law on this occasion.

During the strategy discussion between the members of the special unit and the operation leader, the wife suddenly intervened. She put the matter into perspective precisely. That day the argument had been about the care and custody of the child. Upon hearing that, the negotiator made the spontaneous suggestion that the 'soft option' should be tried and the husband engaged in a conversation. "I could tell him that I am from the court and that I need to clarify something about awarding custody." The unit's operational team agreed that the negotiator should try to speak to the husband. Since the team had arrived at the village in civilian clothes, and were only going to change into uniform when the operation began, nobody in the street knew that the men were members of the special unit Cobra. The negotiator was a middle-aged man. The identity he intended to put over in his conversation with the husband matched his appearance: he had a smooth voice, was skilled in rhetoric and had a cool approach. The aim of the conversation would be to get the husband to open the front door. As soon as that happened, agents positioned left and right of the door would burst into the house and subdue the man. For the assault, the operation leader chose colleagues with experience in close combat methods. The first attack had to be perfect and lead immediately to the desired objective.

The negotiator went to the house with his attaché case. His disguise worked perfectly. He went up the ten steps to the entrance and knocked on the door loudly. Shortly beforehand, four of his colleagues from the operations team had taken up their positions left and right of him. Everything then proceeded very quickly. The husband asked the negotiator from behind the closed door who he was and what he wanted. The negotiator answered in a routine manner. As discussed, he said that he came from the district court and had some questions regarding the divorce and the custody of the child. The husband was surprised and asked why somebody had come from the district court right now. He was not prepared. The negotiator remained businesslike and spoke to the husband calmly, as he had been trained to do.

Finally the husband opened the door; at the same instant the negotiator stepped back to make way for his colleagues. In a split second they entered the house, seized the man and overcame him. They identified themselves as members of the Police Tactical unit EKO Cobra. A matter-of-fact attitude and respect for the law are to be maintained constantly. What follows has been laid down officially for similar situations: "Police." "Lay your weapon down." "Lay yourself down on the ground" and finally: "We have the situation under control." Their commands are spoken so as to not be misunderstood. The sentences are purely functional, with clear diction and no friendly 'please' or even 'thank you'. The perpetrator must be clear that he has no chance of defending himself or escaping, and he must have no possibility of struggling or reaching for his weapon. He would be handcuffed and led away silently to the operations vehicle, the door shut, and the vehicle driven off.

The unit commander entered the house with the wife to see the child. Both also inspected all the rooms. They found the child playing peacefully in his room on the first floor. He had not seen the arrest of his father and ran happily to his mother's arms. The members of the operation team thought that all had gone well.

In the follow-up debrief next day, the operation commander reminded his team how important it is to act out of conviction. One can only be sure if all eventualities have been considered and examined. If not all of the team members are convinced, it is important to convince those who have any misgivings concerning the tactics and mission. The spectrum of possible solutions on every special unit mission is large. It is important to remember that having responsibility means being solution-orientated when working on a mission. However, the showpiece solution is not always the right one, nor is the violent method always the right one. The more information made available to the members of a special unit in the run-up, the more effective their strategy for the operation will be.

Another aspect to remember in this case is that the village of Strasshof should not be regarded as a small crime-filled town. There is a solution to every dispute and it does not always involve violence.

Attack on the Vienna Opera Ball – 2004

The white envelope lay beneath a batch of letters on the writing desk of the Cabinet leader at the Foreign Ministry. It bore a colourful stamp with the portrait of the female recipient.[2] The envelope appeared harmless, only the stamp was spectacular. "For Benita" it said, but the contents of the letter were more than explosive. There were no details as to the sender. The author had an old-fashioned style of writing and had used a blue Lettera 32, an Olivetti cult-typewriter from 1963 designed by Marcello Nizzoli and much sought after by collectors today.

The author had divided his letter into three sections, coming to the point in the last. The Cabinet chief read: "Dear Madam, I have the highly esteemed obligation herewith to notify you formally that you will not leave the Opera Ball this year alive. I shall approach you on the grand staircase with a smile and you will not realise that I am your murderer. Then you will very quickly meet your death on the stairs." It was the second threatening letter of this kind within two months. The Cabinet leader immediately reached for the telephone.

It was 12 February 2004 and barely a week before the Vienna Opera Ball; the traditional meeting place for prominent personalities from international politics, business and culture at the Vienna State Opera. According to tradition, after affairs and political strategies had been discussed, in the evening the end of the ball season was celebrated. For the organisers, the ball involved around 6,000 visitors, including 200 journalists from all over the world who would be reporting live from the Austrian capital, and receipts of around €3.4 million. Added to which an attempt on the life of the then Austrian Foreign Minister and first female candidate for the office of Federal President, Benita Ferrero-Waldner, was planned. Or at least that was what the ominous letter had foretold.

Politicians all over the world live dangerous lives. The risk in Austria might be considered a little less, due to the fact that according to the most recent Global Peace Index, the country is amongst the six safest in the world. For a politician here to receive a death threat via a letter was very rare, Austria being a peaceful country. Nevertheless, the threatened assassination of a popular politician in the framework of a major event with 6,000 guests required special protective measures. For this reason, the Anti-terror Staff was required to develop an extraordinary strategy, and so the best profiler, the criminal-psychologist Thomas Müller, officials from the Foreign Ministry diplomatic protocol, their colleagues from the Federal Office for the Protection of the Constitution and Anti-terrorism, the police and the tactical unit EKO Cobra, sat together at a table in the Ministry of the Interior to discuss a strategy against an unknown and extremely dangerous would-be assassin.

In his first letter, the author had put forward his own theory that it was easier to kill a minister than a president: "If you become president, I shall no longer be able to kill you because then you will have round-the-clock police protection." For some reason he had decided not to keep this to himself. While scientific experts at the police station examined the second letter for traces of DNA, wheels were set in motion of which even the Minister herself – for security reasons – did not know the full details until later.

The Anti-terror Staff initially considered all possible scenarios for the murder attempt and the different solutions needed to prevent it. The conditions in and around the Vienna State Opera House were looked at carefully, as well as the number and position of the emergency exits. Furthermore, the minister's route to and from the Opera House was planned out, taking into consideration all possible crisis scenarios. Once they had agreed upon a plan, the Anti-terror Staff appointed the teams.

The first concern was the immediate daily personal protection for the minister. Six Cobra agents would now accompany her every day from morning until late at night, from her house near Vienna to the Ministry in the city centre, to her appointments, her weekly press conference and evening meetings. Another six agents were stationed in and around her house. She used a chauffeured, armoured limousine, which now had to follow a different route each day, and was itself driven between two vehicles from the counter-terrorist unit. From the moment Benita Ferrero-Waldner left her house she would have the personal escort of EKO Cobra. Her home and offices would be searched daily for explosive devices and the security controls in the Foreign Ministry would be stepped up.

Personal protection does not mean that a person is protected for just one day and that's it. In this case, personal protection meant developing a planned strategy for the day of the Vienna Opera Ball. That equally applied to the protection of the guests at the ball and Opera House. For this reason, days before the event, everyone involved in the preparations for the ball were vetted by the police. As many of the suppliers had worked on 'Project Vienna Opera Ball' for years, their workers were known and regularly screened, but this time the search was widened to include all co-workers – from ushers to cooks, parquet-layers, croupiers, bartenders to waiters – all of whom were subjected again to close screening. Every corner and floor of the building itself was constantly searched by security from the Federal Ministry of Internal Affairs up to the beginning of the ball. The security exits, roof and cellar were also subjected to close scrutiny; a bomb can be hidden anywhere.

Nothing happened in the week before the Opera Ball; no wild pursuits through Vienna, nothing found of note in the minister's house or offices. The officials were hopeful. Profiler Thomas Müller warned, however, that the assassin was dangerous.

Finally the special day arrived. The Vienna Opera Ball takes place traditionally on the last Thursday in Shrovetide – therefore on the Thursday following Ash Wednesday. The Vienna State Opera is closed for two days beforehand for conversion work, as all the rows of seating have to be removed and a special parquet floor laid on the ground floor, thus creating an even surface with the stage of about 850 square metres. Another thirty-four stage boxes have to be added to the existing seventy-six dress circle boxes. Due to the many international guests, the Vienna Opera Ball is one of the largest social events in Austria, presenting quite a challenge for the security forces.

It had been planned that the minister should wear a special protective vest under her ballgown. The vest would contain ceramic plates that would protect her against bullets, as well as any knife attacks. When the minister showed her protectors the dress she had chosen for the ball that evening, they were bewildered; it was a sea-blue, dark green dress with lace trimming on the upper part. It would not be feasible to wear a protective vest beneath it, meaning the minister would be unprotected on her upper body. Recognising the seriousness of the situation, the security men decided that they would have to close in to protect her against possible attack as soon as she entered the building.

The Minister didn't know that the three ambulances parked outside the State Opera House that Thursday in February were there specifically for a possible attempt on her life. The 100 police officers in uniform and civilian clothing in front of the building were there to form a 'transport corridor' for the Minister to escape, if necessary.

The male agents wore their protective vests beneath their frock coats and tuxedos that evening, the female bodyguards wore theirs under their ballgowns. Their equipment for the evening consisted of a pistol, radio apparatus, transmitter and cabling, all glued on in order to have the apparatus ready to grasp at all times. It was obvious that the protective vests would create a lot of body heat. More importantly, not to mention worryingly, was the knowledge that the assassin could be lurking anywhere in the building, ready to launch his attack. The public would not notice the bodyguards, because they made up the usual retinue surrounding a politician like a cabinet minister's co-workers.

AUSTRIA

With a police escort and in one of the three armoured limousines, the Foreign Minister and her husband were driven in convoy towards the Opera House. The route there was changed several times, the special unit selecting for this evening the rather unusual route over the vineyards into the city. Its members were prepared for any eventuality. In all, twenty members of EKO Cobra, together with police and paramedics – all in frock coats and evening dress – accompanied the minister. The convoy halted at the side entrance to the building and not – as was usual – at the main entrance. It was the tactic that evening for it not to be known in advance when and where she would enter. It was meant as a surprise for the assassin, something he had not reckoned with in advance. The minister and her husband had to walk a short way with their protectors, then the party entered the building proper, Benita Ferrero-Waldner and her husband walking slowly arm-in-arm from the foyer to the grand staircase. Among their party were the members of EKO Cobra. This was the most difficult moment of the entire evening. Political colleagues, friends, acquaintances, as well as guests of the ball and journalists jostled around the minister, everybody wanting to speak to her or touch her. It required enormous powers of instinct on the part of the bodyguards to guard the couple. Anybody in the crowd could be the assassin.

Unnoticed by the ball guests, a so-called security ring formed around the minister and her husband in which the bodyguards placed themselves very close to the couple, 'discreet and decent but effective' as the motto says. None of the people near the Minister could break through this ring on the staircase. If anybody tried he would be fended off in a split second. In the foyer numerous police mixed in with the guests to observe the various comings and goings, even a number of waiters were disguised as executive officials. Anything was possible, so the maximum degree of security was in force.

The ball guests were stood everywhere, but were mainly lined up on the left- and right-hand sides of the grand staircase. The minister's husband had suggested in the car that he would precede his wife on the stairway: "I am the elder of us both, if he wants to kill somebody, let it be me." The Cobra agents went up the stairs, knowing with every step that the assassin was somewhere either in front of them or behind. The throng on the staircase had grown, and now journalists and cameramen tried to approach the minister for an interview, but in vain. In a friendly and elegant manner, the members of the special unit turned them away. The minister could be filmed, but not interviewed, as the assassin could be disguised as a journalist. She had to leave the staircase as quickly as possible. Every guest came under scrutiny by the unit and was analysed in a fraction of a second. Every movement, action and look by guests were noted and evaluated. Eye contact was very important for forming character assessments; the eye is the window into the strength or weakness of an individual. The team worked from experience gained from many other missions, communicating with each other via eye contact and body language. Each member of the unit also had constant eye contact on Benita Ferrero-Waldner and her husband. The security forces had spent a whole week working closely with her, knowing exactly when it was becoming too much for her, or when she was getting anxious, but she remained brave and went up the staircase step by step with her famed smile on her lips.

The agents kept an eye on the body language of the guests on the staircase. There are many ways to decode non-verbal signals, and in fractions of a second the members of Cobra looked at mimicry, gestures and body language to answer the following questions: Who is attempting to go particularly unnoticed and by doing so makes himself noticeable? Who is looking in the other direction, even though the minister is standing nearby? Who is staring at her? Facial expressions, gestures, body posture and movement can betray an aggressive person immediately. Body tension among the guests was also looked for. Even the smallest detail could give a clue. The security people were in contact with each other by radio and wore earpieces. As soon as the assassin got near to the minister – depending on the circumstances – the command 'Exit' would be given, meaning that the person being protected has to be evacuated at once. 'Gun' was the order to draw their weapons, and 'act' or 'attack' were the orders to fire. Should the worst occur, the police would hurriedly form a protective corridor to evacuate the minister. The police officers in the foyer analysing the ball guests would report at once to their colleagues if anything came to light.

One step more and they were off the grand staircase. However, over on the left, a man was standing below a rounded arch. He had an adhesive plaster on his neck, was sweating visibly, and gave the impression of being tensed up and strained. The minister's female bodyguard notified her colleagues by radio at once. Unnoticed by the guests, four officers requested the man to accompany them. The bustle grew no less that evening. The whole ball was filmed and all photographs evaluated the next day by the Interior Ministry.

The minister had now reached her box. In a few minutes her first guests were expected; the Spanish Foreign Minister Loyola de Palacio and her

Latvian office colleague, Sandra Kalniete; the Croatian Foreign Minister Miomir Zuzul; the Bulgarian Foreign Minister Solomon Pasi; the Algerian Foreign Minister Abdelaziz Belkhadem; the Andorran Foreign Minister Juli Minoves-Triquell and the actor Miguel Herz-Kestranek. No guest would enter the minister's box unobserved; the agents placed themselves inside the box and outside it for the duration of the ball. If the minister wished to visit the washrooms, these would be cleared beforehand. In a friendly but firm manner, the agents would request the women already there to return to the ballroom for security reasons. Only once did the minister dance with her guests, and even then the bodyguards were unobtrusively close by and dancing themselves, all the time keeping their eyes on the minister.

The evening ended for Ferrero-Waldner and her husband towards 4 am. At this hour there was little activity on the grand staircase and it was easy work for the protection detail as the minister and her party descended the steps. The unit breathed a sigh of relief as the convoy set off to the minister's home, once again following a different route. Their colleagues were already in position awaiting her arrival. There were no incidents on the way. The evening had gone off well; the members of the police tactical unit EKO Cobra were satisfied.

Next morning the members of the special unit meticulously analysed the evening of the Vienna Opera Ball. In the Personal Protection Report, which included all observations required by the Interior Ministry, the agents remarked that a man standing at the end of the grand staircase was taken away by police. The suspicion that this man might be the would-be assassin was considered unfounded after interrogation. The letter to Benita Ferrero-Waldner was deposited for safekeeping in a secret area of the Federal Ministry of Internal Affairs for security reasons. The letter is still there to this day.

Chapter 9

Jordan

Hunt for Criminals in the Kingdom

Unit: Special Gendarmerie Unit 14

Arrest of Dangerous Drug Dealers – December 2012

Friday, 28 December 2012: four days until the New Year and in Jordan, as in Europe, the streets were predominantly quiet. Nevertheless, the police at this time of year are particularly watchful. The commander of Unit 14, the Jordanian police's special unit, received a telephone warning in the early hours of the day from his counterpart in the Anti-Drug Department, advising that dangerous drug-dealers were preparing a drug transport near the capital city, Amman. They must be arrested as quickly as possible so that the drugs would not be allowed to enter circulation. Colleagues at the Inland Secret Service had identified a house outside Amman in which the suspects lived. It was where they grew hemp, cocaine and opium plants at a farm nearby and at a second farm a kilometre away.

The first step was to film and photograph the house and two farms, allowing the special unit to analyse the building very carefully to see how many floors it had, how many windows, which drug dealers were active in which rooms, where they spent the night, who stood guard at the entrance and when. All possible intelligence about the suspects and buildings in which they lived or worked was assembled and after all the material had been looked at, Unit 14 drew up its plan of attack.

The plan was for snipers to be positioned at strategically higher points in the surrounding area, from where they could ensure that the police at ground level were not exposed to any risk of gunfire from the suspects. Furthermore, specialists were to be located around the house ready to infiltrate both it and the two farms simultaneously. The suspects were to be given no chance to flee or engage in a shoot-out. Arrest was the primary objective of the operation.

During the operation one unit member would film and another photograph everything that took place. Based on this plan, the commander coordinated the mission with his Anti-drug Department colleagues and set X-hour for 6.30 am on Saturday, 29 December 2012. Long before sunrise that morning, Unit 14 was in position; snipers positioned in the buildings opposite observed every movement in and around the house and its farm. Meanwhile, the operations' leaders crept up on the house, accompanied by the agents who would break in.

Suddenly shooting began in the vicinity of the house. The gunfire was coming from another dwelling occupied by a suspect's cousin. He was firing warning shots into the air in the hope of forcing the special unit to pull back. Unit 14 was not put off, however; snipers kept watch on the incident and communicated what they saw to their colleagues on the ground. This communication within the unit was very important to avoid any accidents occurring. While the warning fire continued from the suspect's cousin, Unit 14 men entered the house and two farms. Everything had been finely planned; every member of the special unit knew how far he could advance towards which room, door or suspect, each had his precise orders regarding what he had to do, when and how. In this respect the photographic documentation had been a great help to the operation by helping to lay out the building and its surrounds.

Inside the house, Unit 14 arrested seven drug-dealers aged between 23 and 35. Numerous weapons, including Kalashnikov assault rifles and a large quantity of ammunition, were seized in various rooms. At both farms the anti-drug unit found various plants and 750 kg of marijuana.

The raid lasted a total of forty-five minutes. Nobody was hurt. Women and children present in the house at the time were separated from the suspects to shield them from harm. The unit is trained to apprehend suspects, but not judge them. Operations of this kind follow humanitarian criteria and are not brutal raids.

Once the operation had ended, Unit 14 returned to its centre of operations. The mission had gone off well, the arrests made in good time, judicial proceedings would follow in due course.

Arrest of a Major Criminal in Amman – 2013

The man was more dangerous than most of the criminals that Unit 14 had had to deal with until then. He had committed several murders, dealt drugs, stolen cars for breaking and spare parts, bought and sold firearms and would trade anything with anybody for money. He was one of the most brutal criminals at large in Jordan. He was mentally ill and his temperament uncontrollable. He had as little respect for the police as he did for anyone else who crossed his path. He was a danger to himself and others. When the Secret Service called Unit 14 headquarters on 20 February 2013, nobody believed he could ever be caught. "Make ready, we have found him," was the terse information given to unit members.

The Jordanian Secret Service had been hot on his heels for five months. It was always the same story; scarcely had he been fished out than he would dive under again. No day passed without some member of the public reporting where this wanted criminal was hiding, but when the police arrived he would already have disappeared and nobody knew where to.

Over time the game developed a system. The 45-year-old led the police by the nose. Whenever he was within reach he would always give the police the slip. At the beginning of February he murdered two people who had challenged him.

Now the Secret Service had his telephone number and could make a plan of his movements, but this proved unsuccessful. He was everywhere and nowhere; he travelled long distances and made short trips. There was no system behind it. He was spontaneous, and it was that which made it so difficult to catch him.

On 20 February 2013 it seemed possible that success was near. The Secret Service had discovered an address in Amman where he was purported to live. They teamed up with Unit 14 for a visit to the address. The house and its surroundings were photographed and filmed, the material analysed at Unit 14 headquarters and a decision taken as to the next step. The same day news came that the suspect had left. "I knew we would never catch him. He is too clever and we are too slow," the men of the special unit agreed.

The following Thursday, the Interior Ministry informed the commander that the man was in the same district, but at a different address; according to the Secret Service, he was at his brother's house. The Unit 14 commander decided to act at once in order to try and capture the suspect. He drummed up a team and told them to be ready for a night operation. To be on the safe side he divided the special unit between both buildings and towards 1.00

am they had surrounded the two locations. Snipers were also in position reporting to colleagues on the activity in neighbouring houses. However, as Amman slept, there was no unusual activity.

At 3.00 am on the Friday, the suspect made a telephone call. He was not planning to leave. Two hours later, the commander gave the order to arrest him and Unit 14 entered both buildings simultaneously. This time they succeeded; the man and his brother were arrested. They had been sleeping and awoke too late to resist.

In a search of both houses the special unit found hidden money and weapons. Both men had a whole arsenal of Kalashnikovs. Upon their arrest neither was repentant, cursing and insulting members of Unit 14 loudly. The money from the robberies was to have provided the brothers with a life of luxury; fine cars, fine women and much else.

The neighbours, awoken by the operation, congratulated the Unit 14 team, happy that the two criminals and their sinister doings had finally ended after so long. The two men were led off to face trial.

Chapter 10

Portugal

Action on the Algarve

Unit: Grupo Operaçoes Especiais (GOE)
Motto: *Última Razão* = The Last Resort

The Bloody End to a Hostage Drama in Lisbon – 2008

It was a hot Thursday afternoon on 7 August 2008 and most people sought the shade. Others crossed the Rua Marques de Fronteira, one of the principal roads in Lisbon, went down to the harbour and then the beach. The road was named after the Portuguese nobleman, Dom Joao de Mascarenhas, the second Count of Torre, who had led the Restoration War between Portugal and Spain from 1640 to 1668, a war which had finally led to the Treaty of Lisbon. There was something noble about this road and today many cars were driving along it for the port. Nobody took any notice of the two men in jeans and dark glasses opening the glass door to the Banco Espirito Santo. They drew their 6.35 mm pistols and, after taking a deep breath, entered.

Nilton Sousa and Wellington Nazaré had come to live in Portugal some time previously from south-east Brazil and had been planning this coup for a while. They needed money desperately. Aged 26 and 32, the guns made them feel safe. They approached the cashier, their weapons covering a 45° angle, and aimed at him. "This is a hold-up. We want all the money you have in the safe. Get it, quickly. Bring your boss here."

The cashier raised his head, his hand moving cautiously to the telephone. "I have to call the two branch managers, Ana Antunes and Vasco Mendes. They are behind me in their offices. Both their doors are shut."

"Then get a move on, thickhead. We haven't got all day," was Nilton Sousa's terse response. His voice trembling, the cashier told his two managers there was a robbery in process and requested they come to the paying-in counter. Within a few seconds they presented themselves and whilst one of the robbers covered the bank's customers at gunpoint, his accomplice covered the cashier and four staff.

"What do you want?" Ana Antunes asked the robbers.

"We want all your money," Nilton replied.

"Our money is in the safe in the back."

The robber pointed his weapon at the manager and her deputy and said, "Then kindly give me the code. And fast. Do it!" Nilton then put his pistol to the head of Ana Antunes and steered her to the safe where he entered the code himself, apparently not trusting the system.

The safe remained closed. "I don't know what's wrong with it, it often happens that the safe door won't open. I'll try it again," she said apologetically. What the two robbers did not know was that if the code was entered hesitatingly, it released a security mechanism which prevented the safe being opened, and the whole procedure had to be repeated. Ana tried several times but failed to get the safe open. Meanwhile, an internal alarm had been triggered and the police alerted. Ana finally succeeded at the fifth attempt and the robbers made her put the money into a sack. At that moment everybody heard a voice coming through a loudspeaker: "This is the police. We know you are in the bank and have taken hostages. Let these innocent people go free at once. Don't let things get any worse for yourselves."

The Portuguese police manner of proceeding in such crisis cases was to seal off a wide area around the bank and position police officers at strategic points to monitor the situation. High-ranking officials from the *Direção Central de Combate ao Banditismo* (the Justice Ministry who fought organized crime), as well as detective officers, were sent to Banco Santo Spirito. The police special unit, the GOE, had already arrived at No 72, Rua Marques de Fronteira with snipers, operational staff and a negotiating team. An attempt would now be made to convince the robbers to give in peacefully. The lead negotiator spoke to the two hostage-takers in a calm and businesslike manner. He was successful; towards 3.50 pm they released four bank staff including one female member who was suffering from a panic attack. By this time, the street outside was teeming with law enforcement and special unit officers. Curious onlookers had also gathered at the barriers to watch events from a distance, although the police had taken steps to mask what was going on by erecting black protective screens.

Despite releasing some hostages, the robbers were firm, and insisted on being given a getaway vehicle and an aircraft to fly out. The negotiator was not impressed by these demands. His aim was to secure the release of the other hostages, the branch manager, her deputy and the bank's customers. Beads of sweat had formed on his forehead. Negotiations with hostage-takers are never simple, he had known that for years. This pair were tough. Meanwhile, the police warned everybody in nearby shops and offices to close up and go home. There could be trouble and the situation might turn nasty.

The two robbers became bolder. After receiving €96,000 from the bank safe, they now demanded more from the police. The negotiator made it clear to them that the Portuguese central bank had a shortage of banknotes at that time and no new notes were being printed. This meant that it would be impossible to meet their demands at such short notice and they would have to think of an alternative. The negotiations with the robbers continued into the night. Journalists gathered at the barriers. Portuguese TV was reporting live from the scene. The two robbers would not listen to the negotiator's requests and were making increasingly unrealistic demands of the police. The negotiations went on for seven hours until four people suddenly appeared at the front door to the bank. It was now 11.00 pm and dark, although the bank was brightly lit. In front of the door were the two gangsters, each using a hostage as a human shield.

Nilton Souza was holding the sack of money in one hand, with a pistol in the other pointing at Ana Antunes' back. Wellington Nazaré covered her colleague Vasco Mendes. The robbers glared at the police. Snipers were in position and ready. The two men looked around for the promised getaway car, but there was none.

"What do we do now? They haven't brought the car to the front of the bank," Nilton said.

"We'll give them some time. Perhaps it's in a traffic jam."

"Don't be so goddamn naive. They're police. They don't get stuck in traffic jams. And definitely not an hour before midnight." While the two robbers were conducting this loud discussion, the special unit crept up, unnoticed.

It was now almost midnight. Nilton spoke frequently to his hostage and put a black shawl around her so that she couldn't be overheard. Suddenly, he threw it behind himself and drilled the weapon into her back. He spoke to her again, her face froze with fear, and wrapped a hand around her throat. Recognising that the situation had come to a dead end, the GOE operational leader now gave the order to finish it. A single shot rang out. Nilton Sousa staggered and fell backwards to the ground, where he lay still. A second later the entrance door to the bank burst open and within seconds at least thirty GOE men had gone inside. Two more shots were heard and Wellington Nazaré was also hit. Both hostages survived. After examination by the emergency surgeon, Nilton was taken away. Wellington suffered a bullet wound to the cheek and was taken to the San José Hospital in handcuffs. A few weeks later he attempted to escape, but failed and was transferred to the Caixas prison hospital.

On 9 July 2009, Wellington Nazaré was sentenced to eleven years in prison for robbery, six crimes of kidnapping and possession of a prohibited weapon, athough this sentence was reduced to eight and a half years following an appeal. In November 2011 his lawyer applied for him to be extradited to a prison in Brazil, so that he could be near his parents, but was refused. After serving more than half of his sentence, he was finally extradited to Brazil in August 2013 and became a free man upon landing. One of the hostages, Teresa Paiva, declared that she hoped he would "seize the opportunity to become a good person".

Personal Protection of Diplomats in Crisis Areas: Congo, Iraq, Chad, 1997–2008

The protection of diplomats in war and conflict zones is one of the most difficult tasks for a special unit. The GOE had experience of this on three separate operations, each requiring various different tactics: the Congo in 1997, Iraq in 2004-2007 and Chad in 2008.

The first Congo War took place between the autumn of 1996 and May 1997 in the territory of the Democratic Republic of the Congo (DRC), which at the time was known as Zaire. It was a civil war in which the dictator, Mobutu, was overthrown by the AFDL rebel coalition supported by several countries. The trigger for the war had been the numerous refugee camps which had sprung up in the east of the country following the genocide in Rwanda.

The first Congo War marked the beginning of a series of wars in central Africa which have persisted to the present day, with only a few interruptions. For this reason, the DRC was a difficult operational area in 1997.

The Portuguese special unit GOE had initially been given the task of protecting the ambassador and his staff following the outbreak of war. The attack on Kinshasa began on the night of 16 May, when the first group of rebels, 10,000-strong, arrived in the suburbs. A day or so before, Mobutu had fled to exile in Morocco. General Mahele, the last Army Chief of Zaire, ordered his troops not to resist and the city fell without a fight. As the situation escalated, the Portuguese Government under Antonio Gutteres decided upon a rapid evacuation of the Portuguese community from the capital, Kinshasa, which would involve around 200 people. Anarchy reigned in the country for three days; those loyal to Mobutu attempted to flee or remained to fight. Meanwhile, the GOE located all Portuguese nationals and conveyed them in secure vehicles to the airport, from where they were flown abroad.

At this time in Kinshasa, the rebels were enthusiastically received by the population, but the war was far from over. The GOE received the order to bring diplomats from nearby Angola, adjacent to the DRC, to the Portuguese embassy in the Congo. The team was made up of eight men in two vehicles, which would pass through areas which had witnessed the heaviest fighting and exchanges of fire. The next day, the GOE organised the additional evacuation of all diplomats from Angola, as well as those journalists sought by the rebels after making anti-rebel statements in the media. The convoy carrying all of these people faced a journey of 30 km along an extremely dangerous road to the airport. The mission was successful. The convoy never came under fire and all escaped harm.

After the rebellion, Laurent-Désiré Kabila made himself President of the Congo by decree and presented his new government. At the end of May he swore the oath of allegiance at a public ceremony in the Kinshasa stadium. His new government failed to bring stability to the country; Kabila had promised national unity and reconstruction, but then outlawed all political parties and demonstrations. By then, however, all Portuguese nationals had been taken out of the country and were able to follow the events as they unfolded in their former country.

The Spring After the Iraq War – 2003

In February 2004 everyday life in the Iraqi capital Baghdad was not as it might have been portrayed. Nine months after the end of the war, the Americans and the Iraqis saw the new state in different colours. There was a Green Zone and a Red Zone separating the city into 'good' and 'bad'. While the Green Zone had high security in the centre of Baghdad set up by the Americans on the west bank of the Tigris after their conquest, and which was barely 7 km/sq in extent, the Red Zone, which is to say the rest of Baghdad, was sealed off from the centre by concrete walls 3 metres high and thousands of kilometres of barbed wire fencing. Soldiers controlled the access roads with tanks and from watchtowers. While the Americans had free access, Iraqis living in Baghdad had to wait half a day until their vehicles had been checked over before they could enter.

The GOE's mission was to protect the Portuguese embassy in Baghdad, therefore the ambassador and his staff. Information was initially gathered by a military commission three months before the real operation began. This was important to determine the necessary security measures required. The operation was particularly difficult as during the reconnaissance, the special unit discovered to its astonishment that neither the embassy nor the ambassador's residence actually had any security precautions. Although most embassies were situated in the Green Zone where they could rely on the protection of US forces, the Portuguese had two rented houses in Al Mansour in the Red Zone, near the embassies of Germany, Spain and the Czech Republic. Many other special units had already suffered the most terrible attacks and loss of life in this zone. One thing was clear to the GOE; this environment demanded discretion, skill, good planning and communication skills for all those involved.

Because the GOE had very good contacts to the other special units, such as the German GSG 9, the Spanish GEO and the Czech URNA, it had their support for its endeavours to improve the security of its embassy. This meant hard work for the GOE in Baghdad. The local population could not be trusted when new security measures were introduced and therefore extra precautions were necessary.

The GOE selected fourteen men for the installation of the new security measures, while the rest of the force protected the area where their colleagues worked. These measures included the installation of a barbed wire fence and sandbagged obstacles, surveillance cameras at all corners, movement sensors, defensive bunkers, communication posts, explosive detectors, metal doors for the buildings fitted with detectors and the erection of a thick wall to surround the embassy and the ambassador's residence. Finally, a very detailed conference was held with all the embassy staff to explain the new measures.

These measures were enormously important for embassy staff. In 2005 the Portuguese embassy was the target of a suicide bomber, after a man carrying 5 kg of explosives parked his vehicle across from the embassy building. That the embassy staff were protected that day was due exclusively to the security measures installed by the special unit two years before in the grounds surrounding the embassy. In 2003 every journey, every route taken through Baghdad represented a risk for GOE members; a kind of Russian roulette. At any moment a bomb could explode killing dozens of people, including themselves.

Personal Protection for UN Special Commissioners in Chad

In March 2008 a personal protection team for the special commissioners of the UN Mission in the Central African Republic and Chad – known as MINURCAT for short – was prepared in cooperation with the Portuguese Government.

The tense situation in Chad, the Central African Republic and the Sudan presented a problem for their citizens, the countless refugees, the dispossessed and for humanitarian support operations. Moreover, it endangered the stability of the whole region. Despite the treaty signed by Sudan and Chad in Tripoli on 8 February 2006 and at N'Djamena on 26 July that year, which was intended to improve the relationship between the two countries, there were repeated bloody clashes involving both regular troops and diverse rebel groups.

The operation was begun after the uprising involving rebels and Government troops at N'Djamena. After the Permanent Mission of Portugal had obtained authority from the UN in New York, the team that was scheduled to fly to Chad was held back in readiness for several days in case circumstances dictated an alternative destination. The GOE team stood by for several days, along with all of their gear and equipment.

The GOE operation was to protect the newly appointed Special Commissioner of MINURCAT, Victor Da Silva Angelo, on his visits to certain regions in Chad, but also to N'Djamena itself, as well as during his daily work around the clock, including visits to ambassadors, ministers and presidents, his own office, the gendarmerie and other UN establishments. The Special Commissioner was to be protected throughout the day by the GOE, especially when he flew to territories such as Iriba, Bahai, Fada, Guereda, Am Timan, Dogdore, Louboutigue, Bongor, Fianga, Farchana, Goz Beida and Abeche. The special unit operation ended after three years, an exciting but extraordinary experience for the men from Portugal, who were certainly more accustomed to dealing with criminals and terrorists.

Chapter 11

Russia

Hunting Terrorists between the Kremlin and the Volga

Unit: Spetsial'nye Otryady Bystrogo Reagirovaniya - Special Rapid
Response Unit (SOBR)
Motto: Faith and Honour Above All

Chechen Terror at the Dubrovka Theatre – 2002

In the second act, the melody reminded the spectators of an era long past.
The composers Ivashchenko and Vasilev conjured up the image of Leningrad
in 1938; five young men in shiny blue uniforms ran across the stage into
the blue of the night, one of them carrying a young soldier wrapped in a
parachute. Laughing, the five soldiers disentangled the young man. Suddenly
they looked up, then all dropped to the floor. The spectators understood this
to mean that they were taking cover from an air raid. When the supposed
bomber flew over and away, one of the soldiers began singing "It's so good
to do five turns…" At that moment a man in black jeans and mask jumped
on the stage holding a Kalashnikov rifle, which he then fired into the air.

The 900 spectators applauded. For a minute, all those present who
had dressed themselves up to the nines, perhaps having saved up for the
tickets to attend this presentation in the Dubrovka Theatre, thought that the
masked man was part of the successful Russian musical *North-East*. But
they were sadly mistaken.

It was Wednesday, 23 October 2002. At exactly five minutes past nine,
thirty-five masked terrorists barged in through the rear entrance of the
Dubrovka Theatre. The building, located around 5 km from the Kremlin,
had previously been the cultural hall of a ball-bearing factory. Masked men
and women from Chechnya, apparently living within a closed political cult,
made their way through the rows of seats, firing their rifles in the air as they
entered the auditorium and saw their leader Mowsar Barayev standing on

stage. The terrorists were equipped with hand grenades and home-made explosive devices. The women amongst them were dressed completely in black and were called 'black widows' by the media. About ninety people, including the musical director and a number of spectators, were able to escape and inform the police. For the many who remained, the hell as hostages now began.

Mowsar Barayev, 23, was the nephew of the notorious warlord Arbi Barayev, the leader of the Chechnyan Wahhabiten killed by the Russian secret service in 2001. After the death of his uncle, Barayev took command of a large part of the group '29 Division', and now he and his followers occupied a Moscow theatre with 810 hostages.

The Russian authorities acted promptly. Within a very short time the area around the theatre had been sealed off by the police and the anti-terrorist unit SOBR had arrived with their secret service colleagues from the FSB and the ALFA and Wympl units. The Special Rapid Response unit was present on this occasion to support the other two units. A number of tanks also rumbled towards the crime scene.

The terrorists had arrived in Moscow from Chechnya several days previously and, unnoticed by the authorities, had brought with them into the Russian capital two lorries loaded with weapons including Kalashnikov rifles, pistols and more than 100 grenades.

The police were anxious to discover the hostage-takers' demands as soon as possible. One of the hostages, Maria Shkolnikova, a heart specialist, was sent out to the front of the theatre to read out a report in which Barayev threatened to kill all of the hostages if Russian troops were not withdrawn from Chechnya, and all artillery and air force activities were not halted next day. The Russian Federation had been engaged in an armed struggle against separatists and Islamic rebels in the partial republic since 1999. Barayev ordered his hostages to call their friends and relations and have them parade in front of the Kremlin demanding an end to the war. He told the hostages, "Your country has deprived us of the right to have our own nation and now we shall take it back. We are not afraid to die." He later repeated this on a video for the media.

Amongst the hostages was a general of the Russian Interior Ministry. The negotiating team achieved their first small success towards midnight when Barayev agreed to release all hostages able to produce a foreign passport. This offer applied to seventy-five of those present, but the Russian authorities decided that either all hostages must be released or none at all. Barayev responded by stating that he would begin killing hostages if his demand to end the war had not been met by the deadline stated. Cones containing explosive devices were now attached to seats in the theatre and the terrorists placed a huge explosive mound in the auditorium. A volunteer from the terrorist group sat on top of the mound so as to ignite it when ordered.

Long after midnight the hostages were tired and frightened, and some attempted to escape. A young man who jumped up and ran for the exit was struck on the head with the butt of a pistol and fell unconscious. Towards 5.30 am, 26-year-old Olga Romanova climbed the police barriers and went to reason with the hostage-takers. "What is the point of this? Let all the people in the hall go." She was led away to a side entrance and shot dead. In the hall some of the hostages began to pray. Barayev justified the murder to the hostages: "We know the tricks of the Russian secret service, she was one of them."

Thursday, 24 October and the Russian President Vladimir Putin broke off an important journey to meet President George Bush and other international leaders. Meanwhile, numerous well-known Russian actors and journalists volunteered to negotiate with the terrorists, amongst them Aslambek Aslachanov, a member of the Chechen Federation Council, and the political economist Irina Chakamada. They had some success, as thirty-nine hostages were released that day. Negotiations were now opened between the ambassadors of European countries and the terrorists in order to free the foreign hostages. Barayev was stubborn and would only agree to this if the head of the Russian administration in Chechnya, Achmat Kadyrov, came to the theatre, but Kadyrov was not inclined to attend.

The Russian special units had fitted listening devices into the sewer system, which involved blocking off a water pipe, thus flooding the basement. The terrorists raged and demanded an immediate repair to the pipe. The police procrastinated.

Friday, 25 October and other Moscow personalities of note, including the journalists Sergei Govoruchin and Mark Franchetti, negotiated with the terrorists. Politicians also intervened in the attempt to make the terrorists see reason. More hostages were released, but still not enough. At midday a group of doctors led by Leonid Roschal went into the theatre to provide the hostages with medication. The Red Cross brought blankets and served everybody with food. Towards the evening, a journalist from the NTW television channel interviewed Barayev, who declared in a loud voice: "Our motto is Freedom and Paradise. We already have our freedom since arriving in Moscow. Now we want to be in paradise. We are here with a concrete objective – to put an end to the war."

At 10 pm that evening, a group of hostages were released and an agreement reached with the terrorists that more citizens of the United States and Kazakhstan would be freed. Barayev also volunteered to release all of the children.

Meanwhile, the anti-terrorist units had been training for their planned assault on the theatre at a similar building. That night they proudly informed the BBC correspondent that President Putin would be coming to the theatre for talks. During this interview, two members of the ALFA unit infiltrated the theatre to communicate to the hostages that an assault was planned for 3 am the next morning. The ALFA men were discovered, came under fire and were seriously wounded but still managed to escape. At 5 am in the morning of Saturday, 26 October, the searchlights illuminating the main entrance of the Dubrovka Theatre were switched off and the special units entered. The main assault was made by ALFA and Wympel, while SOBR secured the flanks and backs of their colleagues. A derivative of the synthetic opioid, Fentanyl, an analgesic of devastating effect used in anaesthesia and therapies for chronic painful conditions, had been prepared in substantial quantity and was now introduced into the theatre through the ventilation shafts over the stage and holes drilled by the special units. Panic broke out amongst the hostages. A female journalist called her radio staff at Echo Moskwy and made a live broadcast revealing that the operation to release the hostages was being made by a gas attack. Some of the terrorists were equipped with gas masks and opened fire on the Russian forces stationed in front of the theatre. It took thirty minutes for the gas to work. Barayev warned the hostages that when the exchange of fire began, they should lean forward in their seats and also protect their heads.

As the gas took effect the hostages gradually slipped into unconsciousness. Many of the terrorists fell to the ground dazed. The special units approaching the auditorium, unaware of the condition of the hostages, stormed the hall and killed all terrorists present with a shot to the head. None of these men and women would ever be able to report on the organisation and planning of their crime, or be called to account for it. The hostages were carried out and taken by ambulance and local buses to clinics in the centre of Moscow.

Six months after the drama, the musical North-East *was staged again in the Dubrovka Theatre. The auditorium had been altered a little and the*

Bordeaux-red seating now had a blue tone. That evening, many of the former hostages from the October 2002 tragedy were present. When the song "It's so good to do five turns..." rang out in the second act, many of the survivors had tears in their eyes.

An Accountant in Fear and Terror – 2009

For days the skies had been grey and it had rained most afternoons. It was not exactly fine weather for Russia in the summer of 2009, although the thermometer reading hovered mainly around the 20°C mark. It was 7 am when the telephone rang in the operations centre of the SOBR special unit. The commander raised the receiver and heard his colleague at the Moscow Detective Centre say: "Good morning, old man. We have a case for you. Towards midday the cash vehicle of a well-known building contractor on its way from Elektrostal will be raided by five criminals. They are known to us and aged between 25 and 27. I have just sent you an e-mail with full details about the suspects, the route to be followed by the vehicle and the contact details of the people involved at the building firm."

"OK, we're on it," the unit commander replied and assembled his team.

Known for its steel industry, Elektrostal is a city about 60 km east of Moscow which was founded shortly after the 1917 October Revolution. Today the former steel city is known more for its chemical industry and sporting prowess; the Kristall Elektrostal ice-hockey team has produced several well-known players who helped obtain good results for Russia in the world championships.

For SOBR the day began with a tactical talk at 7 am. First the operational staff considered the most likely place for the assault; the point of least resistance. Everything was done swiftly and without discussion, as the accountant would be carrying 40.7 million rubles (€1 million). It was the beginning of the month and payday for 200 co-workers; in addition some inter-firm accounts had to be settled. An informer at the construction company must have given the five-man gang details as to the above-average amount of cash that was to be carried on this occasion.

An in-depth survey revealed one likely place for the raid – a stretch of the A107 Moskovskoye Maloyekol'tso road, which led directly into woodland. At one particular bend the vehicle would have to slow down, giving the perpetrators the opportunity to make their attack at that point. SOBR had the time of departure, worked out the time when the raid would occur and how the perpetrators would be trapped. Based on this detailed timetable, the SOBR team set out to make its arrangements.

At the same time the construction company's accountant was being given a protective vest as he climbed into the armoured car at Elektrostal, members of the unit were preparing themselves in the wood far ahead. At the assumed spot for the raid, there was a swamp to the right-hand side of the A107, with thick woodlands on the left. The tactical team placed a service vehicle with crew at the beginning and end of the dangerous bend, which were naturally hidden out of sight in the woods. Meanwhile, a large number of unit members wearing special camouflage spread out in the woods.

The teams were in position by 11.30 am and awaited the armoured vehicle. The accountant inside it felt none too happy because the detectives had told him that he must be brave; the Russian special unit was known for its professionalism and they assured him nothing would happen to him. All the same, the accountant was sweating. His driver tried to take his mind off the danger by telling him stories about the company, who did deals with whom and what crazy building projects were being drawn up next. None of it helped. The nearer the armoured car came to the woods the more nervous the accountant became. The driver was honest with him. "Listen, it's going to get a bit turbulent now, but we'll both come through it all right. Trust me and trust the SOBR. They're capable of rising to any challenge and won't let us down. We must be strong now." As he finished speaking they reached the wood. Only a few metres more and they would come to the dangerous bend.

A small, dark car came towards them, a Skoda Octavia. Four men jumped out and halted the armoured car, gesticulating wildly with hand guns and shouting at the driver and accountant, "Both of you, out! This is a hold-up. Give us all the money at once. €1 million. We want it now. Quick! We haven't got all day!" The accountant froze with fear. The driver also felt very uneasy, but gave nothing away to his companion. "Stay sitting here, don't move from the spot. The SOBR will appear soon," he whispered.

Two of the perpetrators had baseball bats, which they began to hammer against the windscreen. The other two fired their pistols at the vehicle, unaware that it was fitted with bullet-proof glass. The two men trapped in the vehicle had no idea how they did it, but they managed to keep a clear head, certain that the special unit would have seen all this happening.

Suddenly, one thing happened after another. The two SOBR vehicles concealed at either end of the dangerous bend now came racing up and stopped almost at the feet of the perpetrators who, seeing themselves in unexpected difficulty, took flight. The fifth member of the gang had waited in the Skoda and now alighted. Because of the swamp on one side of the road, of which the criminals were aware, they had no choice but to run into the woods as fast as they could in the hope of outrunning the men from the special unit.

As they ran, they glanced back to see how close their SOBR pursuers were. To their surprise, they saw that they had stayed on the road and were merely watching. They kept running, and then the incredible happened, rather like a scene from Tolkien's *Lord of the Rings*. Some of the trees that had previously been standing still suddenly began to move. They yelled out to the criminals, "Hands up, Police! Get on the floor! It is over. No one's getting out of here. We're the special unit SOBR and you're surrounded."

Horrified, the five criminals looked at the talking trees before stooping and finally lying down on the floor. They were so shocked that they dared not make any sound. They waited for more orders from the special unit. The twelve members of the SOBR who stood around them smirked. "Well now, don't you have anything to say anymore? You'll be taken away and taken to the Police Department."

The five men were removed and placed in two emergency vehicles. With blue lights flashing, the two special unit cars drove back in the direction of Moscow. The accountant and the driver had watched the operation in amazement. They were very happy that nothing happened to them and that everything had gone so well. "You see, I told you that the SOBR wouldn't let us down," said the driver. The accountant nodded, wiped the sweat from his forehead with a handkerchief and replied, "You know what? Once we have delivered the cash to the bank and parked the vehicle back in Elektrostal, I'll invite you for a glass of vodka."

"Make that two," the driver said, and grinned.

Chapter 12

The Netherlands

Terrorists in the House of Orange

Unit: Dienst Speziale Interventies (DSI)
Motto: *Praeparatus Esto* = Be Prepared

Terrorist Occupation of a House in The Hague – 2004

The Dutch film producer Theo van Gogh was considered the *enfant terrible* of his art, and the nature of some of his films and his critical attitude towards Islam became his undoing one November morning in 2004. A few days earlier his most recent short film, *Submission*, the theme of which was the repression of women by Islam, had had its premiere. Van Gogh now received death threats. He did not believe that anybody would do anything to him and so rejected the idea of any personal protection. "Nobody kills the village idiot" was his motto.

On 2 November, while on his way to the studio, he was followed by a man on a bicycle who suddenly opened fire on van Gogh and then cut his throat. Next the murderer used a knife to inscribe a five-sided signature on the lifeless body – all at 8.45 am in the centre of Amsterdam.

The murderer, Mohammed Bouyeri, a member of a radical Islamic cell, was tried and sentenced to life imprisonment. He was part of a network calling itself the 'Hofstad Group', which was composed of young Dutch Muslims, most of whom were Moroccan in racial origin. The Dutch police had investigated a number of people of this network; the members were mostly in their early twenties, had a criminal history and were known to the local police. The mentor of the terror cell was a Syrian, constantly on the run, with connections to an Egyptian terror group.

Besides Mohammed Bouyeri, two other members of the Hofstad Group had been under surveillance by the Dutch secret service AIVD (*Algemene Inlichtingen en Veiligheidsdienst*). Jason Walters and Ismail

Akhnikh were amongst the founding members of this cell, and both had undergone special courses and firearms training for terrorists in Afghanistan and Pakistan. The two young men were being watched, and so AIVD were aware that both had rented a house in Antheunis Straat, in the Laak quarter of The Hague, where they lived inconspicuously. Appearances were deceptive, however, as the terrorist pair were actually planning their next attack – a fact that didn't escape the attention of the secret service, and one day an order of arrest was issued for preparing an imminent terrorist attack.

It was 2 am when the members of the police special unit DSI arrived in Antheunis Straat and took up positions around the house. In the case of dangerous terrorists, the unit always took along all their specialists: technicians, information technologists, explosives and munitions experts. Snipers were posted on the roofs of the houses opposite, numerous police stood by, and no vehicle was to be permitted to enter the area for the next few hours. All members of the special unit, together with police colleagues, were at the highest state of alert as it was not known exactly what kind of weapons and explosives the two terrorists had stored in their house. In this job, one must be prepared for everything.

At about 2.30 am when the DSI were at the front door and preparing to break into the house, a loud explosion wounded four police officers. It was initially thought that the front door had been fitted with an explosive device, but it was later discovered that one of the two terrorists had thrown a hand grenade at the officers. The wounded men were taken away by ambulance. The situation was gradually becoming more dangerous and the commander, along with the operations leader, decided to evacuate the innocent occupants of the house and its neighbouring buildings. These people had to be removed as quickly as possible from the line of fire using a ladder and staircase, and were then taken to the auditorium of The Hague University to await the end of the operation. The commander also decided to prohibit all aircraft from flying below 700 metres over the area and within a radius of 4 km. The only exceptions were the police helicopters, which circled overhead watching out for every movement or unusual activity. The streets around the housing block were to a large extent cordoned off to avoid any further injuries from possible explosions later. Additional snipers were brought in. This time the commander decided to go all out. Following all the experts' advice, he launched an attack at the house. He was unsuccessful; the terrorists drove back the police with hand-grenades and firearms.

It was make or break time for the mission. Politicians became involved; President Balkenende of the Netherlands appeared on television to explain that the numerous fires started in recent weeks in schools and churches were the work of these very terrorists. The authorities had to act now before they could inflict more harm.

Numerous television stations worldwide sent reporters to The Hague in order to report live on the DSI operation. Their vehicles blocked the view of the house to onlookers. Journalists mocked the failed police raid, with the Spanish press in particular comparing it with a similar failed raid by their own police after the Madrid attacks.

Crowds began to gather behind the police cordons. Thousands of local people had come to the Laak quarter to see what the outcome would be. Meanwhile, the operations staff conferred in a special police vehicle on how to terminate the spectacle as quickly as possible. The criminals were armed with hand-grenades, hand guns and machine-pistols. They were highly aggressive and ready for anything. They also fired occasionally at members of the special unit and had already wounded two DSI team leaders.

The operations staff now decided on tear gas as a simple solution to the problem, which is commonly used to quell rioters at major demonstrations. The operation began at 4.30 pm. The DSI stormed the house from several sides to prevent the fugitives from escaping. This time Walters and Akhnikh had little chance of attacking the DSI because they had been so affected by the tear gas that they were forced to take to the street. The DSI were faster and captured them both, with Akhnikh receiving a bullet to the shoulder. As the two terrorists were led away by members of the special unit, wild scenes of fighting broke out on the street between Muslims and native Hague citizens, which required police intervention.

A few days after their arrest it was officially announced that the two men had been planning to kill congressmen Ayaan Hirsi Ali and Geert Wilders. Ali, a champion of women's rights and a critic of Islam, as well as for his cooperation with Theo van Gogh in the film *Submission*, and Wilders for being an outspoken opponent of Islam as a politician and chairman of the Freedom Party. On 10 March 2006 Jason Walters was sentenced to fifteen years' imprisonment, Ismail Akhnikh to thirteen years.

Some time later it was made known that the house in Antheunis Straat had been rented to the two terrorists by a man calling himself Ed Aarts. The true identity of Ed Aarts was never made public, but it became known that the man's visiting card bore the telephone number of the AIVD secret service.

Chapter 13

Hungary

Magyar Power Play in the Underworld

Unit: Terrorelhárítási Központ (TEK)

Arrest of the Major Criminals of Miskolc – 2011

Zsolt, Laszlo and Marton had been planning a major robbery for some time. They had it down to the smallest details: the weapons and equipment, the jackets, trousers and shoes they would need, the vehicle to be used, the places to be targeted. They had observed the shops and obtained plans of the rooms which contained the items of interest. Everything had been carefully planned for a long time; there had to be no mistakes for they needed the money urgently. The coup was to take place today. Calmly they packed everything in their SUV and set off. The three men were each known to the police and had served time on several occasions for firearms offences. On this outing they were also armed.

They needed to stop and refuel at the petrol station in Budapest's Soroksari Street. While parked, the vehicle's registration plate was routinely filmed by a security camera and checked by police. It was noticed that the registration number was puzzling and therefore probably false. The officer informed his police colleagues and just as the three suspects were about to drive off, a police patrol car arrived. The officers got out, approached the vehicle and requested firmly, "Please get out of your vehicle and show your papers."

The documents were provided and the police shone a torch into the faces of the three men. At that instant all three sprang out of their vehicle and opened fire wildly at everybody standing or moving nearby. Police and innocent bystanders took immediate cover. The whole affair lasted only a few minutes and the exchange of fire was used by the three criminals to effect their escape. With a squeal of tyres they drove off into Soroksari Street, where a wild pursuit began.

The men were aware that they had made a grave error. They had not retrieved their documentation from the hands of the police. Firing wildly, they disappeared into the night. The police returned to their headquarters with the papers and obtained information from the central computer regarding the three suspects and made their report. What they discovered made them act swiftly. It was a relatively rare event in Hungary for criminals to randomly open fire on the street; while these men remained at large the risk was too great that the situation would be repeated. The police had seen their criminal records; one was serving a fourteen-year sentence and had been allowed out on parole. Three days later, one of the suspects walked into a police station and surrendered voluntarily. A first success. The other two men were lost to the wind. After interrogating the third man, the police decided that the other two were so dangerous that they needed to call in the special unit, TEK. The latter analysed the situation and with the cooperation of the local authorities, it was discovered where the pair would be hiding out. The decision was taken to act during the night of 25 November 2011.

Members of the special unit TEK left in several tactical vehicles for Miskolc, a town to the north-east of Budapest. The operation would be difficult because the two men had occupied a small flat in the third and uppermost floor of an apartment building. The flat was not only small, but dark, and had a sitting occupant who must not, under any circumstances, be put in any danger by the special commando during the operation.

Protected by shields, a TEK squad took up positions on the third floor of the house while colleagues secured the rear of the building. Then an attempt was made to break down the door of the flat. This proved more difficult than had been expected and a special drill had to be called for to cut a hole in the wall. The method was efficient but took time. [There was access to the terrace from the suspects' flat.]

At the rear of the building TEK saw one of the fugitives on the terrace calling his accomplice to the balcony. A voice called through a megaphone: "This is the police. Come out with your hands up!" They received a burst of gunfire in reply. Resistance to the power of the State could be costly in the long run. A TEK member confronted the two from the doorway to the terrace, a colleague covering his back. The criminals did not mean to give themselves up voluntarily. A powerful lamp was shone into the eyes of one of the criminals, temporarily blinding him. Service dogs, who had no fear

140

of criminals or weapons and were even trained to attack an armed suspect, were brought in to help with the capture. TEK men now entered the flat and made the first arrest, while his accomplice was caught on the terrace. Large-calibre firearms and machine-pistols were found in the flat. The two men were then taken to Budapest.

TEK police are often threatened at gunpoint as part of the job, but this time the situation was very tricky. A TEK officer was directly threatened with a firearm on this occasion: "I know that all of us have experienced fear during an operation at some time, and whoever denies it is lying. Today I was able to overcome my fear when the criminal aimed his weapon directly at my head," he told his colleagues assembled in the Budapest Counter-Terrorism Centre. Everybody in the team understood what he said; they are a homogenous team and were all 'in the same boat'.

Chapter 14

Slovakia

Gangsters in the Detroit of the East

Unit: LYNX Commando

The Prison Break at Leopoldov – 1991

After the Iron Curtain came down, the mood in the prisons of Eastern Europe increasingly deteriorated, especially in the West Slovakian district of Leopoldov, which has the oldest prison in Slovakia. It is a fortress-like building built in the seventeenth century, and after the Second World War it suited the Communist regime as a high security prison, primarily for political prisoners.

On 1 March 1990 an unprecedented revolt broke out in which 217 inmates barricaded themselves in a wing of the institution, known by the inmates as 'the Castle' as it housed the third and fourth regiments, and demolished the entire wing. On 15 March several hundred inmates set up barricades again and finally, on 28 March, set fire to the prison roof with flamethrowers and Molotov cocktails.

Over a year later, at about the time when the special operations unit LYNX Commando was founded in Slovakia, on 23 November 1991 six prisoners aged between 20 and 30 initiated a fresh revolt. Included amongst their numbers was Tibor Polgari, a murderer six times over who was now serving thirteen years' imprisonment for extortion. Polgari was the instigator and leader of the prison rebels. On the day in question, the gang of six waited until the security staff had finished their shift and then began killing the first wardens in cold blood with makeshift knives, before putting on their uniforms and starting to free other prisoners. At the main gate they killed four more wardens, taking their uniforms and machine-pistols. After this assault they felt so confident that three of the gang returned to free another inmate. Finally, as they left they took a warden hostage with them for free passage. The whole incident had lasted half an hour at the most.

In the town of Leopoldov the gang stole a green Skoda, abandoning the hostage as there was no room for him in the vehicle, and made off at speed. During their escape they had an accident and crashed the car. They stopped the first suitable-looking substitute car they encountered, a Lada 1200, and left its owner seriously injured. They drove on towards Trnava, about 15 km from Leopoldov, where the Lada ran out of petrol. They decided to continue their escape by train from Trnava, but in the excitement took a train going back to Leopoldov.

Five of the seven escapees got out at Leopoldov, the other two remaining aboard the train and continuing on to Piestany. Meanwhile the police had been informed and began the hunt by searching the station at Leopoldov. The five escapees saw the officers and took to their heels, hiding in a large haystack in a field where they proceeded to spend the night.

The local media were given information regarding the incident and provided comprehensive news about the break-out by the seven men. The whole country was put on alert. The inhabitants of the village near where the five escapees had gone to ground told police that they had seen heads in the haystack. When they awoke next morning it was too late to flee; the five men were surrounded by members of the LYNX Commando unit and gave up at once. The LYNX team had approached silently, and it's possible that the escapees had heard the military vehicles beforehand and decided that resistance was useless.

The other two escapees who had remained on the train disembarked at Piestany, a town in the northern uplands of the Danube on the river Waag. While debating which way to go next, they were seen by police on the platform. They ran away, but the police gave chase. The two escapees responded by firing at the police with the stolen machine-pistols and then headed for the industrial estate. The police now informed the special unit LYNX and requested reinforcement. During a search of the area, the escapees continued firing and wounded a police officer, who fell to the ground. The exchange of fire continued.

Meanwhile, members of the LYNX Commando unit had arrived at the industrial estate and saved their wounded colleague. The two fugitives now withdrew into an empty building and concentrated their fire on the unit. One of the men suddenly ran from the building aimlessly, driven by panic, and was arrested by the members of the unit. The other man continued firing and was hit twice; once through the jaw and the other in the stomach.

The special unit entered the building and searched it swiftly, finding a huge pool of blood but no victim. It was 7 pm and already dark. The unit members knew that they had only two possibilities; either the wounded man would surrender, or they could wait until morning and probably find him dead from his injuries. It seemed as though the earth had swallowed him up, however, and the LYNX unit – which included many young cadets who had just finished their final examinations at the police academy and were now experiencing their first mission – decided to wait it out until morning, taking the easier option and giving the last fugitive the chance to surrender.

Towards daybreak, at 5 am, the Commando unit silently entered the building and found the man in the central part lying in a pool of blood. The paramedic had him transported to hospital at once, but he later died from the two bullet wounds.

The other six escapees were returned to Leopoldov penitentiary and received additional periods of imprisonment at their subsequent trial. The ringleader, Tibor Polgari, received life imprisonment. The LYNX officer who was shot and wounded later returned to work.

Henrich Masár's Last Hostages – 2003

The young man drove along the Bratislava main road at high speed. He was sweating and very uncomfortable. He scratched his neck constantly. His movements were fidgety, nervous. He was repeating as though it were a mantra: "I had to kill them. I simply had to do it. There was no other way." He had just brutally stabbed to death Margit Sajtlavova and Peter Hantak, from Hlohovec, and Maria Dananyova from Trnava, and their blood covered his hands. He needed the money they had kept saved and hidden in order to get his next fix. He couldn't go on much longer without heroin. His pupils were already as tiny as needle points. "I must get out of here, I must get out of Bratislava quickly," he told himself. So he drove as fast as he dared.

The two police officers at the edge of the highway had not stopped a vehicle for some time. It was 17 July 2003, a wonderful summer's day. Most Slovakians used the day to visit a lakeside. "This will probably not be a lucrative day for us," the Bratislavan officer said, handing his colleague a mineral water. As the silver Opel appeared on the horizon, they both knew at once that it was speeding and prepared for a routine stop.

144

"I must find my dealer. I need a fix desperately," Henrich Masár recited. He was 28, but heroin had him under its control for a long time. So much so that hardly anything else mattered, not even the two policemen who held up a stop-sign, requiring him to pull in to the edge of the road. He had no time for this. The two policemen got into their service vehicle quickly and began to pursue the Opel.

Henrich Masár was sweating even more. "What do these two guys behind me want?" Somehow he managed to make out the police car, but didn't understand why they were chasing him. So what? His speed was now 180 km/hr and it wasn't difficult to outrun the police car. He didn't see the vehicle which appeared as if from nowhere in front of him. As the two cars collided, he heard the impact, but kept going for a few metres before the engine of the Opel gave out. Behind him was a man in a Volkswagen Polo. Henrich stopped it and fired at the man, threw him out of the car and climbed in. He sped onwards towards the village of Kaplna, about 50 km from Bratislava, where he changed cars. He now had to find a refuge to inject the small reserve of the drug he kept for emergencies, but he was still desperately short of cash. He looked about him like a hunted animal, trembling and panting, then ran along the street and found a house with open windows and doors.

It was the home of the Rovensky family, who were in the process of redecorating the whole house. After the death of his wife and eldest son, Mr Rovensky had hesitated for a while about changing anything, but after a year of mourning, his younger son had convinced him. With the support of the son's girlfriend, the three of them had decided to repaint all of the rooms in a strong golden-sun colour. They had just started on the living room when Masár entered the house wielding a bloody knife. "I need all of your money. Go and fetch it. And then close all your doors and windows. You are now my prisoners." They all knew straight away that he wasn't joking. After they had shut up the house and stood trembling before him, he indicated with his knife that they should all sit down. Then he pointed to the telephone and told them to make an emergency call to the police.

The special operations unit LYNX Commando arrived in front of the Rovensky house within thirty minutes. The negotiator stepped out of his VW-Combi and had the local police brief him with all the details. Who was present in the house? Who was the hostage-taker and what did he want precisely? The last item was a mystery. "OK, I'll find that out," the negotiator promised them.

In conversation with Masár, it was soon clear to him that Masár could not accept authority, and had never done so. He was searching for a way out

145

of society, having been unable to find his own way. He was not willing to accept responsibility to lead his own life. The only way for him to get along in the world was by taking drugs. It was clear to the negotiator that Masár had no tolerance or respect for others. He lived a life of irresponsibility every day as a heroin junkie.

The negotiator first attempted to get Masár to release the hostages. He didn't ask for the release of any person in particular, but knew that there were two men and one woman in the house. When Masár replied, "None of them wants to leave," the negotiator didn't understand the reason at first. Only after his co-workers had made some enquiries about the Rovensky family did he understand the background; the family was traumatised by their loss and wanted to remain together under any circumstances. The negotiator made it clear to Masár that his situation was hopeless. The house was surrounded, there was no way out. If Masár didn't free the hostages soon, the LYNX Commando unit would storm the house.

Henrich Masár understood the seriousness of the situation and suggested that he would set one hostage free if he were supplied with enough heroin for one 'golden shot' [a lethal dose], which he would inject himself. The crisis management team debated what should be done next and decided to supply Masár with the drug. The father of the family was released; Masár still holding the son and his girlfriend hostage. After two hours a member of the Commando unit returned with the drug, which had been sufficiently adulterated so as not to be a lethal dose.

When Masár tested the drug he immediately noticed that the police had deceived him as to its quality and couldn't be used for a 'golden shot'. As a result, he would kill the hostages. Thanks to the negotiator's psychological tactics, a second drug handover was agreed. This time a female friend of Masár's, who apparently knew drug dealers he trusted, would administer the last dose. The police went along with the deal. It was shortly after midnight when she reappeared with the 'goods'. After checking the heroin again to confirm that it didn't amount to a lethal dose, the police allowed the lady friend to pass the heroin over. On learning that she had the drugs, Masár released the son's girlfriend, retaining only the son as security in case the police attempted to trick him again. Instead of placing the heroin package on the windowsill as agreed, she leapt over it and entered the house. She was also a heroin addict and wanted to share the fix with Masár.

In a further telephone call the negotiator wanted to convince Masár that the supplied drug was 'pure and good'. Masár didn't want to keep receiving these telephone calls, perhaps suspecting what the unit might be planning, but the negotiator persisted and meanwhile members of the special unit infiltrated the Rovensky house. Finally Masár realised that the assault had begun, called his ladyfriend to his side and called out, "Kill us both or neither."

These theatrical words invited several rounds of police fire. The police were not precision marksmen, but one round was accurate and hit Masár in the head. Though wounded, he survived and was taken away at once by paramedics. The members of the special operations unit LYNX Commando had done well. The last order came: "Unit please return to headquarters."

After a stay in hospital and a subsequent period in an institution for rehabilitation, Masár received a sentence of life imprisonment.

Extortion of the Tesco Supermarket chain – 2003

Banska Bystrica is a town between Bratislava and Kosice, and in the Middle Ages had been the most famous mining town in Slovakia. In 2003, its Tesco supermarket became the target for an attempt to extort a large sum of money.

It was not the first time that Tesco had been the target of an extortionist. The British supermarket chain was very popular with young and old. With branches throughout the world, including many European countries, within a few years Tesco had risen to be the third most successful commercial chain after the US giant Walmart and the French supermarket, Carrefour. The British chain had been present in Slovakia since 1996, and the average supermarket floor surface in Slovakia was 15,000 square metres, offering gigantic purchasing opportunities for the first time. You could find everything at Tesco, from sports equipment and clothing, to electronic and household equipment, not to mention toys, food and drink, and many favourably-priced own brands.

On Wednesday, 28 May 2003, the manager of the Tesco supermarket in Banska Bystrica could hardly believe his eyes as he read the brazen letter he had just received: "I want 12 million Slovak crowns or I'll blow up your supermarket. You have three days to get the money." The sum demanded was equivalent to €400,000. The manager dismissed it as a hoax; probably children having fun just before the holidays.

Explosives were detonated on the Saturday morning. A few shelves were damaged, but fortunately there were hardly any customers present and there were no injuries. Since nobody had responded to his threat, the perpetrator had clearly decided to show he meant business, no doubt wanting to intimidate the manager into giving in to his demands. The threat was unmistakable, and now the manager called the police.

Within half an hour the investigators arrived and examined the letter. The crime scene was immediately sealed off by forensic analysts. Police investigators worked quickly and efficiently. First the Tesco telephone lines were tapped and the lead negotiator and his team occupied rooms which had been set aside for them to use. They didn't have to wait long; in his letter, the extortioner had stated that he would call after three days, which he did. The manager's telephone rang. The blackmailer's voice sounded dry, but firm. "I wish to draw your attention again to the fact that I want 12 million crowns transferred into my account, or else something terrible will happen. The small bomb is only the beginning." He added that his intention was to blow up the entire supermarket.

The lead negotiator engaged the man in conversation, hoping to obtain information about his life and the motives behind his demands. No information was forthcoming and what he wanted the money for also wasn't clear. He repeated his threat to blow up the supermarket 'in the near future'.

The supermarket manager was aghast. He had never experienced such a situation before. In a sweat he telephoned the managerial staff in Britain. That Saturday the telephone line at Cheshunt in Hertfordshire was hot. The British managers advised him how he should deal with the situation. For some time they weighed the pros and cons of paying the demand. Finally, it was decided to follow the path of least resistance and pay up.

When the extortionist rang the Slovakian manager's office on the Sunday, the chief negotiator stated that, in future, they should speak by mobile phone for his security. The latter agreed and then dialled the number he had been given, then the negotiator informed the perpetrator that the money was being prepared for handing over. At the perpetrator's suggestion, it was agreed the drop would be made at a specific place in a wood along the E77 road to Ulanka. The money was to be brought by helicopter and dropped in a sack, enabling the blackmailer to take it without any trouble and make his getaway.

The local Tesco manager informed the bank where the money was being packed in a thick tear-resistant sack. At the same time as the negotiations were taking place, in the background the special units were laying out their standard plan of action. The team sealed off the drop zone over a 500 metre radius and took up positions in and around the wood. Naturally, all those involved were in contact with each other. When it was time, four members of the LYNX Commando unit set off in the helicopter with the sack of money. It was not long before they reached the drop zone and, as agreed, threw out the sack. The helicopter then pulled away.

The special unit and police waited three hours for the extortionist. When he failed to appear, the operational commander gave the order to end the mission. Everybody withdrew, the sack being retrieved and returned to the bank.

On Monday, the extortionist rang the negotiator as if everything was in order. He was basically playing with the officers. He had wanted to see if they had done as he had asked. The past weekend had only been a test to see if the word of the negotiating team, the police and the special unit could be relied upon. Now he demanded that the operation be repeated at the same place on the following weekend. The lead negotiator agreed and said he would see to it. On the Saturday, the bank officials packed the sack again and the four unit men set off with it once more in the helicopter. The police took up their positions in the woods and waited for the blackmailer. They were all linked up by radio and had the road under observation.

This time the negotiator tried another tactic and kept the extortionist in conversation on the mobile phone the whole time. This distracted the man and made him less watchful while the telephone link betrayed his position. The trick was successful. When the unit members burst into his flat, he was still on the phone discussing the money drop with the negotiator. He collapsed when they surrounded him and he heard the sentence uttered so often in television crime programmes: "Police. Hands up. It's over."

The Tesco extortionist was still very young, around 30, and surrendered without a fight before being led away by the LYNX Commando unit.

The sack with the money was taken back to the bank. The manager of the Tesco branch at Banska Bystrica was relieved that the affair had had such a successful outcome, as were his superiors in Britain. During several days of interrogations, the extortionist revealed that he was member of a group of Tesco-extortionists. Four other members were mentioned, but he refused to say more and didn't disclose their names.

The Dramatic Capture of Two Police Officers – 2010

It was 10 pm on a July Tuesday in 2010. Two police officers, a male and a female, were making routine stops of vehicles on the main highway at

Nitra, in the west of Slovakia, 80 km from Bratislava. Nitra is one of the oldest cities in the country with a magnificent fortress and many churches built on a hill.

The man and his male friend were in a Skoda Felicia car and had reached the town of Šal'a, about 18 km from Nitra, when they were signalled by the two police officers to pull off the highway into a lay-by. The driver, a 28-year-old man, had a rap sheet as long as his arm. He was a notorious cross-border thief and murderer, who had served several prison terms in the Czech Republic and several years in Slovak prisons. He knew this area well, having worked there doing casual jobs and thieving since his youth.

"I'm never going to prison again," he had promised himself. When he saw the two police officers waving him in, he saw his dreams of 'never again' were at risk. "I am not going back there, please not prison again," he murmured and stepped on the gas. The police gave chase. The Skoda went faster, left the road on a bend and collided with a telephone pole. The driver and passenger survived the accident unharmed, and abandoned the wrecked Skoda and made off on foot. While the police pursued the passenger in their vehicle, the driver grabbed the machine-pistol he had hidden in the driver's door panel and ran to an empty farmhouse. He took up an attacking position and gritted his teeth, determined to fight to stay free. As the police approached the house he threatened them with the gun: "Hands up and go back to your car. We're going for a drive," he told them, "I am not going back to prison!" After handing over their guns, the officers had no prospect of escaping the situation, and so did as he said. 'Do not invite aggression from a suspect. Remain calm' had been hammered into them at the Bratislava police academy. The male officer was forced to drive with the barrel of the gun pressed to his neck. The female officer sat beside him in the passenger seat. The perpetrator toyed with the three guns on the back seat. Both officers feared the worst. The man felt the same intoxicating feeling of power as he had when he burgled houses. Yet something irritated him. Where should he go now with these two hostages? He forced them to drive him to Nitra. He felt safe there. The vehicle had a full tank and so they drove around the outskirts of the town.

Meanwhile, since the officers had no freedom of movement, the car radio was not answering the messages from their colleagues at the police station. Concerns were now being raised about the vehicle's disappearance. During the random drive, a patrol car at a crossroads saw the missing vehicle pass by. It had three occupants, and a man was gesticulating wildly on the back seat. He was holding something in his hand. After informing their base"Car Z15 found," the officers in the patrol car decided to follow it. It was now clear that the two officers had been taken hostage, and the kidnapper was directing affairs from the back seat. When the patrol car approached close enough to identify the weapon held by the back-seat passenger, the man held it through a window and began to shoot. It was obvious that the situation could only be resolved with support from the professionals of the special operations unit LYNX Commando.

The initial contact with the kidnapper was made via telephone by the LYNX Commando lead negotiator. He called Car Z15 and asked the police officer who was driving to pass the mobile phone to the kidnapper. Once contact had been made, he began a conversation attempting to discover why he had committed this act, what his demands were and whether or not he wanted to give himself up. The negotiator was given short shrift; there was no dialogue and the kidnapper had no demands to make. He just wanted to be left in peace and required neither money, an aircraft, nor a faster car. All he wanted was never to return to prison in his lifetime."So what's the problem? Why would anybody want to put you in prison?" the negotiator enquired.

"Because Slovakia has an arrest warrant out for me," he answered briefly. That marked the end of the conversation.

For the police, the two main problems of this kidnapping were that the stolen police car never stopped and just continued to circle around Nitra. They were also unable to approach it too closely as otherwise the kidnapper would open fire. After four hours, the driver informed his colleagues that the kidnapper had exchanged the female officer with his ex-girlfriend, who was also a police officer.

The LYNX Commando unit was required to find the correct strategy of dealing with this violent and unpredictable criminal as soon as possible. It was assumed that he must have a plan, but his conduct suggested that he didn't. The major risk was that he might seize more hostages. The plan was to arrange a meeting with the kidnapper, who agreed to this relatively quickly. Several locations were suggested and although he was amenable and went along with the proposals, he then broke off the negotiations and never turned up at any of the sites.

Making things more difficult were the delays to the information received by the negotiator. As soon as it arrived, it would be mostly obsolete. The kidnapper constantly altered the direction of travel and kept the entire negotiating team on the run. It was no longer possible to work out where and at what time he would pass by. Car Z15 even stopped at a petrol station so that his ex-girlfriend could buy a bottle of vodka, but this information still only came in after a fifteen-minute delay.

As the kidnapper swigged the vodka and laughed, the police driver saw his chance and said he was tired. It was four in the morning. "We should stop for a rest," he said. "I've been driving for many hours and am tired and can't concentrate. I can't keep on driving." He convinced the kidnapper to finally allow him to pull into a meadow near the village of Nitriansky Hradok. This enabled the special unit to get close to the hijacked police car.

The team decided to bring in snipers to prevent the vehicle escaping. The command centre wanted at least one more hostage freed. The kidnapper kept the pistol against the head of the driver, with the other weapons laid out on the back seat. He agreed to free the driver, who got out of the car and walked around the vehicle. The kidnapper's ex-girlfriend got out of the front passenger seat and joined the perpetrator on the back seat. The members of the special unit followed this spectacle closely from their positions behind the car, as they waited for events to unfold.

The sniper commander gave his men the order to prepare to fire. When such an order is given, a member of the operational commando counts down loudly from five to zero, the word 'zero' being the order to fire. In this case, when the commander had reached 'two', one of the snipers called out, "Stop, stop, we can't fire!" The commander now saw that the ex-girlfriend was in the line of fire with the kidnapper. The risk of killing the wrong person was too great. The negotiator contacted her and said "Go to one side." She understood at once and now the countdown began again from 'five'. When the commander got to 'zero' several shots rang out. Blood spurted inside the vehicle. It was hardly possible to see through the windows.

As the members of the unit approached the vehicle they saw that the kidnapper had been mortally wounded in the head, his skull having burst. Blood covered everything, including the face and clothing of the ex-girlfriend who lay curled up and crying on the back seat of the car. At first the officers feared she had also been hit, but after a quick check by a paramedic it was determined that she was only suffering from shock.

The officers helped her out of the car. The negotiator, a qualified psychologist, handed her a cup of tea and took her aside for a quiet talk. Then, wrapped in a blanket, she climbed into an ambulance from where she heard the commander's final order to his team: "It's over now. Please return to headquarters."

Chapter 15

Lithuania

Operation in the Baltic

Unit: Lietuvos policijos antiteroristiniu operaciju rinktine (ARAS)

The Kidnapper from Panevėžys – 2001

It was a cool day at the beginning of October 2001, and the inhabitants of Panevezys, a large town in Lithuania, the most southerly of the three Baltic States, needed to dress up warm when they went out on the street. The local police were keeping a lookout for two criminals: 25-year-old Virginijus Savickis and his close friend, 31-year-old Romas Zamolskis. They were both wanted by Interpol for shooting at police at Vilnius and Kaunus, and at Russian soldiers in Kaliningrad. They had also assaulted and wounded a money carrier from the Lithuanian Farmers' Bank, the largest banking institution in the country.

On 7 October the two men were spotted by local police passing through Panevezys; during the attempt to arrest them, they opened fire on police and wounded several of the officers. Romas Zamolskis was hit three times and ran into a school, pursued by police. The officers would not be able to shoot inside the school building and therefore conducted a search of the school premises and found traces of blood along the corridors. There was no sign of Zamolskis; he had taken the opportunity to slip away from the school unnoticed.

While Zamolskis, who was still bleeding, went to ground in Panevezys, his accomplice, Savickis, was cornered by police near the school and took a 13-year-old pupil, Aleksandras Spilevjus, hostage. Using the boy as a human shield, Savickis entered a nearby apartment block and, still holding the boy pressed close to his body, climbed to the third floor where he forced his way into one of the flats. The owner was 60-year-old Bronislava Varnyte, who was in poor health and bed-ridden. She peered at the two figures standing before her, then got the shock of her life when she finally realised that they were the kidnapper and his victim.

From the outset, Savickis told his two hostages he would treat them well, but would kill them should the situation demand it. The whole time he was in the flat he kept the loaded pistol aimed at the boy. Meanwhile, the police, who had pursued Savickis to the apartment block, alerted their colleagues at the Anti-Terrorist Operations unit ARAS, and sealed off the area around the building. By the time the unit arrived, they already knew Bronislava Varnyte's delicate medical condition, and the operational leaders knew that this would have to be kept in mind during the mission. Her doctor had warned that any kind of stress could lead to her death. Two things were causing the unit a particular headache; the kidnapper had barricaded himself inside the third floor flat and blocked the door, and the medical condition of the female hostage limited the use of some of their equipment (they could not use dazzle-grenades, for example). ARAS' hopes therefore rested initially on the skill of the lead negotiator, who was a very experienced officer in this line of work.

Communication was established by telephone, the negotiator speaking to Bronislava first, who then handed the receiver over to Savickis. After talking with her family members and doctor, the negotiator suggested to Savickis that he should allow medicines to be sent up. Some time later, once this was all agreed, Savickis requested food and drink for himself and his two hostages: pizza and coca-cola. The police agreed to this request.

The curtains at the windows of Bronislava's flat masked the view of the interior, and Savickis avoided approaching the windows at any time. The members of the unit designed a plan of attack by using a similar building in the neighbourhood. They scouted the house very carefully in order to identify possible escape routes a fugitive might take; this time the hostage-taker would have no chance to get away.

Savickis, who was in virtually constant conversation by telephone with the negotiator, made it clear that he would not free his hostages, stating that he was capable of anything, even killing them. He demanded a jeep for his escape and 1.5 million Litas (about $550,000), although the sum was then negotiated down to $50,000. The psychiatrists who had been called in had no doubt that Savickis was mentally disturbed and they thought it was possible he would carry out his threat to kill the hostages if he did not get the jeep and the money. Meanwhile, sixteen hours of tough negotiating with a mentally unbalanced individual had gone by and the situation was now coming to a head.

A shot was heard inside the flat. In order to protect the hostages, the ARAS commander gave the order to storm the flat immediately. The assault troops attacked from two sides: from the third floor window and through the blocked front door. With a loud crash, nine men entered the flat. "Police, lay down your weapon." Savickis didn't want to surrender even though he knew he stood no chance against the anti-terrorist unit, and he resisted. The boy Alexandras and Bronislava, who were seated at the table, instinctively ducked as the special unit opened fire. When the hostages looked up, they saw Savickis lying in a pool of blood.

The ARAS officers brought out the two hostages, who were unhurt apart from bullet splinters in the boy's arm, and handed them over to the waiting ambulances. The body of Savickis was also carried out. It became clear a few days later that in a moment of madness, Savickis had been on the point of killing them.

Chapter 16

The USA

The President's Praetorian Guard

Unit: Special Weapons and Tactics (SWAT) and US Secret Service

The US President: A Terrorist's Target in Austria – 2006

US Presidents live dangerous lives. The risk of assassination is far greater than dying of a heart attack in office. Attempts to assassinate the sitting US President have been made on twenty-one occasions and the venue has been mostly Washington DC, the seat of office. In total, four Presidents have been killed.

1. Abraham Lincoln – shot from behind with a 44-Derringer by John Wilkes Booth on 15 April 1865, at Ford's Theatre during a presentation of *Our American Cousin*. The President had no bodyguard in his personal theatre box.
2. James A. Garfield – murdered four months after taking office on 19 September 1881 whilst boarding a train. His killer was the mentally-ill Charles J. Guiteau, who used a 442 Webley British Bulldog revolver.
3. William McKinley – shot dead by the Polish anarchist Leon Czolgosz on 14 September 1901, during a visit to the World Exhibition at Buffalo, New York.
4. John F. Kennedy - shot whilst riding in an open limousine through Dallas, Texas, on 22 November 1963. His assassin was allegedly Lee Harvey Oswald, who fired several rounds from a 6.5 mm Mannlicher-Carcano rifle.

Nearly all US Presidents have experienced assassination attempts. Often an attempt was frustrated because the Secret Service overcame the would-be assassin(s) in time. For this reason, the protection of US

Presidents by special agents from the Secret Service, and on certain journeys by SWAT teams, is needed around the clock. If a US President is paying a state visit to a foreign country, it means the local police, security services, the special police units and the Secret Service have to be on the highest state of alert.

The US President ranks highest on the scale of priority for protection. An assassination attempt or terrorist attack against him and his staff is possible at any time. This means that on any state visit abroad, nothing is left to chance. George Bush was the fifth US Head of State to visit Austria after J. F. Kennedy (1961), Richard Nixon (1972 and 1974), Gerald Ford (1975) and Jimmy Carter (1979). Bush was to attend the EU-USA Summit at the Hofburg (the former principal imperial palace of the Hapsburg dynasty) on 21 and 22 June 2006. This visit was considered a high point for Austria, which chaired the EU Council at the time. Though Bush was numbered amongst the most endangered people in the world, according to a threat analysis by the Austrian Interior Ministry, there was an 'abstract but no concrete danger' for him.

The preparations for the visit of George Bush had begun four months earlier. First, the Security Attaché at the US Embassy in Vienna met with senior officials of the Interior, Foreign- and Defense Ministries, political officers and the Chief of Protocol. They discussed all details for the organisation of the EU-USA summit, including for example the conference venues, who would be attending, means of transportation both there and later to the state banquets. Here they worked out the 'common thread' and together visited all of the venues for the conferences and other scheduled meetings. In the following weeks, the officials met very often and when one or another decision was changed, the protocol was amended accordingly in writing.

About six weeks before the arrival of the US President, the operations leaders of the SWAT snipers arrived in Vienna to lay out a plan for the two-day programme with their colleagues from the Austrian elite police tactical unit, EKO Cobra. They scouted the roofs in the immediate vicinity of the conference locations and looked around the surrounding buildings for suitable observation posts. At the beginning of June, the first SWAT sniper teams arrived at the rate of four to ten per day. After meeting with their Austrian counterparts they were paired off; one SWAT man to one Cobra.

Similarly, the first small Secret Service team arrived and, with colleagues from the Interior Ministry, looked over the conference venues, such as the Hofburg, as well as those places Bush and his wife wished to visit, such as Schönbrunn Palace, St.Stephen's Cathedral and the Vienna State Opera.

The two hotels in which the President, his wife and the approximately 900 White House staff would stay were closely inspected. The InterContinental Hotel would be home to most of the party, and be closed to other guests over the period. The remainder of the Bush team would stay at the nearby Hilton Hotel. Traditionally, heads of state stay at the 5-star Imperial, but the Rolling Stones were in Vienna and had already taken up residence.

Extra security measures were taken at the InterContinental such as additional bullet-proof window panes in the presidential suite, something which would be impossible to do at the Hotel Imperial, a building that dated from 1892.

Four days before the arrival of George Bush, a section of the White House Press staff was already present in the InterContinental. The team set up its computers and installed several gigantic satellite dishes on the roof. Kilometres of cable were laid for the secure White House telephone lines, which had the same telephone numbers as they did in Washington.

A total of 2,600 km of tunnels are considered passable in Vienna, and parts of this huge network were protected by the Vienna special police unit, WEGA. Its team of specialists systematically combed the entire area during the state visit, looking for suspicious objects, bombs and weapons, as well as preventing any unauthorised access to the underground passageways and detain any suspects found there. The secret catacombs of the Hofburg were also inspected in the company of the *Burghauptmannschaft*, the authority responsible for the administration and upkeep of the Austrian Republic's historical buildings. The welding of manhole covers, as required in Germany, was not an issue in Austria.

One advantage of being US President is never being stuck in a traffic jam, not to mention having a service limousine. Cadillac One, also known as 'The Beast' to White House staff, was converted to a mobile fortress by the firm *O'Hara Hess and Eisenhart* for more than $3 million. The armour-plated doors are 10 centimetres thick and can withstand anti-tank missiles, while the windows are made of bullet-proof glass – if the President wishes to work in the car he has to turn on the lights – and the tyres cannot burst. These are just a few details from the long list of security precautions. Three virtually identical Cadillacs were delivered to Vienna airport a few days before the President's arrival. The drivers and the Viennese police went over three different routes from the airport to the city's Old Town.

On 20 June a very special 'present' awaited him. In the early morning, the Viennese police discovered four makeshift bombs placed at sensitive locations in the Old Town; one in front of the hotel in which George

Bush would spend the night, another in the Stadtpark (city park) facing the InterContinental, a third on one of the approach routes and a fourth on the *Burgring* (the circular grand boulevard that serves as a ring road surrounding the Old Town). All four bore the label 'Gift for George W.' Shortly before his arrival, the bomb squad disarmed them.

Around 2000 WEGA officers and police from all over Austria had been in position for hours, along with 200 members from Cobra, 600 Secret Servicemen and SWAT snipers. The Austrian Army took responsibility for guarding the airspace with F-5E-Tiger IIs armed with Sidewinder missiles. While several helicopters containing Cobra men with rifles circled above the runway, the Austrian politicians' blood ran hot and cold when an aircraft with blue and white livery and the words 'United States of America' on the fuselage touched down at Vienna International Airport. This was not the aircraft bearing the President, but the protocol aircraft, a forerunner for the presidential aeroplane, Air Force One, which followed shortly afterwards and landed fifteen minutes early at 9.15 pm. Bush and his wife disembarked to be welcomed by the Federal Chancellor. Secretary of State Condoleezza Rice was also with the party. After that, providing all-round protection, a troop formed to escort the guests to three similar Cadillacs, all fitted with the presidential shield and the flags of the United States and Austria. George Bush got into one of the limousines, his wife and Rice into another. The vehicles then headed for Vienna. Preceding and following the limousines were hundreds of bodyguards and delegation members, even an ambulance. The helicopters with Cobra men aboard followed the forty-six vehicle convoy, which included a technical vehicle with recovery and decontamination facilities, SWAT teams from the bomb squad and White House staff.

No problems were encountered on the run into Vienna. The police were stationed strategically every 100 metres along the autobahn in order to prevent would-be suicides from throwing themselves in front of the presidential vehicle. As it passed each control point, the location was reported to the next police control ahead. On the approach to Vienna, members of the Secret Service awaiting the President in front of the InterContinental heard a loud explosion from the nearby city park. Guests celebrating a wedding there had obtained permission to set off fireworks on that day, but the Secret Service had not been notified. At the same time a fire alarm went off in the presidential suite. A Secret Service agent advised his colleagues at the hotel entrance that it might be a false alarm. When he entered the suite to investigate he smelt burnt plastic; a colleague who had been testing the hotplates in the small kitchen during his last rounds

159

had forgotten to turn them off. A plastic cup that had been left on top had begun to burn and had filled the room with fumes. The alarm went off at the Vienna fire brigade headquarters, but because of the protective layer of bullet-proof glass covering the windows, they could not be opened to air the rooms and so the President was forced to spend the night in a room with an acrid plastic odour.

After a four-hour journey, the President and his staff now occupied their rooms at the InterContinental and Hilton Hotels. It was known that the President liked to go to bed early and hundreds of Secret Service and Austrian police stood guard while the President and his wife relaxed behind closed doors. The InterContinental had been converted into a fortress; a no-go zone of concrete blocks had been laid around the hotel to prevent rogue vehicles entering, as police patrolled in front of it.

Next morning, immediately after breakfast, George Bush left the hotel in his Cadillac. The other two limousines followed and also turned off for the Hofburg. The President occupied the centre vehicle flanked by the other forty-six vehicles carrying his bodyguards and followed by eighteen police motor-bike outriders. In order to prevent bombs being detonated remotely by radio or mobile telephones, a vehicle from the Special Observation Unit accompanied the presidential convoy and controlled the frequencies.

On rooftops, SWAT and Cobra snipers kept an eye on all passers-by down in the street. All traffic lights were set to green, and the city fell very quiet. Meanwhile in the Hofburg, Austrian President Heinz Fischer received his guest, the next appointment being half an hour later with Chancellor Wolfgang Schüssel and then the EU-USA summit would take place.

While George Bush was talking world politics in Vienna, his wife Laura visited St Stephen's Cathedral. For that reason, the whole of the inner city was sealed off and hundreds of police provided her with protection. Museums and businesses were also shut down, and all private planes was prohibited from flying over Vienna. Meanwhile, in the morning and again in the afternoon, around 15,000 people demonstrated against the US guest and his policies. Hundreds of police monitored the protests and kept the demonstrators in check. At the time, Bush was in his Cadillac on the way to the National Library where he was presented to students at a debate and also met the Vienna Boys' Choir. Then the convoy with the President, his wife and Condoleezza Rice headed back to the airport and took their leave. When Air Force One took off safely and left Austrian airspace, it was not only Austria's security services who breathed a sigh of relief.

As a sign of their gratitude, the US Embassy in Vienna organised the traditional 'Wheels Up' party at the Hilton for Cobra members, the police and ministries involved. That evening, while the celebration was in full flow, at Bush's next stop, Hungary, the same security hustle and bustle was just beginning.

Devastating Explosion at the Boston Marathon – April 2013

Units: FBI, ATF, CIA, NCTC, DEA

Patriot's Day is a special day in American history, and is an official holiday celebrated in Wisconsin, Maine and Massachusetts on the third Monday in April. It is to remind Americans every year of the beginning of the War of Independence, particularly the Battles of Lexington and Concord in 1775, an armed struggle against Great Britain and the thirteen colonies. A marathon is held every year on this day and passes through the finest streets of Boston. For this reason the holiday is also known to locals as Marathon Day. It is one of the oldest marathons in the world and attracts around half a million people every year from all over the world and is the most popular event in New England in terms of spectator numbers. Only eighteen runners were at the start line for the first race in 1897, but by 1996 the number of competitors had grown to 38,708. On 15 April 2013 there were more than 23,000 registered runners.

Security for the runners and spectators of this great sporting event is the responsibility of the city administration. For this reason, numerous security officers from the FBI's Anti-Terror Task Force were already in position before the start. Sniffer dogs were at the start and finish lines, and numerous security personnel were on the roofs of buildings from the time when the race began. In 2013 the date of the marathon coincided with the day when the Inland Revenue Service allowed an extension of the deadline for tax returns.

It was a wonderful, sunny April day. The joy of the marathon seemed to be in the morning air. A man stood amongst the throng of spectators holding the photograph of his son, Alexander, who had been drafted as a Marine in the Iraq War and was killed in action on 25 August 2004. Members of many veterans associations run the marathon every year in his honour. Parents, friends and relatives position themselves near the finish line every year with flags in order to cheer the finishers home. Just as the son of a spectator was crossing the finishing line and his father waved the

American flag with joy, the unbelievable happened. At 2.49 pm local time when 5,600 runners had yet to complete the course, an explosion occurred at the finishing line in Boylston Street, near Capley Square in the Black Bay district, transforming the city's spring ritual from a triumphal occasion into terrible scenes of unceasing horror and butchery.

A pressure-cooker bomb, filled with metal splinters and hidden in rucksacks amongst the masses of marathon spectators, had exploded. People behind the barriers opposite the Boston Library began to shout loudly while before their eyes an enormous cloud of smoke billowed upwards. Then the first spectators began to flee the danger zone and get as far as they could from the great cloud of smoke. One of the runners, 78-year old Bill Iffrig, was thrown to the ground by the force of the blast. When the explosion occurred, the majority of competitors had already passed the finishing line; the two winners, Lelisa Desisa and Rita Jepoto, had actually finished two hours earlier. Many onlookers had been standing behind the barriers and were now laid on the ground bleeding, several of them having lost body parts. Legs, arms and hands lay scattered in the pools of blood and you could even smell the blood of the victims from the other side of the barriers. The first responders were quickly at the scene and together with onlookers tried to remove the barriers so that the rescuers could get to the victims as quickly as possible. Those on the ground were crying or silent; in shock after being hit by shrapnel or losing a limb.

It was a scene from a nightmare, and the second attack was not long in coming. Thirteen seconds after the first, a second explosion occurred barely 100 metres away, farther along Boyston Street on the same side, but on the course. It was exactly the same kind of explosive left in a rucksack on the ground. Rescue units and medical personnel were present, as on previous marathons, to render First Aid. Additional police, fire brigade and ambulance services were requested from the surrounding towns, and private nursing staff from the entire state.

The two bomb attacks killed three people: 23-year-old Chinese student Lu Lingzi, 29-year-old Krystle Campbell and 8-year-old Martin Richard, whose 6-year-old sister lost a foot. Their mother was slightly injured. The explosive cost 29-year-old Jeff Bauman both legs. 'The man with the hat' as the media called Carlos Arredonde, a voluntary helper with the American Red Cross, found Jeff lying in a pool of blood. He heaved him into a wheelchair, then ran him to hospital. He had lost a lot of blood, was in shock, and was just staring ahead, his face grey and unable to speak. His chances of survival were very poor, but thanks to the swift actions of

Carlos, and the incredible professional work of the Boston surgeons, he pulled through.

Around 264 spectators and runners were injured that afternoon and were treated in twenty-seven local hospitals. At least fourteen people required amputations, some suffering 'traumatic amputation' (i.e. limbs lost in the initial explosion). Chaos broke out as panic-stricken runners and spectators who were attempting to flee collided with emergency personnel arriving from the opposite direction in order to attend the dozens of mutilated and injured, some of whom had already lost limbs. A large number of the injured had metal splinters in their legs because the explosive devices had gone off at ground level. Some of the injured runners had taken part in the marathon for the victims and bereaved of the Sandy Hook Elementary School horror, after a local radio station had made a charity appeal on behalf of the school.

In accordance with emergency plans already in force, the police diverted the runners to Boston Common and Kenmore Square. The Lennox Hotel and several other buildings near the crime scene were evacuated and the police closed off a fifteen-block area around the site of the explosions. Boston Police Commissioner Edward F. Davis recommended that the public stay off the streets. Bags and packages that had been abandoned by people in the crowds fleeing the explosions raised the possibility of other bombs. At first the police had assumed there would be more and for this reason many suspicious items were simply blown up. The FBI swiftly discounted rumours that there were more bombs which had not gone off. A fire which broke out at the John F. Kennedy Presidential Library and Museum was at first thought to have been caused by a bomb, but the police soon dismissed this assumption.

On Monday afternoon, the FBI took over the lead role in the investigation. Richard DesLauriers, the Special Investigator responsible for the case and the head of the FBI's Boston Bureau, made it clear to the media that it was a "criminal investigation and a potential terrorist investigation." As one of its first security measures, the FBI decided to secure the state of Massachusetts by closing down the airspace and cancelling all flights from Boston's Logan International airport. As a precaution, the FBI used warning-intervention vehicles along the entire Eastern coast and as with a domino effect, security was gradually upgraded throughout the country, especially in New York and Washington DC, where Pennsylvania Avenue between the White House and the Capitol was closed to traffic. The transport authorities in Massachusetts halted local services in Boston for two hours and all mobile phone providers were forced to shut down temporarily because of the extreme overloading.

The White House Press spokesman announced that President Obama had spoken to the Governor of Massachusetts, Deval Patrick, and the Mayor of Boston, Thomas Menino, and promised government help. In a televised address, the President stated that the explosions occurred on Patriot's Day and represented an act of terrorism. He ordered that as from 16 April 2013, all flags at the White House and on all public buildings throughout the country, as well as at all military bases and embassies worldwide, were to be flown at half mast for four days. A second measure to help friends and relatives of the marathon runners was the hotline opened by the Boston Police Department. Additionally, the Google hotline service to search for missing persons, developed for such disasters, was activated and the American Red Cross was urged by the authorities to help those families and friends retrieve information.

In parallel the FBI now began a fervent hunt for the criminals and involved officers from the ATF (Alcohol, Tobacco and Firearms), CIA, the NCTC (National Anti-terrorist Centre) and the DEA (Drugs Enforcement Agency). The FBI, CIA and NCTC rated the bombing as a terrorist act. The devices were described as 'unconventional explosives'.

A manhunt was immediately set in motion in the form of a dragnet to apprehend the perpetrators. Civilian routine was disrupted by stopping public transport, closing schools, universities and businesses, while the public was asked to remain at home for their own safety. Fragments of evidence that had been found around the two crime scenes were sent to the forensics laboratory, where it was determined that the devices had been chrome pressure cookers filled with gunpowder, nails, steel air-pistol pellets and ball bearings to increase the explosive effect. One of the characteristics of this type of bomb is that it is easy to make. The components are readily available and instructions for making the bomb can be found on the internet. Both bombs were put together by the terrorists themselves. The authorities stated that the perpetrators could have read instructions for how to make the bomb in Al Qaeda's *Inspire* magazine, which is published on the Arabian Peninsula. One of the two criminals had also bought firecrackers in New Hampshire. A deformed lid from one of the pressure cookers was found on the roof of a nearby house. Later, the remains of two black rucksacks used to transport the bombs were found. The bombs themselves had been detonated remotely by a control for model cars.

Because they had no clues yet as to the identity of the perpetrators, the FBI decided to involve the public in the search. People were requested to send the FBI all photographs and videos from the time of the attacks. Police Commissioner Ed Davis justified this to the media by explaining that "the crime scene was not only one of the best documented, but also one of the most complex crime scenes we have ever had." It was a brilliant move by the police; the public reacted very quickly and sent in a host of photographs and videos of the Boston Marathon and any suspicious-looking persons. This documentary evidence was then quickly examined by the police and online social networks.

The FBI stated that this had been done primarily to protect those innocent people who had been falsely identified as possible perpetrators via social media. One video showed the two suspects had stayed on the course to observe the chaos caused by the explosions. The two men didn't leave the scene until later. Meanwhile, there was some very important information received from a key witness, Jeff Baumann. He had been standing close to one of the two bombers and had lost both his legs in the explosion, before having to go through a further operation to remove fluids from his body as a result of the trauma. After he had woken up from the anaesthetic, he wrote to the authorities that he had seen one of the terrorists, "Saw the guy, he looked straight at me." Baumann was then immediately questioned by the FBI and it was his report which helped to significantly limit the number of suspects in the photographic and video evidence. He was able to provide a detailed description of the bomber, which then made it possible for the FBI to identify him in a photograph.

It was a phenomenal success for the investigators. On the afternoon of 18 April, the FBI, using the image analysis and several witness statements, presented images and videos of the two suspects to the media. Both men had been at the Boston Marathon carrying rucksacks. The bombers were 19-year-old Dzhokar and 26-year-old Tamerlan Tsarnaev, of Chechnyan and Avarish origin. They had grown up in Kyrgyzstan and emigrated to the United States with their parents in 2002, settling in Massachusetts. The family seemed to find itself in the gulf between the two cultures; the brothers suffered from an identity crisis, megalomania and a complex family breakdown, which in turn led to their violent actions.

Five hours after the FBI had published the 'Wanted' pictures of the criminals, 27-year-old Sean A. Collier, seated in his police patrol car near the Stata Centre at the Massachusetts Institute of Technology, was shot six times by the two killers as they tried to steal his service weapon. They were thwarted in their attempts because they didn't know how to release the weapon from its holster. The officer died a few minutes after the attack.

The two bombers now decided to steal a black Mercedes-Benz M-Class SUV in the Boston Allston-Brighton district so as to be able to move on quicker. The vehicle's owner, Dun "Danny" Meng, a Chinese engineering student at North-Eastern University, was taken hostage and the two men told him that they were responsible for the Boston Marathon bombing and had just murdered a policeman. Fearing for his life, Meng obeyed Tamerlan's instructions and drove the vehicle with a gun pointed at his head. Tamerlan and Meng were in the SUV, followed initially by Dzhokhar, who was driving a stolen green Honda, but later decided to join the other two in the SUV. The two brothers were apparently planning to drive to New York and bomb Times Square. After an hour driving around Watertown, the two criminals forced their hostage to withdraw $800 from an ATM since they were short of cash, before putting certain purchases into the SUV. Tamerlan now made Meng sit in the passenger seat. Meng was afraid he would be killed and thought that "his last day on Earth had come."

Next, the two murderers spontaneously decided to stop at a Shell petrol station. While Dzhokhar went to buy a few snacks and fill up the tank, and Tamerlan worked to disconnect the vehicle's GPS system, Meng unbuckled his safety belt, opened the car door and ran across the street to a Mobil petrol station to alert the police. They took his call seriously and from then on concentrated their search on Meng's stolen SUV. He had thoughtfully left his mobile phone in the vehicle so that the police could track it. This was the turning point in the three-day hunt for the two terrorists.

In the early hours of 19 April, the fugitives drove the SUV through the dark, narrow roads of Watertown. It was now their fourth day on the run and so far they had gone no more than a few miles from the scene of their crime.

Following the stolen SUV's GPS system, the police tracked the car to Dexter Avenue. Watertown police chief Joseph Reynolds was nearby when the phone call came at 12.30 pm. The hunt for the most notorious terrorists since 11 September 2001 was now approaching its end.

During the course of the day, hundreds of law enforcement officers conducted a door-to-door search for the fugitives in more than twenty streets. Boston residents were asked by the authorities to remain indoors while the search for Dzhokhar and Tamerlan continued. The same day the FBI, West New York police authority and the Hudson County Sheriff's Department went to the flat of the terrorists' sister in West New York, New Jersey, and seized all of her computer equipment.

Shortly after midnight, Joseph Reynolds, whose shift as patrol leader was just beginning, identified the two suspects, one in a Honda Civic, the other in the stolen SUV. Reynolds had turned into Dexter Avenue and saw the SUV heading slowly in his direction. He reduced his speed so as to see the registration plate clearly and glanced at the driver, whom he recognized as the older brother Tamerlan. They exchanged looks. Reynolds decided to follow the SUV. He was advised by control to wait for a back-up unit, but he continued to take up a position two car's length behind the SUV as it turned left into Laurel Street. Then the SUV driver's door opened, Tamerlan got out and immediately began shooting at the police car. Reynolds ducked below his dashboard and put his Ford vehicle into reverse. He called into his radio, "I have to shoot!" Police reinforcements were already on the way and Watertown Police Sergeant John MacLellan arrived with a squadron of cars. As soon as he turned into Laurel Street, a bullet went through his windscreen. He joined in the firefight by heading for the two armed brothers. Dzhokhar Tsarnaev had now appeared to assist his brother and they began throwing explosives. Reynolds and MacLellan took cover by a house as Dzhokhar threw a much larger explosive at them, this time a pressure cooker stove. A wild exchange of 300 rounds of fire now took place between police officers and suspects in Laurel Street, the latter also hurling hand grenades.

According to Watertown Police Chief Edward Deveau, the brothers had prepared a vertible arsenal of weapons. However, Tamerlan was soon out of ammunition and threw aside his empty pistol. Suddenly, Dzhokhar drove the stolen SUV towards his elder brother. With great presence of mind the police attempted to pull Tamerlan clear, but Dzhokar ran him down and dragged him some distance along the street. A half mile farther on, Dzhokhar abandoned the SUV and fled on foot into the night. His brother Tamerlan didn't survive the accident and succumbed to his injuries at 1.35 am in a Boston hospital.

Towards 6 that evening, after the authorities had allowed residents out of their homes, David Henneberry went into his Watertown garden to inspect his boat *Slip Away II*. He was sure that two of the oars had fallen through the cover which protected the boat in winter. In checking he noticed that the strapping was looser than usual and returned indoors, but decided a few moments later to go back for a closer look. When he rolled back the cover he noticed a large amount of blood on the floor of the boat and a message scrawled on the planking. As he looked towards the engine he saw the figure of a man lying there motionless. He couldn't see the man's face.

Henneberry reacted swiftly, climbed back down the boat's ladder and ran to the house to call the police, who responded in record time. An officer accompanied Henneberry and his wife to a neighbour's house before the police surrounded the Henneberry house and a wild shoot-out began. At 8.15 pm the authorities announced that a man believed to be Dzhokhar Tsarnaev had been arrested and taken to hospital.

Returning to his boat Henneberry found a strange note written by Tsarnaev, who called the victims of the bombing "collateral damage" and compared them to the civilian victims of US military operations. One of his more obscure declarations read: "Whoever attacks one Muslim, attacks them all." At 8.58 pm the Boston Police Department tweeted: "CAPTURED!!! The hunt is over. The search is done. The terror is over. And justice has won. Suspect in custody."

While the streets of Boston remained eerily empty for hours, the police could claim a victory in that, although wounded, one of the bombers had been taken alive. He would have to answer for his actions and would also be able to help the US special units, and all other authorities involved, understand the background to the terrorist attack. While the 19-year-old survivor supplied information from his hospital bed, the pieces of the jigsaw were gradually pieced together until everything made sense.

On 22 April 2013 Tsarnaev was charged with using a weapon of mass destruction which caused death and premeditated destruction of property and using explosives which also caused death. Two days later, on 24 April, the FBI and the Department of Homeland Security reported that their investigators had reconstructed the two bombs and discovered that they had been set off using a remote control normally used for toy cars. US Government officials maintain that they received no Secret Service reports indicating that a terrorist attack was to be made. However, Peter King, a member of the US Secret Service Committee, stated that he had attended "two top secret briefings regarding the current threat levels in the United States a week before the attack, but there was no evidence to support it."

The father of the two bombers later stated that the FBI had been watching his family and that they had interviewed his sons five times at Cambridge, Massachusetts, regarding possible explosions on the streets of Boston.

It was made public that in March 2011 the FBI had been warned by the Russian Interior Secret Service (FSB) that Tamerlan "was a supporter of a radical Islam"and was planning to visit Russia in order to link up with "background groups", but after questioning Tamerlan and his family directly, they found no evidence of this. However, the FBI had him included on the Customs and Immigration warning list, in the well known communications system for the financial authorities TBCS. When the Russian Secret Service made further enquiries to the CIA, there was no mention of a Tsarnaev in their databases, although they did enter him in a warning list, namely the Terrorist Identities Datamark Environment (TIDE).

On 1 May 2013 three young men were arrested in connection with the bombings. Azamat Tazhayakov, Dias Kadyrbayev and Robel Phillipos were associates of Dzhokhar Tsarnaev and were accused of helping their friend after the attack. Federal prosecutors alleged that the trio removed items from Tsarnaev's bedroom after the bombings to throw police off the scent. Azamat and Robel were sentenced to three and a half years' in prison for removing vital evidence from Dzhochar Tsarnaev's room in the wake of the deadly attack on 15 April 2013.

Tamerlan Tsarnaev was buried in a Muslim cemetery in Doswell, Virginia, in May 2013, after all cemeteries in Massachusetts and its adjacent states refused to allow his burial there. At the end of May an FBI agent shot dead Ibragim Todashev in Orlando, Florida, while questioning him about his relationship to Tamerlan Tsarnaev after mobile phone records had linked the two men. Todashev informed the agent that Tsarnaev had taken part in the drugs-related murder of three people in 2011. Todashev was shot dead after suddenly pulling a gun on the officer.

On 8 April 2015, Dzhokhar Tsarnaev was found guilty on all thirty counts and sentenced to death on 24 June 2015. The nature of the charge, using a weapon of mass destruction which led to the death of several persons, together with the attendant circumstances, made the death sentence appropriate under the US justice system.

Epilogue

What else you should know...

Terrorism has a history. Whoever looks closer at this history will see a 'red thread', namely the terrorist's struggle for a new world view. Analysing the brutal steps in retrospect, one notices that whereas terrorist groups of the 1970s, such as *Action Directe* in France, the *Rote Armee Fraktion* in Germany, the *Brigate Rosse* in Italy or the IRA, embraced violence as a political weapon, the attitude of the newer groups changed from the outset of the twenty-first century. They were far more radical than their predecessors. From 2001 the Pakistani Osama bin Laden became motivated by a belief that US foreign policy in the Middle East had set out to repress Muslims, and deliberately kill or harm them in other ways. He expressed his view by the phrase "They hate us for what we do, not for what we are."

It is becoming clear that terrorist organisations have risen up, sustained by the writings of the Islamic author and thinker Sayyid Qutb, who preaches that the Muslim world is no longer Muslim due to the lack of Sharia Law and has returned to pre-Islamic ignorance. In order to restore Islam, a progressive movement of right-thinking Muslims is necessary in order to establish 'true Islamic states', re-introduce Sharia Law and free the Muslim world of all non-Muslim influences and concepts, such as socialism and nationalism. According to Qutb, the enemies of Islam include "traitorous Orientalists" and "world Jews" who set up conspiracies and spread "wicked lies" against Islam. This inevitably leads to the modern-day terrorists who strike not only in Europe, but across the globe in order to build their world view, therefore their Caliphate and with it the leaders of their religious movement and rulers of the sphere of influence in which this belief is lived to the full. Jihad serves to lead them in the struggle against other belief systems and so achieve their goal. This is the background to the attacks of recent years which are portrayed in this book.

On my visits researching for this book to special unit commanders of those countries involved, when I asked them what their message would be for people today, they answered without hesitation, "Tell them they should be more watchful in future." They don't want to foster any more fears among the general public, but rather to warn them to keep a closer watch on their surroundings. When I asked for their advice on what to do when an attack took place, the answer came again without hesitation, like a mantra: "Run, hide, tell."

If one looks at the anti-terrorist policies of most countries, one notices that the protection of citizens, the infrastructure and the lessening of vulnerability to attack are amongst the most important aims of any country. These include key measures such as securing the borders, improving road safety, protecting strategic targets and reducing the vulnerability of critical infrastructures. The European Union is working to better monitor terrorists planning attacks and then bring the perpetrators to justice. Anticipating attacks, and controlling and minimising the consequences of any attacks, is a further aim in the fight against terrorism.

What is clear, however, is that the fight against terrorism must work on a global level. The security of Europe is closely linked to the situation elsewhere, especially the neighbouring countries. The relationship between the EU and Third World countries has improved over recent years due to political dialogue and subsequent high-level security and intelligence exchanges. In those countries where major attacks have recently been carried out, e.g. France, Belgium and England, the fight against modern-day terrorism will continue to shape and define them.

In all I spent two years with the teams from the world's best police special units. My conversations and experiences with them have provided an authentic behind the scenes look to which nobody, except those professionals involved, had ever been granted previously. Knowing that missions are carried out every day – many of them under conditions of the strictest secrecy – of which we will learn nothing about is exciting. I now understand much better why certain details are not filtered through to the public, and why police raids and certain operations must remain secret. On the one hand, the suspected perpetrators and their families might be warned and then try to flee. On the other, the constant criminal and terrorist activities would simply threaten to overwhelm us. Just as technology continues to advance, so does the form of the threat from terrorist cells. For this reason, the response of countries to threats, such as the equipment used in the struggle against terrorism, must be constantly redeveloped.

However, we should never forget that terrorism is based on the terrorists' misconception that democracy will eventually give way to bombings, hostage-taking or blackmail. Their narcissism cannot harm us, because in truth, only democracy offers the necessary protection against their exaggerated vanity. A state's democratic principles are therefore amongst the most powerful armaments in the struggle against global crime. The special forces teams do their upmost to defend democracy and stop terrorist activity with all means at their disposal; the more carefully contrived the technologies, the more refined the means of protecting the people will be.

In the struggle against terrorism, our interests and values must be in the foreground. Criminals must be made aware that there is retribution and that no nation will allow them to lead it by the nose. Governments and also the citizens of a country deserve respect. The fear of retribution should be enough to prevent criminals from committing monstrous crimes such as terror attacks. The world can be constantly improved with new technologies and developments, with industry and ambition, but not with ill-will and weapons. For this reason, criminals must be taught that they can run, but they can't hide, because there is no escape. Everywhere in the world there are people who will ensure that every criminal receives his just deserts.

I know now that an enormous amount of work goes into planning the perfect elite police tactical unit. These dedicated men and women, who cannot imagine themselves in any other line of work than what they are doing, are team-orientated and work in unison, calmly and cautiously, using tactics and strategy. Their operations play out extremely swiftly, and I have been able to witness this with my own eyes.

Much of what I had heard about them I now see differently. When I read how the two suspects in the Boston Marathon bombing were caught after barely three days of skilful photographic analysis, file comparison and countless interviews, then I know that my book is more relevant than ever and that it coincides with the spirit of the times. That kind of successful conclusion to an investigation is only possible when authorities and units work in harmony. When I learn today that this or that suspect has been apprehended in Austria or abroad, then I know that the commanders and their teams that I interviewed have triumphed again. That's how it should be. After all, their mission is to guarantee not only the security of a nation's citizens, but also to ensure justice: the ideal state of social coexistence.

Acknowledgements

This book could never have been written if I had not been in the extremely fortunate position of having a strong international network of people who have supported me over the years. My special thanks and respect goes to those governments who have responded positively to my book project and supported it in the spirit of democracy, security and peace in this world.

I would also like to express my heartfelt thanks to all the commanders and members of the special units from those sixteen countries who generously gave me a behind the scenes look at their work, and spent much time and energy supporting me over several years. In particular I would like to mention the British unit SCO19, its commanders and the whole team for the insight afforded me on a recent visit. Thanks guys!

I am also very grateful to my British publisher, Pen & Sword Books Ltd., for their confidence in me, and the enormous support I received from the whole team – above all from Heather Williams and Paula Hurst – for the numerous useful conversations, great ideas and the extremely productive cooperation. It gives me great pleasure to know that my book will now appear in English and be available to a wider readership.

I extend my thanks to my agent Lars Schultze Kossack and his team for their great work and many conversations which pointed me in the right direction. Thank you, Lars!

At this point I would like to say a warm hello to all the British men and women whom I got to know during my time in London and with whom I discussed this subject. Most of them were unaware of my research, but they gave me a great deal of insight which I found invaluable for this book.

Last but not least, a big thank you is due to all my family and friends at home and abroad who helped me with many ideas and suggestions as to how best to proceed with this updated version of my book.

Endnotes

Chapter 1: United Kingdom

1. The police later stated that the intention might have been to dispose of the diamonds through the Russian mafia. At their trial the following year, Betman and Cockram received eighteen years' imprisonment apiece, Adams and Ciarocchi fifteen years, Wenham four years.
2. The first doctor believed to have been on the scene was off-duty consultant anaesthetist Dr Michael Daley. In recognition of his bravery there, his name was entered in the Book of Valour of the British Medical Association in June 2017. See BMA: Awards of Honour (bma.org.uk)

Chapter 2: France

1. A revivalist movement within Sunni Islam supporting the implementation worldwide of the Islamic Sharia law.

Chapter 3: Belgium

1. Dolecki and Wagemans were tried at the Liège correctional tribunal and sentenced in June 1990 to ten to eleven years and nine to ten years' imprisonment respectively. Wagemans never regained full use of his legs. *Le Soir*, report by Alain Lallemand, 16 June 1990.

Chapter 5: Germany

1. Grenzschutzgruppe 9 (border protection group).
2. The Bundeswehr naval frogmen were seconded to GSG 9 on detached duty where they were subject to the orders of the police commander. Therefore the approval of Parliament was not required.

ENDNOTES

Chapter 7: Israel

1. A Sunni-Islamic Palestinian organisation whose aim is to overthrow the State of Israel using terrorist methods.

Chapter 8: Austria

1. On 2 March 1998, Natascha Kampusch (b. Vienna 17 February 1988) was abducted on her way home from school by Wolfgang Priklopil and held captive in a cellar measuring 2 x 5 metres at his home in Strasshof. After eight years she escaped on 23 August 2006. Her abductor committed suicide by throwing himself in front of a train.
2. The Foreign Minister, Benita Ferrero-Waldner (born Salzburg, 1948), at that time also a candidate for the office of Austrian President, had designed her own postage stamp for her electoral campaign. Normally in Austria only stamps bearing the likeness of deceased politicians are printed.